2531979
AAM-2764

56496
io

Allen

·y's

ONE MORE
DAY'S JOURNEY

The Education of Black Folk:
The Afro-American Struggle for Knowledge
in White America

ONE MORE DAY'S JOURNEY

The Story of a Family and a People

by ALLEN B. BALLARD

AN AUTHORS GUILD BACKINPRINT.COM EDITION

One More Day's Journey

The Story of a Family and a People

AN AUTHORS GUILD BACKINPRINT.COM EDITION

Published by iUniverse, Inc.

For information address:

iUniverse, Inc.

2021 Pine Lake Road, Suite 100

Lincoln, NE 68512

www.iuniverse.com

Originally published by McGraw Hill

"The Southern Road" by Dudley Randall is reprinted with the
author's pemission from Dudley Randall, *Poem Counterpoem*,
Broadside Press, 1966.

"Evenin' Air Blues" copyright 1951 by Langston Hughes. Reprinted by permission of Harold Ober Associates, Inc.

ISBN: 0-595-31802-9

Printed in the United States of America

*For my mother and father
and
for
Aunt Alice
Uncle Jerry
and
Aunt Hilda*

ACKNOWLEDGMENTS

This book, reflecting as it does the lives and histories of Black Philadelphians and South Carolinians, owes everything to them. As I list the acknowledgments, it will become clear that this book is the outcome of a collective effort. I feel honored and privileged to have been assisted by so many people of goodwill.

Leon Johnson did vast amounts of newspaper research in 1977 when both he and I were at the Moton Center in Philadelphia. I also thank Juanita Alexander, Sadie T. M. Alexander, Gwen Baber, Leslie Berger, Craigmore Boles, Anna Bouie, Ruby C. Boyd, Courtney Brown, Lawrence C. Bryant, Mamie Ballard Bunn, Mr. Chipley, Louise Coursey, Mr. and Mrs. William Dorsey, the Dowdy family, Martin Fields, Estelle Freeman, Celia Gibson, the Grimes family, Willie Hanniford, Dean Harrison, John Hatch, Dell and Jose* Hayles, James Hinton, the Reverend Joseph L. Hinton*, Percy Holmes, Tessie Jamison, Leonard Jeffries, the Reverend Ed Johnson, Roland "Tad" Johnson, the Reverend Joseph L. Joiner, Delores Jones, Floyd Logan*, Betty J. Melvin, Robert N. C. Nix, the Reverend Carl P. Ogden, James G. Spady, the Reverend William P. Stevenson, Ray Trent, Marie D. Watson, Carol Wells, David Wills, Harvey Wilson*, Flora Young, and the Young family of Danville, Pennsylvania.

Granting extended interviews were Charles Ballard, Lula Ballard*, Maude Bell, Alberta Blackwell, Mabel Brady*, Hughsey Childs, William P. Duckrey*, Arthur Huff Fauset*, Robert

*Deceased.

Acknowledgments

Gardner, Willie Hatcher, Firman Hopkins, Clarence P. Jenkins, Ralph Jones, Ella Mae Logan, W. Logan, Milo Manly, the Reverend Frank Mitchell, Rosa Moragne, Chief Inspector James N. Reaves, Alice Rhodes, Jack Saunders, Stephen Simpson, Eloise Fickland Spencer*, Dorothy Warwick Taylor, Howard E. Townes, M.D., Wade Wilson, and June Wiggins*. Their willingness to be interviewed and their endless patience and understanding shored me up and emboldened me at many critical times in the writing and researching of this book.

It would be presumptuous of me to single out any one of the dozens of relatives in Greenwood or Abbeville counties for thanks. They took me in like a long-lost son and extended to me a welcome that I shall never forget. I thank them all.

Helping in the typing were Juanita Alexander, Georgia Capels, Karen Carrol, Cynthia E. Edwards, Gardenia Hobbes, Delores Jones, Madeline Moyer, Jan Paxton, and Rita Serrett. The book could not have been completed without their assistance.

Elias Blake, Kenneth B. Clark, John A. Davis, Christopher F. Edley, George Fischer, Charles T. Hamilton, Timothy S. Healey, John Monroe, Nell Irvin Painter, Jewell Cobb Plummer, Franklin Williams, and Stephen J. Wright all responded graciously when I needed references for the grants necessary to do the research and writing of the book. The late Charles P. Davis of Yale was also strongly supportive of the work.

I used the facilities of the Temple University Urban Archives where Fred Miller, Peter Silverman, and Karen Galloway extended themselves beyond the call of duty. The staffs of the Historical Society of Pennsylvania, Archives of the State of South Carolina, Pennsylvania State Archives, South Carolina State, Claflin University, the Schomburg Center for Research in Black Culture of the New York Public Library and the South Carolina Collection of the University of South Carolina were all helpful, as were the staff at the National Archives and Phillip Lapsansky of the Library Company of Philadelphia.

A one-year stay at the Moton Center, then in Philadelphia, in 1976–77 was crucial in my ability to do indispensable field research. A one-year fellowship at the National Humanities

Center in 1980–81 gave me the repose and quiet needed to write the book. Their staff, particularly Corbett Capps, Patricia Perry, Rebecca Sutton, and Alan Tuttle and just about everybody else there made my year one easy and uninterrupted stream of writing. A grant from the Ford Foundation, arranged through Benjamin Payton, helped to support me during that year. I thank all these institutions, and add that they are in no way responsible for the views expressed here.

Finally I would like to thank Earl E. Thorpe—he was the first person to read the manuscript and was generous in his comments—Geoffrey Blodgett, Eric Foner, John Hope Franklin, Reginald Hildebrand, Iris Hill, James Olney, Akos Oster, and Nell Irvine Painter. Busy with their own work, they nevertheless took time to make helpful comments on my manuscript. Without hesitation, I can say that this is a much better work because of their constructive criticisms. Of course, they have no responsibility for the content of this book.

I'd also like to acknowledge my debt to the contemporary community of scholars of Black history at large. Their hard work has made this the most exciting area of contemporary American historical investigation. In addition to those cited above, I have profited greatly from the research of Herbert Aptheker, Lerone Bennet, Ira Berlin, John Blassingame, Joseph Borome, Leonard P. Curry, George Fredrickson, Eugene D. Genovese, Herbert G. Gutman, Vincent Harding, Theodore Hershberg, Nathan I. Huggins, Winthrop D. Jordan, Lawrence W. Levine, Leon Litwack, John Lovell, Jr., James McPherson, James Oakes, Benjamin Quarles, Albert J. Raboteau, George Brown Tindall, Joel Williamson, and many others. Of course, I differ with some of them on some of their interpretations.

I would also like to note that Professor Hershberg—while working on the same subject as I—was kind enough not only to open his data to me, but to permit his research aides at the time, Henry Williams and Robert Ulle, both outstandingly knowledgeable about Black Philadelphia, to assist me in deciphering the census data on Black Philadelphians. I need hardly add that the works of W.E.B. DuBois, Carter G. Woodson, Alrutheus A. Taylor, Benjamin Mays, E. Franklin Frazier, St.

Acknowledgments

Clair Drake, Horace Cayton, J. A. Rogers, Rayford Logan, and Charles S. Johnson have been central to my intellectual development, for I read their books in my youth. Of particular importance was an early work by Carl T. Rowan, *Go South to Sorrow*, which I read and re-read in my college years. Likewise, I read innumerable times Howard Fast's *Freedom Road*.

I also owe a debt to Alex Haley, for in 1969, in my official capacity as dean of the City University of New York, I introduced the then well-known, but not yet famous, Haley to a conference of librarians. His talk on his search for his African forebears had an immeasurable impact on me. So powerful was his speech, and so great his enthusiasm, that before my eyes he was transformed into an African. I am almost certain that the "roots" of this book were planted on that occasion.

While this work rests on a bedrock of knowledge, it owes much to James Baldwin, James Cleveland, Otis Redding, Mahalia Jackson, Sam Cooke, Jim Brown, Muhammad Ali, Malcolm X, Odetta, Ralph Ellison, Richard Wright, Paul Robeson, Nina Simone, Joe Louis, Leadbelly, and Martin Luther King. In short, I have tried to be true both to the spirit of our people and to the discipline of history. The reader may judge how successful that effort has been.

Alfred Prettyman saw the merits of an early version of this manuscript and acquired it for McGraw-Hill. His trenchant and wise comments guided me in the early revisions of the manuscript. He was kind enough to comment upon the manuscript even after he had left McGraw-Hill. Upon his departure, Elsa Dixler became responsible for the final editing of the book. She was a godsend. I can't express enough to her my appreciation for her meticulous, careful, and judicious editing. She is truly a professional.

Over the past ten years, my family—my brothers Forrest and Walter and their wives Geraldine and Irene—have helped me in innumerable ways. I thank all of them. And I think this is an appropriate place to thank Hilda Ballard, my stepmother, for almost fifty years of love.

My son John, and Willa Cook, my companion and best friend throughout the writing of the book, were supportive even when the logistics of writing became disruptive to their lives. I hope that the result justifies their loving sacrifices.

To make the book more accessible to the general reader, the footnotes have all been placed in the rear of the book.

In a work of this sort, which involves so many people, it is easy and indeed inevitable that someone who helped will be overlooked in the acknowledgments. If this is the case, be sure that this is not intentional, and so I thank you too.

CONTENTS

Contents

One more day's journey
And I'm so glad!
One more day's journey
Well, I'm so glad!
One more day's journey
You know I'm so glad!
For the world can do me no harm.

Traditional Black Spiritual

Part I

OLD PHILADELPHIA

"A Sunday Morning View of the African Episcopal Church
of St. Thomas"
(*Historical Society of Pennsylvania*)

Chapter 1

LINKING SOUTH CAROLINA
AND PHILADELPHIA

I know moonlight, I know starlight
I lay this body down
I walk in the moonlight, I walk in the starlight
I lay this body down
I know the graveyard, I know the graveyard
When I lay this body down

Traditional Black Spiritual

The two places, Philadelphia, Pennsylvania, and Greenwood, South Carolina, are connected on the map by long red lines that run parallel to the Appalachian Trail. From 1917 to 1923 large numbers of Black people came up the line by train, in an event called the Great Migration. Among them—having sojourned awhile in Greenville, South Carolina—was my paternal grandfather, whose son was to marry my mother. I am but one of the thousands of Black people of Southern background who grew up in Northern cities, and thus became part of the modern Black community. While the trains from the Carolinas, Georgia, and Virginia ran to Philadelphia, New Brunswick, Trenton, Newark, and New York, other trains from Mississippi, Alabama, Arkansas, and Louisiana were running to Detroit, Cleveland, and Chicago.

My mother never let me know much about the South

because, being of pre-Revolutionary Philadelphia lineage, she knew little of it, and what she did know, she did not particularly like. And my father was just plain ashamed of the South: I recall how he told me to please shut the hell up once when, mowing the lawn, I sang some Mississippi chain-gang songs I had learned from listening to records. My father was really just a country boy, but brilliant, ambitious, and hungry for success in the Northern world and in the Northern class that my mother represented.

But my sweet and loving grandmother from South Carolina used to sing softly, "Glory, Glory, Hallelujah, when I lay my burden down," as she ironed the clothes she took in to keep the family going. And one night, so hot that the sweat dripped over my eight-year-old body so that I couldn't tell the difference between it and the crawling of the bedbugs, a man named Roger sat with eight others on the corner across from my uncle's home. Roger's voice began to rise up in a song from a church in the Southland. The voice quavered, steadied, moved on up to glory, then broke just on time for the others to join in as they each were moved. For an hour they sang, for an hour I listened. Something was carrying me back to a place I had never known. And I knew someday I would find the place that could create such powerful and beautiful music, and a person like Roger. The next morning, they took Roger away to the penitentiary for killing one of his singing companions of the night before. With a razor. Over dice.

So what I have done in this book is to take two places and many people, both quick and dead, and show how they are related to each other. I've tried to make some sense of the forces that formed me and most other Black Americans. I decided to focus on Philadelphia and South Carolina. But first I had to find out what I was looking for, and where to look. So I began a journey of exploration into the past. Temporarily abandoning my customary role—for I am a college professor— I began to search the memories and ways of people in both locations. Later there would be time for books.

4

Some Old Philadelphians

Go to Bob Gardner, everybody said. Cousin Bob is a fast-talking, sophisticated graduate engineer who has spent most of his seventy-odd years as a handyman and a house painter. He is a light-skinned Old Philadelphian whose walls are covered with superb watercolors. He painted every one of them, and his learning and knowledge would do credit to any evening gathering in Cambridge, Massachusetts, or Princeton, New Jersey. Gardner knows everything about Black athletes and can recite, on request, the winners and times of all the one-hundred-yard dashes run at the annual Penn Relays. The exploits of Duke Slater, the great Black Iowa football guard of the 1920s, halfback Brud Holland of Cornell, and Paul Robeson of Rutgers may be forgotten by many, but Bob can trace the line from them to O. J. Simpson, and never miss an All-American.

One day, he gives me a letter. It is about the line of descent of his and my maternal family. At the head stands John Emory. The name marks the first step of the journey, for Emory, along with Richard Allen, Absalom Jones, and two other Black men, were pulled from their knees by force by white deacons from the segregated St. George's Church in 1788. They left that church and founded the Free African Society, the first chartered Black institution in the country, and the precursor of both the African Methodist Episcopal Church, and St. Thomas, the first Black Episcopalian church. Further down the list appeared the name of Jean-Pierre Burr, the image of the portraits of his father, Aaron Burr. Jean-Pierre Burr, a barber and one-time laborer, was a member of the Underground Railroad, a signer of many protest documents, a founder of the Moral Reform Society, and a member of the Banneker Institute, all foundations of the Black intellectual and activist tradition in the 1830s and 1840s. I was dumbfounded—first, because I felt forced to live up to that heritage, and second, because without even moving out of my cousin's room, I had been introduced to the major institutions of the Pre–Civil War Northern Black community. Jean-Pierre's grandson was Raymond Burr, a colonel in the post–Civil War Black militia and a pallbearer at the funeral of the Black martyr, O. V. Catto. In this quiet house in Philadelphia, certain that he can do anything with his hands or mind, sits an offspring of the Burr line. He has maintained the records to pass them on to me.

He directs me to a distinguished-looking house with white porticoes. A sign on the enclosed porch says, "Come with a whoop, come with a holler," and then trails off, "or don't come at all." A holly bush stands there, and on it a wreath that says the "House of the King." It refers to Christ, of course, but it just might refer to the owner's deceased father, Dr. William Warrick, physician, about as distinguished an Old Philadelphia name as I can think of. Someone once had the nerve to call his daughter a social climber. With ice in her voice, she said that one might as well call Queen Elizabeth a social climber. She meant every word of it, she assured me. Now this daughter sits alone in the house, and wants to know what I am after. I blurt out, now much aware of my South Carolina blood, that I am after the making of the Black community in Philadelphia and that she and her family were central to that process. She understands that particular fact far better than I do, and proceeds, for hours and days, to pull out paper after paper, treasure after treasure of our history. She led back to William Still, and to the Underground Railroad in Philadelphia, and ultimately to a block in Philadelphia where, miracle of miracles, both her forebears and mine lived a few houses from one another in the period before the Civil War. It was an area frequently devastated by white rioters. Gradually she pictures for me a complex social, economic, and political hierarchy, based on merit, wealth, and generations of freedom. The absence of traceable white antecedents raised one's status in this society.

One day, I went to an elegant apartment house in Central Philadelphia. Here I was received by a cousin in poor health, but living literally on top of the world, the wife of a Black doctor. I tell her I am in search of information about a mutual relative, and as I talk to this cultivated woman, I again feel the Southernness in me. Her husband had come out of the

South and, by sheer force of will, built a practice and married into the Black upper class. My cousin was herself important. In the 1930s she had been a journalist, political activist, and arbiter of the social who's who. Despite her graciousness, I couldn't help but wonder why the group around her, including my mother, spent so much time going to parties in the midst of the onslaughts against Black people in the South. Although many of them actively engaged in protest, I felt, at bottom, they were just not serious enough. Not many people are.

One Sunday shortly thereafter, while stalled in my research and troubled in mind, I went to an African Methodist Episcopal Church—the church of Richard Allen—and an anchor of the community. The preacher said that we don't read the Bible enough, and asked everybody to bring a Bible the next Sunday. I said to myself, "But I have no Bible." The next morning I received a long-awaited call and was told to come collect not one, but two Bibles. They led me back in space to Maryland and Delaware, and in time, a century and a half. When I saw them, a spiritual rocking began in my soul, something like the movement one sees among the choir members when the first chords of "Leaning on the Everlasting Arms" are played, an anticipation of grace to come. As I turned the carefully written pages listing the births, weddings, and deaths of my mother's family, I saw not names but a chain that had held despite blows, heat, cold, and curses. It would not break.

The pictures that accompanied the names were shaded from African black to American white, but the older the pictures, the blacker the faces. The people named in the Bible had lived in Altoona, Pennsylvania, Kansas City, and Camden, New Jersey, but most were unmistakably African. It was just where I thought I had come from. How came it to be, then, that their descendants in 1939 had been able to peer with haughty eyes across the table at me and say, "the child really has no manners." What the Old Philadelphians were saying was that these damn South Carolina kids have no manners. I strained as I read the Bible to reconcile the class and color snobbishness of some Philadelphia Blacks with the inescapable Africanness of the noses, cheeks, and lips of the faces

7

before me. Surely one great-grandfather, an escaped slave from Maryland whose back was scarred from whippings, had taught my mother to have no color attitudes toward others. She'd taught me the same thing, and yet she and her people had absorbed some of the poison that infected white society. The Northern-born Philadelphia Blacks of old lineage had a tradition of protest, but they also disdained their own. It was the major weakness in the institutions that made up their community.

The Bibles, and some other information, led me to Maryland, just two states up from South Carolina. Looking at the map, I tried to understand what forces had differentiated the two communities of slaves. Those differences must have been great indeed to prevent the Africans from one place from recognizing the Africans from another when they came together in Philadelphia. It almost seemed to me as if the oppression had to be repeated all over again, in the new place, Philadelphia, in order for them to become one.

I Move South

Since my childhood, South Carolina has meant fear and darkness. When there was thunder and lightning, my South Carolina grandfather would tremble and grow fearful, saying that "the Lord is in His Holy Temple, let all the Earth be silent before Him." We grandchildren would sit motionless, or as close to it as a child can come, until the storm passed. My grandfather's fear was transmitted to me directly. And like many other second-generation immigrants, I was ashamed that my people came from a place of terror and ignorance. As a child, I imagined the South as a battlefield where the forces of evil held sway.

By 1930, over two-thirds of all Black Philadelphians had been born in the Southern states of Virginia, South Carolina, Georgia, and North Carolina. And one out of every ten of them had been born in South Carolina. In fact, between 1917 and 1923 almost one out of every two Blacks leaving South Carolina and heading North went to Philadelphia. Thus, the South Carolina tradition was transported from one state to another. I wanted to explore that tradition as it affected Philadelphia.

I went to visit my cousin Doris. Everything was wrong with her Philadelphia house. The plumbing didn't work, the pipes leaked, Doris and her family were freezing. A few weeks later the house was featured in a newspaper story as an outstanding example of neglect by landlords and the city. Doris, rheumatoid and near to her appointed time, was out of South Carolina and close to me in blood and mien. Sitting there, I asked myself, paraphrasing Malcolm X, "What do you call a Black man with a Ph.D. from Harvard?" Answer: "A fortunate African." What do you call somebody from South Carolina on welfare? Answer: "An unfortunate African." For in Doris's living room hung a picture of a fierce-eyed woman with African-Cherokee face, our great-great-grandmother. She had been married to a man who, it was said, bought her and her children out of slavery in South Carolina. Doris mentioned a town called Greenwood, South Carolina, and another town, Abbeville, nearby. She insisted that there was something vaguely French in the family background. Two ancient aunts, she said, survived in Greenville. Years later, after Doris's death, I found a monument to the Huguenot settlers who had come to Abbeville County, South Carolina, in 1755.

The aunts in Greenville were over eighty, and the one on crutches was taking care of the other. Greenville, the second largest city in South Carolina, is a textile town in the far northwestern corner of the state. It is fifty miles north of Greenwood, on the edge of the Piedmont range. On a spectrum of historical cruelty to Blacks, Greenville would be yellow, Greenwood blood red. Between the two cities are towns called Woodruff, Easely, and Anderson, the last names of many of my childhood friends. My aunts had spent most of their lives teaching, first in those towns, and then in Greenville itself.

My aunts are spunky and loyal. Their brother, also over eighty, lay in a Philadelphia hospital, having suffered a stroke. When he could be moved, Aunt Ella—with her broken arm in a sling—boarded a plane for the first time in her life, went to Philadelphia, and brought him home. In a vacant lot across the street from her house, neighborhood children assembled at night to play their tape recorders. Hearing that federal money was available for community gardens, she secured a grant to start one on that noisy lot. Since then the children congregate elsewhere at night, but only after they have tended their garden. Gentleness and strength characterize this woman, but had she been transplanted to the North forty years ago, she would have been ignored by the upper stratum of Blacks. Despite her degrees from Western Reserve and NYU, her soft lilt and her coffee-brown skin would have marked her as "Southern," and therefore socially unacceptable to some Philadelphia Blacks.

The sisters are part of a professional class who stayed at home in the South and served through the "Trouble Times." The women drove in buggies up in the mountains and down dusty trails on hot summer days to teach the children who did not go North. So little Josh White down the street was taught by them, as were Peg Leg Bates, and the Reverend Jesse Jackson.

First Impressions of Greenwood

Greenville had been relatively good to my family. My grandfather's blacksmith shop there had prospered and he had been able to buy a house and an automobile. But in 1918, about to be drafted into a segregated labor battalion, he headed for Philadelphia and employment in an essential war industry. Yet Greenville had not instilled the terror-stricken look in the eyes of my grandfather—a man who could fell a stubborn mule with one blow of his fist—Greenwood had. My mind remained fixed on that place, so I had to leave my aunts and move down the road to Greenwood. My ancestors kept me from bearing down on the accelerator as I drove; I did not go over fifty-five as I passed the lynching tree at Clinton and finally arrived in Greenwood. As it turned out, a state trooper had been on my tail for the last ten miles. Abbeville, the town with the French name that Doris had mentioned, lay over on my right in the wooded hills, and somehow I felt the danger came from that direction. I was wrong: the danger lay all around me. I remembered that the place I was entering, the place that made my grandfather shake and tremble, had been called Abbeville County until 1900—encompassing not just a town but a whole countryside.

Greenwood, bordered now by superhighways, has a McDonald's and a Holiday Inn. Yet the first morning of my stay there, while I was jogging, a carillon played "Near the Cross," the family burial song and one of the most beautiful hymns of the Black church. Later that day, in a wooded and vine-filled graveyard, behind the crumbled Cedar Grove A.M.E. Church, I found the tombstone of my great-grandmother, Alice Logan. She'd been born in 1859 and died in 1902. While I sat softly talking to those who had gone before, guns went off, bodies hung from trees, songs rose up out of the ground, great Black arms—like those of all my male line—brought down hammers on anvils, and I knew that I had found the heart of my search. In Greenwood, the railroad built by convict labor still runs through the center of town. Not far off is Morris Chapel Baptist Church. The church, the center of the community, stands on ground that was owned by my great-great-grandfather, John Ballard, ex-slave blacksmith from the Aiken plantation in Winnsboro, South Carolina. Ballards were among the founding members of the church. Across the street is Mount Pisgah A.M.E. Church, to which many Black Philadelphians belonged.

Soon I grew familiar with the town. On Main Street is the hotel where Mr. Williams worked as a headwaiter in the early years of the century. He was such an important Black man that the town elders named a street after him when he died. Away from the center of town, white houses line the quiet tree-covered streets. Mr. J. C. Self, the lord of this fiefdom in the early 1900s, built houses for the cotton mill hands. The houses still stand and would easily sell—the ones that belong to whites, that is—for close to $85,000 in a New York suburb. Mr. Self built houses for Black workers too, but they were made of wood, not brick. Some of the men and women who lived in those houses were my cousins.

In the stores of downtown Greenwood I was courteously served, but the feeling in my body was like the one I experienced when I ate lunch at the Hotel Lux in Moscow. The Lux was where foreign Communists, recalled to Moscow in the days of the Great Purges, were housed before they were taken off to be shot. In Greenwood, you looked up at a street sign and realized that the name of the road was Phoenix. It led directly to the scene of a bloody race war in 1898.

The area south of Greenwood, I decided, would be the locale for the examination of Black rural life prior to the departure for the cities of the North. I knew all the objections of my fellow academics: "Did you test for the validity of your sample? How typical is this of other rural areas? Was there not something special about the Greenwood experience?" and so on and on. But Greenwood had enough suffering, battling, and triumphs to serve as a prototype of the Black rural past. It would do as well as any.

The cotton fields are gone, but the churches that demarcated the boundaries of the Black community are still there. Their names are Damascus, Mount Moriah, Pine Grove, Oldfield Bethel, Big Mount Zion, and they are tied together by family and shared history. Streams named Hard-Labor and Cuffee Town run through this land. You can lay out a map of the United States in 1880, shade it for the various Black religious sects, then shade Black churches in urban areas in 1930. Lines drawn between similar colors would give an accurate representation of the sources of the Great Migration.

The Black people of Greenwood formed a natural community with the towns of Hodges, Due West, and Ninety-Six to the North; Edgefield County to the East; and to a lesser extent, the towns of Honea Path and Anderson along the railroad toward Greenville. To the South the biggest city was Augusta, Georgia, connected to Greenwood by a railroad that ran through Bradley, a small village some ten miles outside the limits of Greenwood proper. Much of my family is from Bradley.

If ten out of every one hundred Black Philadelphians as of 1930 were born in South Carolina, it is safe to assume that at least ten percent of these were born in this county. And today, in the hamlets that comprise the former Abbeville County, there is not one family that does not have close relatives in Philadelphia. It's always Philadelphia, and if you ask where their kin first lived, it's always in the same four or five square blocks. The Abbeville Blacks were all impelled toward Philadelphia by the same set of political and economic upheavals in their home county.

Abbeville County had comparatively few incidents of armed conflict between Blacks and whites during the Reconstruction compared, say, to the rest of South Carolina. But the violence of the 1898 race riot shaped the lives of hundreds of future Black Philadelphians. Abbeville County was also the site of major unrest and countless lynchings. Each of these events propelled clans of Blacks into motion toward Philadelphia and the North. No understanding of the urbanization of Black Philadelphians can exist without knowing what took place in that county with the French name. One Abbeville native resident who came to Philadelphia in 1918 was moved to say that maybe "God intended it to be this way, that we be forever scattered through the earth as speckled birds."

Making Specific Connections

One Sunday in Greenwood I asked a cousin which church to attend. She said that the A.M.E. Church was more famous, but had lost many of its congregation, and that maybe I should go to the Baptist church next door. As I entered they were singing the "Old Ship of Zion," the old song that tells of the ship that has transported "many a thousand" from slavery into the freedom of death. The faces of the choir were Black, the robes white, and the voices full of the dirt, sweat, and gravel that Abbeville County's Black history had come to mean to me. They sang of the triumph of will over terror, and I, who had grown weary with reading of these things, wept, my tears adding water to the river Jordan over which the Zion ship must pass.

A year later, home near Philadelphia, I read Benjamin Mays's history of the Black church. Mays told how, during the Great Migration, a congregation had not only moved from South Carolina, but had given the name of the home church to the church in the new place—Philadelphia. The name of the church was Morris Chapel Baptist, where I had worshipped in Greenwood.

The next morning I went to Morris Chapel Church, Philadelphia. It stands in the northern section of the city, on the border of the area that was the first home to the refugees from Greenwood in 1918. As I looked around me, I saw the images of the people I had seen in the churches, homes, and stores of Greenwood. The saunter was the same, as were the reddish tinge of skin, the obesity from the fatty diet, and the pitch of the softly exchanged "howdies." Listening to some teen-agers wolfing at one another on the street, I understood—really for the first time—that some of my people had come North and never lost the voice or ways of Abbeville County.

The minister's very first words to me—"But you're a Philadelphia Negro, aren't you?"—sounded the theme of this book. Born and raised in the South and only recently come to the church, he felt an instinctive aversion to me and anyone else who had had the effrontery to be born in Philadelphia. That meant, said the minister, that you had forgotten the needs of your people. Particularly if you had a light skin. Told that this church came out of my place, he quieted, and asked how he could help. I was directed to a woman who, knowing my family's reputation in the Baptist music circles in Philadelphia, gave me further endorsement and the name of Hughsey Childs from Greenwood, South Carolina. Childs, a retired chef, was among the first members of this Philadelphia church. He is still actively involved both with present-day Greenwood and with the natives of that town now resident in Philadelphia and he knew, from his parents, the story of the race riot at Phoenix in 1898.

Hughsey Childs unfolded a tale only Homer could do justice. He anticipated my questions, wanted to know why I had not asked others, and added pieces to the historical jigsaw puzzle. When shown a map of the Phoenix area, he nodded at God's power to bring to light those things that were done in darkness. He agreed not only to talk about the darkness, but also about the founding and the formation of Philadelphia's Morris Chapel Church.

Childs made it clear that the Greenwood connection in Philadelphia is so vast that there can be no end to the task of a scholar who attempts to trace the offspring of those born there who came to Philadelphia in 1918. Greenwood's progeny are numberless. Are you looking for the Tolberts out of the Damascus section? Their relatives live right around the corner. Are you seeking some of the Jones family, those "bad dudes" who started the trouble down there? Some of them live ten blocks away. And in the next block, and the next block, lived people interspersed with my own familial connections.

After awhile, Greenwood people were so numerous they could no longer live in the same houses or rent places next door one to the other. They became part of the community. They lost contact with many of their friends, married people not of Greenwood or of South Carolina, and made friends on the job with people from different regions of the South. People from the dozens of Greenwoods in the South were trying to acclimate themselves to Philadelphia. But, through it all, a continuity with the South was maintained. I know, because years later, without realizing it, I married someone whose people were also from Greenwood.

In an Old Philadelphia Church, South Carolinians Are Found

Having searched Philadelphia for clues to the Southern past, and traveled to Greenwood to track them down, I thought to end my journey in the heart of Philadelphia's original Black community, Mother Bethel A.M.E. Church. Both the site of the Liberty Bell and the home of Betsy Ross are close by the church founded by Richard Allen in the last days of the eighteenth century. No Black institution in Philadelphia or elsewhere can match the history of activism of the bishops and clergy of the African Methodist denomination. Mother Bethel *is* Old Philadelphia—or so I thought before I entered the church one hot July afternoon to find that much of the congregation was from South Carolina.

Three women who sit on the historical committee of the church listened to my plan to examine the interplay between the Northern and Southern Black communities. When I had finished, one of them told me that her mother had been a childhood friend of my grand-aunt. That must mean, I said, that your mother was from Greenwood, South Carolina. Not Greenwood, she said, but a small town near there called Bradley. She was the granddaughter of the chief minister of the A.M.E. Church in the Greenwood district. He had left after a lynching in 1916. Beside her sat another woman, also of South Carolina, and the mother of Judith Jamison, the former leading dancer of the Alvin Ailey troupe. The third woman was from Virginia. Before long, I was sitting with a pile of letters documenting the transfer of people from the churches of Greenwood to this mother church in Philadelphia in 1918. The letters had the addresses which had become so familiar to me—Weston Chapel, Mount Pisgah, and Pine Grove. Even my great-grandmother from Greenville, I discovered, had been a long-time congregant of this Philadelphia church. In the very heart of the Northern Black community, I had found my Abbeville people.

The Journey We Take

To study the history of Black Philadelphia is to open a long-festering wound. It must be drained of the infection of violence. As the existence of Black Philadelphians has been marked by injustice and oppression, so has that of the Black residents of Los Angeles, Detroit, Newark, Durham, or Chicago. Our focus is on Philadelphia, but it might just as easily have been any other Black city. The story will begin with the formation of the Black community in Philadelphia before 1900. We'll look at its attempts to fashion a life for itself. Then we'll journey to Abbeville, South Carolina, observe the lives of Black people during slavery and Reconstruction, and travel with them to Philadelphia. Finally, we'll show how our modern Black community is a mixture of the Southern and the Northern traditions, and how it has both withstood and been shaped by oppression, both North and South.

Chapter 2

AT THE BEGINNING

Nobody knows the trouble I've seen
Nobody knows my sorrow
Nobody knows the trouble I've seen
Glory, hallelujah

Traditional Black Spiritual

There are no "Old Philadelphia" Black families if by *old* you mean "always free." Any Philadelphia Black who makes that claim—as some do—must sooner or later confront the ship manifests of the seventeenth and eighteenth centuries. The Black Philadelphians came from Barbados, Nevis, Antigua, Saint Christopher, and Anguilla. Most had been transshipped from Africa, although some had been in the islands for a generation or more. Nobody knows how many African captives were brought to Philadelphia before the American Revolution, but the estimates run from two to ten thousand.

Quakers and the Slave Trade

As early as 1685, three years after Philadelphia's founding, a Quaker—a man who wore the same hat of peace that sits on William Penn's head on the statue atop Philadelphia's City

Hall—brought six slaves directly from Africa. Another Quaker asked his brother in Barbados to send him some slaves, since he knew there would be a labor shortage when he arrived in Philadelphia. A famous old white Philadelphian, Jonathan Dickinson, brought ten slaves with him when he arrived from Jamaica.

Philadelphia, then, stood fully astride the developing economy of slavery. Its merchants firmly established themselves as provisioners for the Barbados slaveholders. In fact, many of the Quaker merchants came directly from Barbados. Samuel Carpenter, for example, had worked there for ten years before he came to Philadelphia. With capital accrued in the islands, he put together a string of enterprises that within a decade made him one of the "wealthiest merchants in the province." This trade that flowed from Africa to England to the West Indies to the Colonies made the Old Philadelphia fortunes. Flour, corn, bacon, iron, molasses, livestock, and stolen Africans undergirded Philadelphia's growth. Shipbuilding prospered and a class of artisans arose to meet the many requirements of commerce.

Many Quakers thought slavery clashed with their religious principles. Some stopped importing Africans, but many subordinated their religion to moneymaking. Such Old Philadelphians as Samuel Carpenter, Jonathan Dickinson, Isaac Norris, Benjamin Mifflin, Samuel Powel, Jr., and John Reynell were slave merchants. The last two were among the "Weightiest Quakers in Philadelphia."

William Penn himself owned slaves whom he later freed. And he was part of the Quaker merchant community that traded "Rumm, Sugar, Molasses, Silver, Negroes, Salt, Wine" to accumulate wealth and power. He outfitted ten ships for this trade of commodities in 1691. Some idea of the nature of this trade can be gained from the fact that one non-Quaker–owned ship coming into Philadelphia in 1701 from Barbados carried twenty-five slaves, over half the value of its cargo. These slaves were sold in Philadelphia.

Slavery in Philadelphia and Pennsylvania expanded greatly during the Seven Years' War in the mid-eighteenth century, a war fought to determine, among other issues, which European nation would have the rights to the raw materials—including slaves—of the West Indies. Various taxes on the importation of Africans were passed, but they were nearly always motivated by the necessity for raising revenue. When an act against the importation of slaves was passed in 1761, some Philadelphia merchants protested. They said that the region had to import slaves to keep the price of labor and, therefore, the price of staples low.

During this period, ships dropped anchor in the Delaware and sold Africans directly to waiting buyers. The ships had names like *Sally*, a schooner that brought African captives to Philadelphia from the river Gambia. The history of Black Philadelphia begins in the entries in ships' logs, which gave the names of captains, numbers of Africans, and the islands from which Black Philadelphians were transshipped. The names of the importers can still be found on the streets, museums, schools, and businesses of Philadelphia. The black people are called only "several Negroe Men, Women, and Boys," or "Sundry Negroes of about 10 or 12 years," or "Parcel of Five Negroes Boys and Girls." Nothing is named after them.

As late as 1800, after the law said you could import no more slaves, a shipment of one hundred Africans was brought into Philadelphia and sold there and into the surrounding counties. In the city "it was a common sight to see the odious spectacle of the drove, tied two and two, passing through the city towards the countryside." Many Africans died from the Philadelphia cold because they arrived naked down at the docks. A Quaker said of one Black woman that "I have put her on cloathes. It not beignt the custom for ym to go naked—people will not buy ym so."

Early Philadelphia

By the time of the Revolution, Philadelphia was the largest city of the American colonies. A foreigner who visited around that time praised "its fine appearance, good regulations (and) agreeable situation" and felt the city could be compared to the "most ancient towns in Europe." It even had street lights, the beginnings of paved streets, and running water from pumps.

The mansions of wealthy Philadelphians matched the splendor of the city. A stroll through the Philadelphia Museum of Art, made famous by Rocky's run up its stairs, gives the viewer a sense of the impeccable taste and high style of those who created Philadelphia. Signs on its exhibits of old furniture claim that "No community had finer mansions facing its streets nor could any equal in magnificence the nearby country estates." Nothing indicates to schoolchildren touring the museum today that those lovely "homes required the care of many Negroes and servants for their upkeep."

Pre-Revolutionary Philadelphia was a major center of colonial trade. The "Great Philadelphia Wagon Road" ran from the city out to the Susquehanna River and from there into the Shenandoah Valley, the Carolinas, and frontier territory. You could reach Burlington, New Jersey, in two hours by coach, and three different routes each led to New York and Baltimore. There were also roads to Annapolis, the major port of entry for Africans into the Virginias and points North. Supplies to feed and clothe the Africans came down the roads from Philadelphia. The forced labor of the Africans, in turn, supplied the Southern slave masters with the money to pay the Philadelphia merchants for these goods.

The accumulation of wealth in Philadelphia led to the creation of a class that lived on the same lavish scale as the Virginia slaveholders or the "Puritan merchant princes of Boston," rode in well-appointed carriages, gardened, and indulged the "pleasures of the table." Of the seventeen wealthiest people in Philadelphia by the time of the Revolution, eight were active Quakers and four had been reared as Quakers. Only five were non-Quakers, and one of these, William Shippen, "owed the basis of his fortune to his Quaker grandfather."

Who were these Quakers? They had come to the New World to create a haven where, in the words of William Penn, they would be free of the "outward cares, vexations, and turmoils which before we were always subject unto, from the hands of self-designing and unreasonable men." It has been said of them that their religion was mystical, their attachment to money practical. They had many good qualities: generosity, benevolence, and an emphasis on self-help. But "inwardly passionate to be helpful, the Quakers, burdened by a reserve that hardened into formalism, were more stiff than courteous, more cold than welcoming." They believed in equality, but thought the lower classes should obey the higher. Indeed, it was a man's duty to lift himself and his family and to enjoy the fruits of his labor.

Philadelphia, a Cultural Capital

A highly urbane culture arose in Philadelphia out of the wealth created by commerce. An almost universal system of education was one of its foundations. By mid-century, students from Jersey, Delaware, Maryland, and the islands came to Philadelphia for study. The city contained many schools, that emphasized classical education, which were run by private tutors for the children of the wealthy. At the same time, the white working classes and mechanics were educated at night schools that aimed at basic literacy. Some language groups, such as the German immigrants, had special schools for their particular needs. It was also possible for some women to get an education.

The city's elite valued intellect, and the educated in Philadelphia were likely to be physicians or public figures rather than ministers, as they were in Boston. Newspapers, tracts, and pamphlets circulated freely, and private and public libraries were built by men of wealth. The Quakers thought that books should be readily available to broaden the minds of both the young and the old, and Philadelphia's great Logan Library is a testament to this belief. The literary climate was vigorous, with many citizens writing history or biography. By the time of the Revolution, many Philadelphians, except the most recent immigrants and most Africans, were literate. A contemporary observer noted "the great taste for books which prevails among all orders and ranks of people in this city."

It was also a city of music, with a large corps of private voice teachers and many musical soirées where one could hear the music of Corelli, Handel, and Geminiani. Wealthy Philadelphians purchased paintings and tapestries from the old cities of Europe and commissioned "self-portraits." You see them now in all the museums in Philadelphia. The rich also sent their children on "grand tours" to Europe. A historian of Philadelphia has argued that the city served as the entryway into the United States for the ideals of Western democracy. He added that the application of these ideals in Philadelphia resulted in an attention to human need "unsurpassed in any other community of this age." Poverty, disease, and cruelty were thought to be bad and socially inefficient.

The city was marked by religious diversity and tolerance. By the time of the Revolution, many Quakers had become Anglicans, today's Episcopalians. The saying was that you could be a "Christian in any church, but could not be a gentleman outside of the Church of England." The Presbyterian church, however, was the largest of the eighteen churches in the town. The congregations were built around distinctive ethnic groups: the Quakers were mostly old English and Welsh; the Anglicans "later" English and Irish; the Presbyterians, Scotch and Scotch-Irish; and the Lutherans, German. These national distinctions were further maintained because each of the denominations had its own separate schools.

A network of ethnically based taverns and clubs formed the basis for social life in white working-class Philadelphia. The Irish set up a "Society of Friendly Sons of St. Patrick of Philadelphia for the Relief of Immigrants from Ireland" and the Germans established a similar organization. Within these groups, there might be a cross-section of all classes: "gentlemen, artisans, laborers—whose paths in their home country might never have crossed, achieved, if not friendship and intimacy, at least a sympathetic understanding based on the powerful, though accidental bond of common homeland and common national traditions." Such organizations influenced not only social activities, but also jobs and political positions.

Some fire companies, for example, were extensions of Irish clubs. Philadelphia was transformed by the flood of immigrants pouring into the city and through it to western Pennsylvania and the frontier. The city became more rowdy as it became a major port of entry into the United States for many Europeans.

Early Blacks and Philadelphia Culture

There were some direct educational benefits for Africans raised in Philadelphia. The Quakers, in a practice they later reversed, admitted some Africans to the Friends' Public School as early as 1737. And Anthony Benezet started a school for Blacks in his own house, which he supported for twenty years until the Society of Friends took over the responsibility. John Emory, my earliest traceable ancestor, studied in that school. Benjamin Franklin was likewise influential in obtaining help to educate African children through a school at Christ Church. And one Sunday morning during the depression of 1763, all the churches in the city preached a sermon to raise money for the distressed Black people.

Our people worshipped at many of the city's churches. Early in the eighteenth century, attempts had been made to convert the slaves. The outcome, some whites thought, was mixed, for it frequently led the converts to become "turbulent and boisterous" and to act as if they were as good as whites. There was much religious mixing, and a Philadelphia Black's instructional class "included some of the poorer white members of the church and he himself appeared before the congregation to be publicly catechized, baptized, and in a word, accepted as a member of the church." That simple ceremony was a powerful stimulus to equality.

Eighteenth-century Philadelphia contained many lessons for a people in slavery. Many wealthy whites worshipped money, building great homes and dressing lavishly. Certainly this surrounding wealth and the upward mobility of Philadelphia whites did infect some Africans with the idea that they could make it in America. Indeed, the writings of some early Black Philadelphians attempt to portray their success in business. Even the most radical among them seemed to feel that the demise of slavery would free our people to participate in the American system.

Philadelphia also held other lessons. Some Quakers believed in humility and social activism and they respected intellectuals. There were so many books around the city that it was impossible to keep them away from the Blacks who resided there. Philadelphia was also a prime example to Africans that organization around collective needs and common ancestry could promote group survival. If the Germans, Irish, and Welsh could organize, why not Africans? Finally, the distinction between American ideals and American practice was especially clear in this city where the Declaration of Independence was proclaimed. Some Black men and women arose in Philadelphia to challenge the slave system. Their actions and thoughts will be our next concern.

Chapter 3

BLACK PHILADELPHIA LEADERS

There is one idea that has often suggested itself . . . in contemplating the condition and progress of these people. . . . It is the nobility of human nature in itself considered.

A foreign observer on Philadelphia Blacks in the early 1800s.

Of all the captives in the New World, American Blacks were in the most precarious position; unlike Black Brazilians or Cubans, who could almost blend into their societies of mixed bloods, southern Europeans, and free Blacks, American Blacks stood out as a distinct minority in a white society. Thus, the leaders of Philadelphia's Black community had to create structures that would insure their survival in an environment that was hostile and sometimes violent. Those leaders may not have been perfect, but we will find that they built well.

The Legacy of Philadelphia's Black Leadership

The long list of institutions built in Black Philadelphia includes many of Black America's first attempts at self-government. Some institutions lasted, others did not. It was in Philadelphia that the Free African Society, generally thought to be the first formal organization of Black people in America, was founded. St. Thomas African Episcopal Church was the first Black church in the United States. Philadelphia was also the birthplace of the first African denomination in the world, the African Methodist Episcopal Church, and of the first African Presbyterian Church. Other institutions that first appeared in Philadelphia included a school for free Blacks in 1770, a literary society in 1832, and a convention movement, first started in 1817.

Each of these organizations has significance. The founding of the A.M.E. Church, for example, was an important step toward the creation of the modern Black community. But it is the range of organizing in Philadelphia that makes its Black community unique. The city's Blacks contributed to the struggle for African survival in the United States. An almost unknown Black historian, William Carl Bolivar, referring to the founding of the Free African Society, said that "the more we have of historical research, the more we realize that the pivotal point in the life of the Colored American hinges at the year 1787 in the city of Philadelphia."

Philadelphia Blacks had certain advantages over Blacks in other communities. Their leaders had early access to education, were raised in a city where slavery was benign relative to the South, and were exposed to the revolutionary ideas and literature that pervaded the nation's first capital. A small number of Philadelphia Blacks, as we noted earlier, were accepted into membership in the Anglican church and literacy in the catechism went along with the conversion. Finally, liberals such as Benjamin Franklin—a former slaveholder—contributed money to the founding of the African Methodist church.

Although the Black community in Philadelphia was not divided between former field hands and house servants—Northern agriculture was not suited to slavery—natural distinctions emerged between those who had been free a long time and those who escaped from slavery with its abolition in Pennsylvania in 1780. Shadings of skin color were important. There were ties among those who had originated in the same rural areas or small towns. These and other differences continue to the present day, but the mark of the Philadelphia community was its consistent effort to unite in the fight against slavery in the South and discrimination everywhere. Racial oppression was the decisive factor in the formation of the modern Black community.

In this chapter, we will focus on the lives of the Philadelphians who led the community until 1900. In subsequent chapters, we will examine the churches, schools, self-help organizations, and systems of thought they developed. Finally, we will observe how violence permeated daily life in this wrongly named City of Brotherly Love.

The Early Black Community

The Black community in Philadelphia was governed, in its formative stages, by a trio: preacher Richard Allen; James Forten, a sailmaker; and Absalom Jones, the founder of the Black Episcopal church. Later, Robert Purvis and William Still served as leaders of the Underground Railroad. The mantle of leadership then passed to O. V. Catto, who was assassinated in 1871. By that time, the basic contours of the community had taken shape. Of these "Old Philadelphian" leaders, Richard Allen was born a slave in Philadephia; Absalom Jones, a slave in Delaware; James Forten, a freeman in Philadelphia; Still, a freeman in New Jersey; and both Purvis and Catto, freemen in South Carolina.

Origins of Black Philadelphians

The Blacks of the pre–Civil War era were a diverse people. Many, particularly in the period before 1825, retained their African culture and were fluent in several languages. On certain African holidays they could be found in a downtown square "dancing in numerous little squads" and singing "each in their own tongue" after the customs of their several nations in Africa. They had strong voices and accompanied themselves with homemade guitars and musical instruments formed out of gourds. Before 1835, many worked as porters. They wore long aprons and "donned the high hats discarded by their employers." Others were janitors or chimney sweeps who spent their spare time congregating around the Continental Hotel and Independence Hall. You could see coffee-colored women from Haiti or Santo Domingo in the early 1800s with peanut candy cakes in trays carried balanced on their heads. In Philadelphia there were "Mestizo ladies with complexions of the palest marble, jet black hair and eyes of the gazelle, and of the most exquisite symmetry" as well as "coal black negresses in flowing white dresses and turbans of 'mouchoir de Madras' exhibiting their ivory dominos, [with an] insouciant walk with a white or creole." Frequently, the women were escorted by "white French gentlemen," both dressed richly in the West Indian fashion. Most of these Haitian refugees lived in the area around Second and Race streets.

The Life of Early Blacks

By 1832 the community had accumulated some wealth. James Forten was worth over $100,000 in that year. The foreman in a sail loft, Forten had taken over the business when the owner retired in 1798. He employed some forty men, both Black and white, and was well-known for the high quality of his sails. At the same time, some Blacks, barred from most commercial enterprises, transformed their roles as servants and cooks for wealthy whites into profitable catering businesses. We dominated the field for the rest of the nineteenth century. Among the most famous caterers was Thomas Dorsey, an escaped slave who was well-known for both the sumptuousness of his table and his financial support of the anti-slavery movement. Blacks were also carpenters, bakers, shoemakers, hairdressers, and mechanics. Many were sailors. In 1810, Black people accounted for ten percent of the city's people. But by 1870, immigration had so swelled the white population that the proportion of Blacks dropped to one thirty-third.

Thus most Blacks lived in abject poverty. An observer, toward the middle of the last century, said that they lived worse than slaves in the West Indies. He said, "No person can conceive of the wretchedness they exhibit." A Quaker study of the Black community in 1848 found dead bodies in "cold and exposed rooms and garrets." Black people sometimes lived in board shanties that were five or six feet high and "as many feet square." They were built on the bare ground, with the wind whistling through cracks in the boards and moisture dripping in. Sometimes the Africans stayed in "cold, wet, and damp cellars with naked walls." Hundreds lived by salvaging food from white people's garbage. This misery was concealed because the poor lived away from the streets, down dank alleys and in filth-laden backyards. The techniques of data gathering were primitive in those days, but statistics show that Blacks had a much higher death rate than whites and "this excess was due largely to bad housing and poor ventilation, consumption and diseases of the chest being the most effective cause."

From the outset, the law was different for Black and white people. As early as 1693, the police could pick up any Black man they found wandering around on Monday morning and whip him. By 1700, white Philadelphians had established a special court for Black people, free and slave, which operated until 1780. In short, Blacks could not vote, were subject to special courts, had no trial by jury, were under constant surveillance, had to carry passes, and had children taken from them to work for whites. If a free Black man made too much trouble, he was put back into slavery.

Pennsylvania was among the first states to outlaw slavery, and the Abolition Act of 1780 held that Blacks should be tried in the same court as whites. It also provided that emancipation be gradual. If you were born a slave before that time, you remained a slave. A slave's children were to be bound until the age of twenty-eight. The mass of Black Philadelphians were thus transformed from slaves into servants, and it was only after 1810 that a large class of free Blacks came into existence. But until the time of the Civil War, *any* Black person's life was precarious in Philadelphia. He or she could always be lured away or kidnapped into slavery.

But there was a strength and vitality in that community despite the oppression around it. One contemporary observer was impressed with the quickness and precision of Black Philadelphians' mathematical calculations and with their "great keenness and intelligence." The historian who has made the most detailed study of the early Black Philadelphians concluded that in the midst of hard trials they still managed to own homes, support their own schools, pay taxes, build churches, and create a viable community. The greatest tribute to them comes from a foreign commentary: "When I see a people pinioned by so many discouragements and bruised under such a complicated and heavy mass of difficulties as these colored people, steadily and surely elevating themselves over their circumstances . . . I am struck with a degree of admiration and amazement that I seldom feel on any other occasion, of the intrinsic strength and infinite tendencies of humanity."

James Forten, Sailmaker

James Forten was born in Philadelphia of a "father who had never worn the yoke." His great-grandfather had been brought from Africa as a slave, but his grandfather had accumulated enough money to purchase his own freedom. The father of James Forten served in the Revolutionary War. Forten himself was a drummer boy in that war, was taken prisoner, and put on board the "Jersey Prisonship." The British offered him his freedom if he would defect from the American side, and threatened to sell him into slavery in the West Indies should he refuse. Forten said, "No, no, I am here as a prisoner for the Liberties of my Country. I *never*, never shall prove a traitor to her interests." Many slaves flocked to the British cause, but Forten had experienced enough freedom to consider himself an American. Yet immediately after the war, he went to live in England for a year, and there became a dedicated abolitionist.

Forten grew into a successful man who declared, modestly, that he had "acquired property, and paid taxes in this city." He was African-featured, dark-hued, and physically courageous. On four occasions he pulled drowning people out of the Delaware near his sail loft. For those acts he was cited by the Humane Society. During the War of 1812, when Philadelphia was threatened by the British, Forten, along with Absalom Jones, enlisted twenty-five hundred Black men to help build defenses. Forten also helped organize a battalion of Blacks who were about to go to the front when peace was announced.

In 1800, Forten, along with Richard Allen and Absalom Jones, signed the Black Declaration of Independence, a petition urging Congress to modify the Fugitive Slave Act of 1793 and enact legislation to abolish slavery. Unlike some abolitionists, Forten declared the Black people equal to the white. He once asked whether ". . . the God who made the white man and the black left any record declaring us a different species." Forten provided the *Liberator* with twenty-seven subscriptions on the day before publication commenced; William Lloyd Garrison, its editor, later said that there would have been no paper without that "timely remittance" from Forten. With the support of Forten and others, Black people sustained the *Liberator* over the first three years of its existence and made up three-quarters of the total subscribers in April 1834. Only the "wealthy New York merchants, Arthur and Lewis Tappan" contributed more to the abolitionist movement than Forten.

Forten was a man of substance who lived handsomely, but dedicated his life to defeating slavery. His home was the Philadelphia center of abolitionists, white and Black. He neither smoked nor drank, and was said to be a "model man, one of nature's noblemen."

Richard Allen—From Slave to Bishop

In his portraits, Richard Allen looks like a man who, at the slightest provocation, would say, "Now, why did you do such a damn fool thing?" Wisdom is set deep in his eyes. He was born in 1760, a slave of Benjamin Chew, the attorney-general of Pennsylvania, who owned a beautiful estate called "Cliveden" (now an old folks home, surrounded by a Black community. The nearest church of his denomination, located in a converted movie theater, is the church of my South Carolina grandfather).

When Allen, whose mother was a mulatto, was seven years old, the attorney general sold him down into Delaware with his father, mother, and three siblings. So he was born into urban slavery and sold into rural slavery. As white Methodists sang and read the Bible, he learned to read. He persuaded his master that a religious person was a better worker, then convinced the man to set him free. The same master had already sold most of Richard Allen's family further south.

Once free, Richard Allen became an itinerant laborer, mule skinner, and preacher. He is believed to have been present at the meeting in 1784 where American Methodism began, and he was so well-known as a preacher that one of the founders of that church, Bishop Francis Asbury, asked Richard Allen to travel through the South with him. This offer Richard Allen declined, knowing better than to tempt the fates. He did, however, travel extensively through Delaware and Maryland, preaching the gospel to both Blacks and whites. He became sympathetic to the Methodist faith, which was natural since John Wesley, another of its founders, had vigorously attacked the slave trade. Yet Methodism was strongly entrenched among the slaveholders of the South. In February 1786, Allen came to Philadelphia, and by 1789 had been ordained as the first Black deacon of the Methodist church.

The founder of the A.M.E. Church has been described as an intelligent statesman who was "modest without timidity" and "brave without rashness." He urged Black people to labor with their hands, be honest, stay away from prostitutes, and "go not to the tavern; the song of the drunkard will soon be changed to weeping and wailing and gnashing of teeth." Richard Allen was generous and bought the Mother Bethel Church for his congregation with ten thousand dollars of his own money. He visited the prisons and the sick, and was like a prophet to the Black people of Philadelphia. Like most great leaders, he was fiercely independent and intolerant of those who did not share his vision. He placed the label "African" on the institutions he founded and fought to keep whites from gaining control of them. After his death in 1831 it was said that "No other African corpse, it is presumed, was ever attended to the place of interment in America by so great a number of more sincere mourners."

The African Methodist church grew rapidly. In the fifty years from 1826 to 1876, the churches grew in number from 33 to 1,833, and their membership from 8,000 to 200,000. Richard Allen knew that resisting white oppression in the church helped weaken its impact in the political sphere. As a historian has noted, if Luther and John Wesley were important figures in the struggle for religious freedom, then Richard Allen "was the apostle of human freedom."

Absalom Jones, a "Singular" Man

The third "founding father" of Black Philadelphia was Absalom Jones, born a slave in Delaware in 1746. When he was a child, whites made him wait on their table. Somehow he saved money and "bought" himself a primer. Reading became important to him and, as Jones declared, through it "I became singular." When he was eighteen years old, his master sold off Jones's mother, five brothers, and a sister, and the boy was brought to Philadelphia. There he was permitted to continue his learning in a night school. In 1770, he took a wife who was also a slave. He worked seven years for the money to buy her freedom, and after repeated supplications to his master, was himself freed in 1784.

Absalom Jones was forty-six when he became the pastor of St. Thomas African Episcopal Church. He was the strong right arm of Richard Allen, and was present at Allen's ordination to the bishopric of the A.M.E. Church. His influence remained local, unlike that of his mentor. He is said to have been a mild, heavy-set, dark-skinned man who often visited the sick. He hated the bondage of his people and warned the whites that if they loved their children they should not burden their heads with slavery. Forten, Allen, and Jones were the leaders of the Black community from its inception through 1830.

Robert Purvis, Black Abolitionist

Robert Purvis and William Still provided leadership to that same Black community in the somber years of struggle with slavery from 1830 until the Civil War. Purvis was a natural fighter for justice whose portraits show nothing but defiance. He looked white, was always impeccably groomed, and moved with style and class. Whittier said that he had "never seen a finer face or figure; and his manner, words, and bearing are in keeping." Purvis was born in Charleston, South Carolina, on November 4, 1810. His father was an Englishman who came to America about 1790 and became a cotton broker. His mother was the daughter of a German-Jewish flour merchant and an African woman who'd been born in Morocco in 1750, spirited into captivity at age twelve, and sold in Charleston. Somehow the African woman achieved freedom and married the Jewish merchant. In 1819, the father of Robert Purvis sent the whole family to Philadelphia. The old man died in 1826, leaving an estate of over $120,000. Purvis was privately schooled, then went to Pittsfield Academy and, briefly, to Amherst College. He was a charter member, at age twenty-three, of the American Anti-Slavery Society and gave freely to Garrison's *Liberator*. He joined the American Moral Reform Society in 1835 and two years later was in Harrisburg, Pennsylvania, for the formation of the Pennsylvania Anti-Slavery Society.

Purvis married Harriet Forten, the daughter of James Forten and herself a strong force in the antislavery movement. Thus, from the outset, Philadelphia and South Carolina were linked. Once, when Purvis applied for a passport, it was denied on the grounds that he was not an American citizen, even though he was freeborn. President Andrew Jackson saw to it that the passport was issued.

Purvis used all means, both legal and illegal, to combat the enemies of his people. He formed the Vigilant Committee in August 1837, composed mainly of Black men who were pledged to help slaves on their way to Canada. In 1840, he voted along with the majority to have the few remaining whites on that committee removed. When white rioters in 1842 made Purvis's home a target of their assault, he moved to a country estate outside Philadephia where his "horses, and carriages, and his personal attendance, were ever at the service of underground railroad members." His home was a place where, the abolitionists said, " 'the wicked cease from troubling and the weary are at rest.' " Purvis was called the "Father of the Underground Railroad" and according to William Still, his successor, he could always be counted in, no matter how dangerous the task.

William Still, Underground Railroad Conductor

William Still himself was cut from the same cloth. He was born in Burlington, New Jersey, the youngest of eighteen children, and received no formal education. At twenty-three he arrived in Philadelphia with five dollars in his pocket, and three years later, in 1847, he obtained a clerkship in the Pennsylvania Anti-Slavery Society. He occupied this post for fourteen years and was, in the time before the Civil War, the president of the Philadelphia branch of the Underground Railroad. Still had great physical courage. He and five willing Black porters once rescued a slave woman from a ship in the harbor; he was arrested for this act. When federal troops were in hot pursuit of the remnants of John Brown's brave band, Still took the fugitives into his own home. When Brown's family came grieving to Philadelphia on the eve of his execution, Still took these strangers in. Virtue has its own reward: in 1850 one of the persons whom Still rescued was his own brother, who "had been separated from his mother, when a child of only six years."

After the battle against slavery was over, Still went into business, yet he remained active in the political affairs of Black people. He donated money to the Black home for the aged in Philadelphia. A Presbyterian, Still wrote *The Underground Railroad*, which remains the best work on that subject. In the preface, he says that he wrote the book so that "the race must not forget the rock from whence they were hewn, nor the pit whence they were digged."

O. V. Catto, Scholar and Activist

During the Civil War, O. V. Catto, the offspring of an elite Black family of Charleston, South Carolina, became the leader of Philadelphia's Black community. Catto's father was William T. Catto, a Presbyterian minister who came to Philadelphia in 1844 when his son was five years old. He eventually became the pastor of the First African Presbyterian Church, of which William Still was a member. O. V. Catto was educated at segregated Black schools, and was a graduate of the Institute for Colored Youth, the nation's first Black high school, where he won high honors at his graduation two years before the Civil War began. In June 1863, when the Rebels threatened Gettysburg, he followed the Philadelphia Black tradition and formed a company of students to join the Union army. They were sent to Harrisburg, issued equipment, and were about to leave for Gettysburg when the army refused to induct them because of their color. Catto later became a major in the First Division of the Pennsylvania National Guard.

O. V., an athlete, believed in "his right to act independently and to forcefully push for improvement of the conditions of Blacks." Whites thought him arrogant for he "always contended that the Black man was equal to the white man in all respects and [that] Blacks could and would eventually be leaders in the nation." He was shot by white political assassins in 1871 because he would not be denied the right to vote and sought to inspire people to do the same.

One who was close to these leaders and to those around them said: "They were truly a spartan band, the colored men and women. . . . These same men stood guard for weeks on end to protect Mother Bethel Church from white pillagers and set up their own trolley lines when the whites refused to let them ride on the trolley car." It is no shame to be called an "Old Philadelphian."

Chapter 4

THE BLACK CHURCH

The Lord is my light and my salvation; whom shall I fear?
The Lord is the strength of my life; of whom shall I be
afraid?

Psalm 27:1

The church and its leaders were the center of Black Philadelphia. Men, weary from work, came at night to paint the walls of the churches. Women spent time and money buying flowers so that the sanctuary might glorify God. And the little ones, dressed in their best, learned ethics there on Sunday mornings. On the journey of exploration into the roots of the modern Black community, the church stands squarely by the roadside.

The Church and the Free African Society

Both the Black Protestant Episcopal Church and the African Methodist Episcopal Church derive from the Free African Society, established by Black Philadelphia families who had come together to aid one another, and then coalesced into larger units. Eventually a Black consciousness emerged. On April 12, 1787, the Free African Society's founders, among whom were Absalom Jones and Richard Allen—the "Free Africans, and their descendants of Philadelphia in the state of Pennsylvania"—proclaimed the goal of uplifting themselves and all Black people. W.E.B. DuBois, in his classic study of Philadelphia's Black community, called this act to be "the first wavering step of a people toward organized social life." These African men, DuBois claimed, had a vision of a society that would function as a substitute for the African tribe. The society, which regulated marriages, taught thrift, and attempted to improve the morals of its members, was the forerunner of similar organizations in Newport, Boston, New York, and Charleston, South Carolina. The treasurer of the Free African Society was Joseph Clark, who was white and a Quaker. His successor, by the rules of the society, was always to be a Quaker.

The critical impetus to the founding of the first Black church occurred in November of the year of the founding of the Free African Society. One Sunday morning, as Absalom Jones and others knelt at prayer in St. George's Methodist Church, an usher asked them to move. Jones replied: "Wait until prayer is over, and I will get up and trouble you no more." The Black men then departed the white house of worship. Richard Allen then tells us " . . .we all went out of the church in a body and they were no more plagued by us in the church. Notwithstanding we had subscribed largely toward the furnishing of St. George's Church." These Black men were able "to soar out of their slavery and recognize immediately that they had to assume an attitude of freedom and take on the characteristics of men conscious of invaded rights." They already had prepared an organization that would help build their own place of worship. The whites became angry with the Free African Society, charging its leaders with draining money from the white church by soliciting funds for their own church. But the Free African Society held its ground. Its first church, called plainly the "African Church," had words from the prophet Isaiah carved on its doors: "The People Who Walked in Darkness Have Seen a Great Light."

The First African Church Is Founded

A decision about the new church's denomination had to be made. Both Absalom Jones and Richard Allen wanted to affiliate with the Methodists. But the Free African Society voted to become Episcopalian and asked Richard Allen to become the first priest, a post he declined. Absalom Jones sublimated his preference to the will of the body and agreed to head the church. Allen, on his part, agreed to defer the soliciting of funds for a Methodist church until the new African Church, St. Thomas, had finished its subscription.

A spirit of cooperation permeated many of the activities of these first Black American statesmen. Cyrus Bustill was "the first to relinquish his claim on the old [Free African] society in behalf of the church." He was born in Burlington, New Jersey, and "traced his ancestry back to a powerful Indian tribe." He bore the mark of the tribe on his ear, and his son and a daughter participated in the Underground Railroad. His daughter, like him a Quaker, finally left the Quakers, saying, " . . . in proportion as we [Blacks] become intellectual and respectable, so in proportion does their Quaker disgust and prejudices." The first man to renounce his share of money in order to build the first African Church was the great-great-grandfather of Paul Robeson.

The congregation of the newly created St. Thomas paid a price for having Absalom Jones as rector. The rulers of the white Episcopal body to which the church belonged said that Absalom Jones was unqualified to become a priest since he did not know Latin and Greek. If the Blacks insisted on having their "kind friend and helper" as their minister, the African Church could not have any role in the "general government of the Episcopal Church." Arguing that Jones's spirit of love and self-sacrifice was more important than knowledge of ancient languages, the people of St. Thomas accepted him as their reader and deacon. The Episcopal church, long after the death of Jones, continued to exclude St. Thomas from any voice in the affairs of their church. It didn't matter how many languages the succeeding priests knew.

The establishment of St. Thomas raised even more serious problems for the future condition of Black people. Elitism was implicit in the founding of the church. Adam Clayton Powell later said that a Black person who was not a Methodist or Baptist had lost the African heritage. And, indeed, the founders of the church were aware that they were patterning themselves after what one of our church historians—in all seriousness—called "the very best and holiest of the white race within their midst." There was a deep-seated antipathy in the members of the Free African Society toward dance and song. In a letter to the Boston chapter, they had said that Black people needed to stop partying and that "it was a shameful practice that we, as a people, are particularly guilty of. While we are feasting and dancing many of our complexion are starving under cruel bondage; and it is this practice of ours that enables our enemies to declare that we are not fit for freedom." Implicit in their argument was the assumption that all would be well if all Blacks acted like whites.

In 1862, the Reverend William Douglass, long-time priest of St. Thomas, said, "Whatever of taste, order, and intelligence being now discovered among the various colored churches here may in a great degree be treated to the stimulating influence of St. Thomas. It stood alone at one time in favor of the education of the ministry and people." The rector admitted that Episcopalianism was not for all Black people. He expressed the hope that someday the emotional needs of the Black masses would fade and that they would become "honest and candid worshippers after truth." In 1900, W.E.B. DuBois declared that St. Thomas Church reflected favorably upon Black intelligence and that despite its aristocratic tone, "the church has nevertheless always been foremost in good work." Indeed, the church was active in establishing schools for Blacks. A school was attached to it from 1804 to 1816. The officers of the first Black insurance company in this country, founded in 1810, were either deacons or vestrymen of St. Thomas.

Influence of Episcopalians and Presbyterians

Although sometimes labeled the "Black bourgeoisie," the truth about the Presbyterians and Episcopalians is more complicated. Many of their ministers were socially conscious. For example, Peter Williams, the first ordained Black Episcopal priest and rector of St. Phillips in New York, was universally recognized as a champion of oppressed Black people. He contributed money willingly to those in need. The great bishop of the African Methodist Episcopal Church, Daniel Payne, tells how, upon his arrival as a youth in New York he saw Williams give tuition money to a poor Black student. "The Reverend Mr. Williams handed to this interesting lad a ten-dollar bank-note, expressing regret at his inability at that time to give more, and promising more assistance at a future day." The spontaneity of Williams's act so impressed Payne that he was touched in the "depths of his soul."

Let Payne tell what happened: "I said to myself: 'Can I also aid him?' I had then but forty dollars in my pocket—all the money I had in the world . . . [but] I took out my purse and gave him two Spanish silver dollars." Later that night, Williams took Daniel Payne—fresh from his native South Carolina—to his first antislavery meeting.

The young man Payne and Williams had helped was Alexander Crummell, the great Black nationalist thinker and founder of the American Negro Academy, who also became an Episcopal priest. Crummell argued that "for men, for societies, for races, for nations, the one living and abiding thing is *character*." With character, Black people would become great. Crummell said in one of his sermons that "While for two hundred and forty years the brutal hand of violence has been at the black man's throat, God has been neither blind nor quiet. . . ." and predicted that this tragic play would end itself "in the lapse of time when the hour is come."

The Episcopal church's influence spread to other parts of the country. In 1824, Peter Levington, ordained by Absalom Jones at St. Thomas, founded the first African Church in the South—the St. James First African Church in Maryland. When he found that the free Blacks there were against mingling in worship with the slaves, his burdens were "greatly aggravated," but he put down the revolt against his policy of mixed worship. It should be recorded that a white bishop aided him in this struggle. William Douglass, the future rector of St. Thomas, was trained and ordained in Levington's church. The St. James Society became a replica of the Free African Society and a point of unification for all Black people in the city.

Frederick Douglass protested against the refusal of St. Thomas to permit the church to be used for antislavery speeches. But the men and women of St. Thomas were actively engaged in the Underground Railroad. History has not left us a record as to why they refused Douglass a lectern, but it was against their policy to hold antislavery meetings in that church.

Richard Allen Founds the A.M.E. Church

The African Methodist Episcopal Church (A.M.E.) emerged from the Philadelphia community at the same time as St. Thomas. The A.M.E. Church was, for a long time, the shield of Black people in their time of trouble and their shelter from the stormy night. No organization has been more central to the history of Black Americans. W.E.B. DuBois called it "by long odds the vastest and most remarkable product of American Negro civilisation."

The founding of the A.M.E. Church was the result of Richard Allen's belief that Methodism was a denomination more suited to the mass of Black people than Episcopalianism. As he said, "The plain and simple gospel suits best for the people; for the unlearned can understand and the learned are sure to understand." He further believed that the discipline of Methodism would be good for Black people. Douglass, the pastor of St. Thomas, agreed that Methodism appealed "chiefly to the feelings and affectations . . . which are always strongest among undisciplined minds." Allen stated that the reading of sermons would never be as effective or helpful to Black people as extemporaneous sermons.

The very strengths of the A.M.E. Church became points of controversy. The twin issues of literacy and emotionalism agitated the church and its leaders throughout the nineteenth century. Some forms of African religion and culture—frequently manifested in song and dance—survived in the United States. Moreover, the destruction of the tribe and the family, and the almost universal prohibition against teaching Southern slaves to read, meant that many Black people did not share the values and styles of European culture. Yet the survival of the African people in the United States depended on their ability to assimilate the techniques and skills of those who had enslaved them.

No Black leader more clearly demonstrated this contradiction than the great Daniel Payne, bishop of the A.M.E. Church and the most influential leader of the church during its period of growth after the Civil War. Trained as a Presbyterian, Payne chose to go into the A.M.E. Church because that's where the people were. He said that he would rather educate his people than be the great Black novelist Alexandre Dumas or even Napoleon. Indeed, he testified that when he was young he had received a message from God saying, "I have set thee apart to educate thyself in order that thou mayest be an educator to thy people." Payne battled for an educated ministry in the A.M.E. Church. At a church conference in 1844 he introduced a resolution calling for educational requirements for ministers. Payne's resolution was defeated, but it was later carried under the influence of Bishop Morris Brown, himself illiterate, but "by nature sagacious, and therefore large-hearted; so that without education his common sense always led him to give a hearty endorsement to it." Payne felt that an "enlightened ministry" would be the instrument of Black liberation. Looking about him, he said, "O, my God, what a work is yet to be done."

Payne told one woman going off to teach in Washington that she had best be prepared to be burned by two fires, the Black and the white. Payne was singed by that fire many times. When bishop, he removed a minister at Mother Bethel Church who refused to permit a white woman to join the congregation.

Payne felt that all persons were equal before God. This same attitude lead him to declare that Martin Delany, the great Black nationalist, had permitted his love of his people to override his love of humanity.

Payne struggled constantly against African traditions in the church. He would not let worshippers sing their "spiritual songs," arguing that they were "corn-field ditties" and had no place in the church. Yet his denial of the songs meant denial of the people themselves. In 1878 Payne attended a "bush" prayer meeting where the worshippers formed a ring, took off their coats, and proceeded to have a good time, with African hand clapping and foot pounding, something that Payne elsewhere called "Fist and Heel" worshipping. The bishop told them to stop. They did, but since the spirit was upon them, they rocked slowly and rhythmically for the next fifteen minutes, singing. Payne told them they were a disgrace to the race and the Christian faith. They told Payne that God acted upon different people in different ways and that "at camp meeting, there must be a ring here, a ring there, a ring over yonder, or sinners will not be converted." (The reader may recall that in Philadelphia on African feast days each tribe danced in its own ring.)

Payne declared that the church would be better off without such worship and that ministers who perpetuated this "fanaticism" were "intensely religious, but grossly immoral." However, attempts to ban such ceremonies drove many worshippers out of the church.

The A.M.E. Church Takes Root

Mother Bethel, the first African Methodist church, was founded by Richard Allen in 1794 as a place of worship for "descendants of the African race." Some of the Blacks who remained in the segregated St. George's Church charged those who left with segregating themselves. The white Methodists attempted to maintain both religious and physical control over Mother Bethel, but it was a confused situation. They hoped to control the Blacks, but did not want them to be part of the governing structure of the white Methodist church. The Blacks, on the other hand, wanted to remain Methodists, but with total autonomy over their church affairs, thus not conforming to usual Methodist procedures. It was not until 1807 that the Bethelites received the right to "nominate and appoint" Black preachers for themselves. By 1813, effort to exercise this right had so galled the white Methodists that they attempted to force preachers onto the congregation. There were physical confrontations in which white preachers were not permitted to enter the pulpit and, finally, in 1816 the Bethelites won a court case recognizing their right to exist as an independent denomination.

Strong reasons existed for keeping Bethel an all-Black church; it was an Underground Railroad station. It was also the chief meeting place of the Blacks of Philadelphia. Mother Bethel's commitment to the struggle was its trademark. One night an escaped slave who had just arrived in Philadelphia went to the church and hid himself in a corner. Standing there, he heard a hymn with words like, "He delivered them when bound, healed their wounds, and turned their darkness into light." Surely thrust by the song back into the darkness from whence he had come, he heard still another hymn and then a sermon declaring that the Lord was good, and that his mercies endured forever. Whereupon the slave got up, praised God, shook off the chains on his mind, walked into the light, and joined the congregation of Mother Bethel.

The pastors of that church, sometimes brave men, sometimes a little bit scared, sheltered Africans escaping from the South. And sometimes they went South to help slaves to escape: "In certain parts of Maryland, camp meetings were allowed, and each year several of our Methodist ministers would go down for the ostensible business of soul-saving, but more to get men and women their freedom. The men especially active in this manner were the Reverend Clayton Durham, Walter Proctor, and Joseph Cox. In the course of years of such pilgrimages, scores of the enslaved were piloted to freedom." Sarah Allen, the wife of Richard, was famous for her courage in "harboring runaways, a dangerous and illegal activity . . . but she continued to do it, donating her time, money, and the protection of her home." There is a Sarah Allen Club today in most A.M.E. churches. Moreover, churches in Philadelphia, as in other major cities, were constantly put to use as meeting places for Blacks engaged in antislavery agitation and Underground Railroad activities. Quinn Chapel, the major A.M.E. Church in Chicago, was a "conspicuous example of providing accommodations for fugitives." Some churches held monthly prayer meetings for slaves, and in others, the pastors used the "greetings of welcome . . . to include runaway slaves." Other Philadelphia churches also participated. Thus, on December 28, 1843, a meeting to establish an Underground Railroad committee took place in the First Presbyterian Church in Philadelphia.

The refusal of whites to let us worship with them had resulted, by the early 1800s, in the formation of independent Black churches in such places as Baltimore and Wilmington, Delaware. By 1816, Methodist societies of Free Africans had been organized also in Attleborough, Pennsylvania, and Salem, New Jersey. Word-of-mouth communication about the "African" churches and pressure by the whites created a Black religious movement that insisted upon its own autonomy. Many of these congregations came together in 1816 in Philadelphia to form officially the African Methodist Episcopal Church and to consecrate Richard Allen as its first bishop.

Allen's consecration was a compromise on the potentially divisive issue of skin color. The delegates initially elected Daniel Coker of Baltimore, a light-skinned mulatto, as their first bishop. But several Black men objected, and he stood down in favor of Richard Allen. Bishop Payne, in his memoirs, stated that color consciousness was so important that Richard Allen, some ten years later, appointed a light-skinned man, Morris Brown, a bishop, and Morris Brown later appointed Edward Waters, a man of black skin. Posts of power were allocated so as to minimize differences.

From 1816 on, the A.M.E. Church spread as rapidly as America's frontiers. Branches of this church were formed in

48

Princeton, Trenton, and Woodbury, New Jersey; New Hope, Pennsylvania; and Bridgeport, Connecticut; then it swept up to White Plains, New York, and to Bedford, Massachusetts, with its large population of sea-going Blacks.

You can see what Richard Allen accomplished if you go up to Mount Gilead A.M.E. Church in Bucks County, Pennsylvania, the last stop on the Underground Railroad before runaways were transported across the Delaware River into New Jersey. In the graveyards of St. Paul's A.M.E. Church in Bellefonte, Pennsylvania, carved on the memorial stones, are the names of Black warriors dead in the liberation of Wilmington, North Carolina, and Petersburg, Virginia, from the slaveholders during the Civil War. And in the A.M.E. Church in Hopewell Village, Pennsylvania, also an Underground Railroad post, you can see names in the graveyard like "Black Kuba" or "Man of Color." Richard Allen's genius is in the Bethel A.M.E. Church of Pottstown, Pennsylvania, where there is a memorial to one of the first men wounded in the Civil War, a Black man. And it is also in the Mount Zion A.M.E. Church in Danville, Pennsylvania, the setting of Toni Morrison's *The Song of Solomon* and the church before the Civil War of my Susquehanna riverboatman great-great-grandfather. Today, the sun does not set on Richard Allen's church.

An important branch of the A.M.E. Church was established in Charleston, South Carolina. By 1821, the branch was brought under the official jurisdiction of the Philadelphia Conference of the A.M.E. Church. By 1822, under the leadership of Morris Brown, the Charleston congregation was up to three thousand, very close in numbers to the membership in Philadelphia. Brown, born free and by trade a shoemaker, helped many slaves to purchase their freedom, and was jailed for a year for "too great sympathy with the slaves." When Denmark Vesey's plot to overthrow the slaveholders was aborted in 1822, the A.M.E. Church was implicated and Brown had to flee to Philadelphia. He was made a bishop there in 1828.

In the territories west of the Alleghenies, Bishop Paul Quinn almost singlehandedly planted the flag of African Methodism. Out of Quinn's efforts, for example, Richard Cain, later A.M.E.

bishop and congressman from South Carolina, was converted at Portsmouth, Ohio. Cain received his education at Wilberforce, Ohio, and honed his leadership skills by serving in the mountains of Pennsylvania, including Danville, in the church of my ancestors. After the Civil War, Cain organized the Black community of South Carolina during the Reconstruction. Another branch of African Methodism, the A.M.E. Zion Church, became a separate denomination in 1822.

The first Black Presbyterian church was also established in Philadelphia. It, too, achieved its independence against the wishes of the white governing body. The founding pastor of the First African Presbyterian Church was the Reverend John Gloucester, a friend of Richard Allen and the father of four Presbyterian ministers. This church, founded in 1807 at Seventh and Bainbridge streets, was also a center of Underground Railroad resistance. It was the church of William Still. After the Civil War, its rolls included the names of Chris Perry, the founder of the *Philadelphia Tribune*, and Louisa Bustill, the mother of Paul Robeson.

The white Methodists organized a Black mission in 1794, which developed by 1797 into the Zoar Methodist Episcopal Church, the forerunner of the Black Methodist churches that remained within the white fold. The First African Baptist Church was founded in 1809. Thus by 1825 a full range of churches had been created in Philadelphia, as was also the case in Boston and New York.

Clear social distinctions existed among those churches. DuBois noted, toward the end of the nineteenth century, that "At St. Thomas one looks for the well-to-do Philadelphians . . . cold and reserved to strangers or newcomers; at Central Presbyterian . . . the older, simpler set of respectable Philadelphians; at Bethel . . . the best of the great laboring class—steady, honest people; at Union Baptist . . . Virginia servant girls and their young men." And, a survey of the churches admittedly based on incomplete data, showed skin complexion was lightest among the Presbyterians and the Episcopalians. But close to forty percent of the Episcopalians were dark complexioned, and better off financially than their light fellow worshippers. By the 1840s, the Baptist churches seemed to have become identified with migrants arriving from the South.

But, again, there seemed to be cooperation. The men and women of the various churches joined together in antislavery activities, literary activities, and sports. And some old announcements tell us that in 1889 the Sunday schools of St. Thomas, Central Presbyterian, and Allen Chapel A.M.E. all went on a picnic together, and that in 1895, the Wesley A.M.E. Zion, First African Presbyterian, Cherry Street Baptist, and St. Thomas Protestant Episcopal Sunday school children did the same thing.

A Black person unaffiliated with a church was likely to be poor. Nonmembers were cut off from a wide range of church activities that could sustain them in a hostile environment. The churches were centers of benevolent societies, learning, contacts with those who knew the city, and in some cases—if Mother Bethel is a good example—regulation of the morals of the congregation. Intoxication and adultery were censured, and suspensions and expulsions from the church could result from continued misbehavior.

Certainly, as DuBois noted, the churches represented a substitute for the shattered African tribe and family. And their establishment resulted, as George Freeman Bragg, Jr., the historian of the Episcopal church, once wrote, in nothing less than the assertion of the "manhood of the black man."

Chapter 5

BLACK EDUCATION

Wisdom is the principal thing; therefore get wisdom: and with all thy getting get understanding.

Proverbs 4:7

The cohesiveness and vitality of the early Philadelphia Black community was due to its early access to education. That access was limited compared to what the whites enjoyed, but it was like a feast compared to the opportunities available to those in rural slavery. For education was the key to African survival here. Mastery over technology, self-defense, and the creation of a collective Black identity were all dependent, to some extent, upon the written word.

First Schools for Black Pupils

We know that Blacks were educated in Philadelphia as early as 1722 and that Anthony Benezet, the Quaker, held a school for Black students in his home in 1750. In the late 1770s, his school was a vital influence in the education of Philadelphia Blacks. By 1789, Quakers had founded the "Society for the Free Instruction of Orderly Blacks and People of Color," an evening school. Many Black women also received an education, and by 1797 some three hundred Black students of both sexes were enrolled in a total of seven Black schools. Attendance at the schools was sometimes low because "of the danger which at times beset any Negro who ventured at a distance from his home after dark."

Unequal from the Outset

From the beginning, our people received little in the way of public education. In 1820, even though the law said that Black students—like the white poor for whom the first public schools were intended—should be educated, school officials refused to appropriate monies for what would have been segregated academies. They finally opened the first public Black school in 1828, both because of a decline in the enrollment of poor whites, and because the Black crime rate had risen, and the city fathers felt—a then prevalent belief—that it was more cost efficient to educate Blacks than to put them in jail.

The schools the Black people received were then, as now, leftovers. Black schoolchildren studied in buildings that had already been used by whites. Likewise, their schools were frequently staffed by teachers who had been cast off from the white schools. One Black woman said that the Blacks had "instructors, who if placed in any other than a coloured school, would hardly be considered earning their salt; but we must be silent, as anyone who possesses a few qualifications is . . . fit to keep a school for us . . . conscious of the unequal advantages enjoyed by your children, we feel indignant against those who are continually vituperating us for the ignorant degradation of our people."

All the teachers in the Black schools were white, and staff turnover was high. By 1838, every white school had an abundance of teachers and assistant teachers, while the Black school had one teacher for 149 boys and two teachers for 251 girls. Nor could we feel secure about receiving an education. In 1840, the public authorities almost shut down the Black schools. Only the strong protests of James Forten prevented this from happening. Black education terminated in the eighth grade. When the first public high school was established in 1837, Blacks were not permitted to enroll in it.

In 1854, for the first time, segregation was legalized if twenty or more Blacks were in a school. The previous informal system of segregation was thus now made formal, the law creating a separate and unequal education. Black schools were only to stay open four months a year, a much shorter time than the white schools.

The official creation of separate schools led to a movement among Black Philadelphians for Black teachers for their children. It also enhanced the growing sense of isolation of the Black community and its consequent drive for autonomy. A historian of the Philadelphia Black school movement indicates that only in Philadelphia of all the Northern cities did the Black community voluntarily accept segregation after 1900. One explanation might be a sense of Black nationalism and self-help that dated back to the eighteenth century.

The Black Community Creates Its Own Schools

Philadelphia Blacks were never content to leave the education of their children to the whites. Soon after the founding of Mother Bethel, a school was established on its premises. St. Thomas also had a school for Black children.

Several excellent private schools were established. One was run by Sarah Mapp Douglass, one of the Bustill family, a member of the Anti-Slavery Society and the same woman who had denounced the Quakers for their racial intolerance. A second school, founded in 1850, was headed by Margaretta Forten, the recording secretary of the Philadelphia Anti-Slavery Society, and a daughter of James Forten. A third school was that of Amelia Bogle, probably a relative of the Philadelphia caterer of that name. There were several other such schools, the most famous being Adam Driver's school, founded in 1850, which had almost fifty students.

Of the Black school population just before the Civil War,

about 1,000 students were in public schools, 748 in charity schools, and some 350 in private schools. The private schools, all Black, were generally the best, so Philadelphia Blacks early identified Black schools as being superior to white. Both the future Bishop Payne and Alexander Crummell taught in those schools at one time. Thus the Black elite, privileged to have their children either with tutors or in private schools with such teachers as Sarah Mapp Douglass, were being separated from poor Blacks even while creating autonomous Black institutions.

Black America's First High School

Indeed, the Douglass school was a preparatory school for the capstone of Philadelphia Black education, the Institute for Colored Youth, the first Black high school in the country. The institute, called for short the ICY, had a faculty that was all Black and highly qualified. Philadelphia's Black community, out of its own degradation, had created an autonomous school system that ran from kindergarten to high school.

The Institute for Colored Youth demands our special attention for its character, and the students it graduated were responsible both for the intellectual tradition of Black Philadelphia and, to a large extent, of modern Black America. It was nearly as influential in the creation of an intellectual tradition as was the A.M.E. Church in the creation of a Black religion. The institute was the result of a bequest by Richard Humphreys, a Philadelphia Quaker and an ex-West Indian slaveholder, in 1832. Blacks had approached the Quakers with a plan for a combined academic and vocational high school. Under the terms of the agreement, the Quakers agreed to supply the money and the Blacks to supply the teachers. Founded in 1837 and chartered in 1842, the institute was first located on a farm outside of Philadelphia. Its real beginning was in 1852, when it was moved to the heart of the Black district at Sixth and Lombard streets. The first teacher hired, in 1849, was Ishmael Locke, grandfather of Alain Locke, who was closely identified with the Harlem Renaissance.

The ICY had strong leadership in its successive principals, Charles A. Reason, Ebenezer Basset, and Fanny Coppin. The first principal at the Lombard Street location was Reason, born in New York, and the son of Haitian immigrants. He was a onetime professor of mathematics at the New York Central College, had been rejected from theological seminary on the basis of his color, and was such an outstanding teacher that Bishop Payne said that he had visited "many schoolrooms in the United States and in foreign lands, and closely watched the methods of many teachers, but I have seldom met his equal, never his superior." Reason was active in the Underground Railroad, a contributor of funds to Black causes and a poet who, bidding people to become active, said: "Then up! Awake! Nor let dull slumber waste your soul's devotion! Life doth bid you haste! The captive in his hut, with watchful ear, awaits the sweet triumphant song to hear, that shall proclaim the glorious jubilee when crippled thousands shall in truth be free."

Reason was succeeded by Ebenezer Basset, a graduate of Connecticut Normal School, who was "especially successful in the coaching of mathematics and classics in which he had excelled while a student at Yale" in 1854 and 1855. He was a strong believer in Black teachers for Black schools, as was O. V. Catto who, while a teacher at the ICY, said that he had "long been of the belief that no white man could so well instruct colored children as could a colored teacher." From 1869 to 1879, Basset was a consul to Haiti and was so highly thought of that he was invited to lecture on the "Right of Asylum" at the Yale Law School. Fanny Coppin, the principal of the ICY over the last third of the century, was born a slave, educated at Oberlin, and so dedicated that her name appears on practically every leaflet sponsoring any Black cause in Philadelphia during her tenure in office.

The ICY's curriculum emphasized the classics. Final exams were given in Latin, algebra, geometry, physiology, and trigonometry (plane and spherical). In 1867, the students were asked to write on such subjects as the "Rosetta Stone," "Rome Under Augustus," "Radicalism vs. Conservatism," and the salutory at the graduation was delivered in Latin by Pliny I.Locke, the father of Alain Locke. A child named "Toussaint L. Martin" read her own poem at the commencement exercise.

The ICY was both a center of Black activism and creativity. In 1862, J. Q. Allen and Jacob White, Jr., graduates of the institute, were appointed to the Robert Vaux School where White, as principal, proceeded to build the first Black public school with Black teachers. By 1890, three-quarters of all the Black teachers in the Philadelphia and Camden area were graduates of the institute. That school was the key to the entry of Blacks into the school system and the basis for a semi-autonomous Black public school system.

The tone of the ICY curriculum was moralistic, revolutionary, and deeply steeped in Black nationalism. The ICY was, of necessity, organized in isolation from the Black masses and under the influence of Haitian Black nationalists—some of whom had come to Philadelphia in the aftermath of the revolutionary upheavals in that country—Underground Railroad fighters, and antislavery activists. The graduates of the school who went into the South during the Reconstruction taught the Black students there about the greatness of Africa and the revolutionary heroism of Toussaint L'Ouverture. They taught different subjects to the Black children in the South than the New England schoolmarms did.

By any measure, the ICY produced an extraordinary crop of graduates. Their graduation pictures show that most of their faces are black in color, not light-bright. Alain Locke's father taught at the ICY, then graduated from Howard Law School before entering the civil service. The first Black graduates of the University of Pennsylvania, including William Hodge Adger, who "by his scholarly and moral deportment made it possible for the door to remain open to members of his race," were ICY students. The men and women who went on to build fine public schools in Brooklyn, New York, Princeton, Newark, Camden, and North Woodbury, New Jersey, were graduates of the ICY. The list also includes the names of those who became ministers to Haiti, Liberia, and organizers of the National Black Academy. Meta Warrick Fuller, one of the first Black sculptors, was a graduate of the institute, as was a doctor named Abele, who ". . . in the examination before the Pennsylvania State Board . . . obtained an average of ninety-seven and three-tenths, the highest known." He was a lineal descendant of Absalom Jones. A famous teacher was Robert Campbell, who was born in the West Indies and taught at the ICY for five years before going to Africa with Martin Delany to explore the Niger Valley. His book about that journey, *My Motherland*, attracted widespread attention.

The graduates of the ICY so dominated the Black Philadelphia system that some schools were almost totally staffed with descendants of old Black Philadelphia families. The ICY graduates, then, were the foundation of the Black teaching corps that was in place in Philadelphia when the migrants swept in from the South. Jacob White, Jr.,'s Robert Vaux School also made an important contribution to Black education in Philadelphia, and was a major supplier of Black teachers to the South in the period after the Civil War. Henry O. Tanner, the artist who painted the picture of an old gray-haired man teaching a child how to play a banjo, was a graduate of that school.

Another school, named Ashmun Institute by its Presbyterian founders, was incorporated in 1854 and began admitting students in 1856. Later called Lincoln University, it, too, had an important impact on Black Philadelphia. By 1900, there were seven Black schools in Philadelphia, five of which were staffed by Black teachers. Philadelphia Blacks had a literacy rate of eighty percent.

Literary Clubs Supplement Formal Education

The education that went on in the classrooms was supplemented by an extensive network of literary societies directed toward the intellectual uplifting of Black people. William Carl Bolivar said, "Our men and women were fired by a tremendous ambition, and equipped themselves so as to be ready for any opening wherein a defense of their race might be necessary." The free people of Philadelphia were once again pioneers in the creation of Black institutions. Historian Dorothy Porter believes that these literary societies were of such importance as to have had an effect on the total educational progress of African people in America.

Nothing came easy to those early Philadelphians. They pointed out that some American whites had the leisure and the wealth that permitted them to make a cult out of literary appreciation, but that Black people were poor and had to work for a living and this "alienated them from the habits and necessities of literary men." They understood that the training of the mind required time, discipline, and immersion in the "dryness and insipidness" of often dull writing. They knew that at the end of a hard day's labor with their hands it would be difficult to concentrate on intellectual matters and therefore they could not expect "in keeping with the laws of nature to make more than a decent resemblance to a literary society." But they washed themselves up after work and came out to literary meetings because they felt that Black people needed a literary tradition. One of these people said that if not tied to action, intellectual training would be a waste. Its true aim was to make us women and men who could be faithful to the burdens history put upon us. Be faithful, said this founder of a Black school in Brooklyn, to yourself, to your people, and to your God, and you will rest in the enjoyment of a rich by-and-by.

A white observer of one society was struck by the "acuteness of reasoning, and . . . elevation and elegance of language." He further noted that members talked about issues that concerned Black people and knew the power of a just cause buttressed by a united people. The emphasis on combating injustice was not unusual. For example, the Moral Reform Society's preamble began: "We have observed that in no country under Heaven have the descendents of an *ancestry* once enrolled in the history of fame, whose glittering monuments stood forth as beacons, disseminating light and knowledge to the uttermost parts of the earth, been reduced to such degrading servitude as that under which we labor from the effect of *American slavery* and *American prejudice*." They were keenly aware of their mission.

A large number of Black literary societies flourished in Philadelphia in the first half of the nineteenth century. One of the first meetings on record is of a society sponsoring William Whipper, a Black Underground Railroad man, in a lecture at Mother Bethel Church. In 1838, the Library Company had a six-hundred-volume library and its one hundred and fifty members met in the basement of St. Thomas Church. Another society monitored the education of Blacks in the schools and wrote histories of the literary societies so that a "historical record of the instruments that were used to elevate the colored people" would exist. One such record, the carefully penned minutes of the Banneker Institute—one of the most influential societies—was kept by Jacob White, Jr.

The Banneker Institute was founded in 1854 in a building at Seventh and Lombard streets and afterward relocated to the corner of Sixth and Walnut. Its forty members, many of whom were ICY students, included O. V. Catto, William Still, and Redman Fauset, the father of Jessie Fauset, the novelist, and Arthur Huff Fauset, educator and political activist. They had an uphill fight. In its minutes we find complaints that some lectures were poorly attended, that members frequently fell behind in their dues, and that some business meetings had to be cancelled for lack of a quorum. Sometimes its officers would complain that it "is an unenviable undertaking to attempt to cultivate a taste for literature among our people." Indeed, in 1857 the institute's president said that the program of public lectures had been a failure, although ten good meetings had been held that year.

The records of the institute show that its members were forging a body of thought about the condition of our people. One of the first debates addressed the subject "Would the Downfall of the Republic of the United States Be Beneficial to the Interests of Black People?" Another lecture was on the "Present Condition and Future Prospects of Haiti." O. V. Catto delivered a lecture on the history of Egypt. The institute was sponsored by the leaders of, and in turn, supported, the Underground Railroad. So it is no surprise to find buried in these Jacob White archives, beneath lecture topics and notes, a sudden explosion of names—W. C. Nell (Boston); R. Morris (Boston); C. L. Reason, W. J. Catto (Washington); W. F. Johnson (Harrisburg); T. R. Chester, E. D. Basset, D. Bustill, L. E. Wears, J. Q. Allen—the major Underground Railroad leaders. The onset of the Civil War brought an end to most of the activities of the institute.

Philadelphia Blacks fought hard in this arena, as in others, to obtain parity with the whites. Jacob White, Jr., eloquently tells how the literary societies of white Philadelphia held a special meeting to decide whether to admit the Banneker Institute to their association. An accrediting committee had visited the institute, heard a lecture, and observed a debate on the "Kansas-Nebraska Act." Afterward, they examined the minutes of past meetings and the bylaws. White tells us that all the white committee members, except one, agreed that the Banneker Institute was of high enough quality to be admitted to the association. But a motion to admit the Banneker Institute was defeated. The institute was Black and, White said, "acting upon this, we were excluded by them."

The tradition of literary societies continued in Philadelphia through the early part of the twentieth century with the institution of the Afro-American Historical Society. Its members included Robert Adger, a friend of O. V. Catto, born in South Carolina in 1837 and a remarkable collector of books and memorabilia about Black people. He gave his great library to the Black Home for the Aged. Somehow it disappeared, and it can be found today at Wellesley College. A second member of that society was William Henry Dorsey, who also assembled a large collection of works on Black people. It was found, several years ago, at Cheyney State College, the successor to the ICY. A third member was William Carl Bolivar, whose writing on early Black Philadelphia provided much of the information contained in this book. The recording secretary of the society was Edward F. Harris, a volunteer for the Battle of Gettysburg. He later enlisted in a Black regiment as a sergeant-major and fought in South Carolina. Afterwood he attended Franklin Institute and served as a first lieutenant in the National Guard of Pennsylvania. Matthew Anderson, a great Presbyterian minister and the husband of William Still's doctor daughter; R. R. Wright, Jr., historian and A.M.E. prelate; and the Episcopalian Reverend Phillips were all members of the society. So were Fanny Coppin and Theophilus J. Minton, an 1866 ICY graduate who earned a degree at the University of South Carolina Law School and became a Philadelphia lawyer.

By the turn of the century, then, Black Philadelphians had created both the teaching cadres and the tradition of intellectual inquiry necessary for the education of the community. Schools and societies alike were conscious of their responsibilities to Black people, and contributed in a variety of ways to that cause.

Chapter 6

SELF-HELP AND PROTEST

May the memory of the giver
In this home where age may rest
Float like fragrance through the ages
Ever blessing, ever blest

Dedication poem by Frances E. W. Harper to donor of "the home
for aged colored people" in *Poems*, Philadelphia, 1900

As early as 1797, Absalom
Jones, James Forten, and Richard Allen petitioned for entry
into the newly formed Black Masonry. The application was
accepted and Jones was made the master of the Philadelphia
lodge, with Richard Allen its first treasurer. By 1815, a Grand
Lodge had been established in Pennsylvania, with four sub-
ordinate lodges. African Freemasonry in the United States,
founded by Prince Hall, a member of the Free African Society
of Boston, was yet another of the threads that wove us into a
community. Hall, who received the Mason charter directly
from England after rejection by American Masons, was a radical who urged Black people to learn the lessons of the Haitian
revolution. Since their founding, besides their obvious social
function, the Masons have been a major force both in integrating Black leadership and in insuring their membership

against personal disasters. Moreover, they have been preeminent in benevolent works in the community.

Helping One Another—The Institutions

During the nineteenth century, Black self-help organizations proliferated in Philadelphia. In 1839, Philadelphia Blacks organized the Agricultural and Mechanical Association of Pennsylvania and New Jersey to help our people move into the trades. They even created an Agricultural Emigrant Association to establish a "settlement in one of the healthy, luxuriant, and beautiful valleys of the Territory of Montana" near the Northern Pacific Railroad. After the Civil War, O. V. Catto and William Still organized a building and loan association for Black people.

By 1900, the city's Black organizations included an Odd Fellows organization with nineteen lodges, a Quaker City Association whose membership was limited to native-born Philadelphians, and organizations of Blacks from Delaware and South Carolina. In addition, caterers and waiters had associations that were both guilds and social clubs. By 1897, Philadelphia Blacks had built their own hospital named after Frederick Douglass. Fanny Coppin, noting the plight of Black servant girls from the South, opened up a "Women's Exchange and Girls' Home" on South Twelfth Street to care for them.

Nor did they skimp on personal benevolence. Stephen Smith, a Columbia, Pennsylvania, merchant and a key Underground Railroad worker, donated property and cash worth $250,000 for a Black home for the aged in 1867. My uncle died in that home, well cared for until the end. A caterer named John Trower was "active in Cherry Memorial Baptist Church, Christian and 16th Street and he personally guaranteed mortgage and loans of the congregation amounting to $75,000." Trower also financed the building of a church in Ocean City, New Jersey, and another, the Mount Zion Baptist Church in Philadelphia. My Greenville, South Carolina, uncle played the organ there and he led the choir in song a few years ago when they buried the man who used to live next door to us. As a child, I walked past that church every morning. Its pastor was a brilliant and learned man who came by especially to talk to me when I was asked to integrate a white college in Ohio. Trower also organized a building and loan association for Blacks and purchased a farm of 110 acres near Downington, Pennsylvania, so that an industrial school for Black children could be built there. He was on the board of trustees at the Douglass hospital, and a major contributor.

Black Philadelphians even formed their own baseball team, the Pythians, captained by O. V. Catto (although William Still denounced the frivolity of playing games while the struggle went on in the South). The Pythians played teams from Washington, D.C., Harrisburg, Lincoln University, and Howard University. The lineups contained members of the Black elite and trips to other cities became social occasions. Wives and fiancées accompanied the teams and visited with friends. The games were another way of solidifying relationships among Blacks in different cities.

On December 18, 1867, delegates from the Pythian Ball Club asked for membership in an association of baseball teams meeting in Harrisburg, Pennsylvania. The whites told a Pythian delegate that it would be better for everybody if he would withdraw his request. The delegate telegraphed home for instructions and received the reply, "Fight." This he did, but the whites still would not accept the Pythians.

Antislavery Organizations

It is almost impossible to draw a distinction between self-help organizations and protest organizations in nineteenth-century Black Philadelphia. While slavery held sway in the South, the fight against it was the ultimate form of self-help. The Philadelphians hated slavery and the community's leaders spoke out against it. Absalom Jones maintained that God had seen the Americans use whips, screws, pincers, and white-hot skin-searing irons on Black people. Richard Allen said that

65

Black people hated slavery, but could not hate the whites as much as "you who have been and are our great oppressors would manifest if reduced to the pitiable condition of slaves." He said, I will tell you how hateful slavery is in the sight of God, and that he has brought low kings and princes for such oppression. Robert Purvis lambasted the slaveholder oligarchy that had controlled the American government as "one of the baddest, meanest, most atrocious despotisms that ever saw the face of the sun."

These leaders were responsible for the national Black convention movement. Its origins lay in the Free African Society and with the 1806 petition of Jones, Allen, and Forten urging Congress to modify the Fugitive Slave Act of 1793. Their petition was rejected by Congress and they were told that protest had "a tendency to create disquiet and jealousy, and ought therefore to receive no encouragement or countenance from this House."

The first Black mass meeting in America was held at Mother Bethel Church in 1817, chaired by James Forten, to protest the plans of the American Colonization Society for deportation of Blacks to Africa. The convention's report stated that "we will never separate ourselves voluntarily from the slave population of this country; they are our brethren by the ties of consanguinity, of suffering, and of wrong." It was followed, in 1831, by the first Black national convention which Lerone Bennet refers to as one of the "ten great moments in Black history."

Richard Allen was the president of this convention, and an important convener was the Episcopal minister Peter Williams, from New York City. Blacks from practically every Middle Atlantic state attended, as well as an honorary delegate from Ohio. The colonization question was debated and the delegates took a position against emigration. National conventions were held from then on, their location alternating between Philadelphia and New York, and then spreading to other cities. They institutionalized protest into forms which could gain a national hearing and serve as a unifying point for all Blacks in the country.

The protests of the Black convention movement preceded the formation of the mainly white Anti-Slavery Society, but Blacks participated in that event as well. Two Black men signed the Declaration of Principles of the American Anti-Slavery Society in Philadelphia on December 9, 1833. That founding document of the abolitionist movement was, moreover, written in the home of James McCrummell, a Black man, while William Lloyd Garrison was his guest.

The Black antislavery movement in Philadelphia confronted many of the same issues as Black organizations in other cities. One of these was the participation of whites. As early as the mid-1830s, William Whipper asked Black people to remove the names "colored" and "African" from their lodges and societies. Philadelphians, led by Purvis, generally were opposed to gatherings that were "exclusive," meaning all Black. They also participated in the disputes that marked the national movement in the mid-1840s. That movement split into two wings: political abolitionists sought the abolition of slavery through the electoral process, while the Garrisonians, or moral suasionists, believed that the political process was polluted by the participation of slave owners and argued that the major appeal should be made to America's sense of morality. Much has been made of the split between the Philadelphians, who remained Garrisonians, and the New Yorkers, led by Henry Highland Garnet. But Philadelphia "moral suasionists" on the Underground Railroad worked with the New Yorkers until the Civil War. And, as we've already noted, Robert Purvis, while opposed to "exclusive" organizations, voted to expel the whites from his Vigilant Committee when it seemed necessary.

Underground Railroad

The Underground Railroad was the core of Black Philadelphia's involvement in the struggle against slavery. At the center of that effort was Robert Purvis, who had created the Vigilant Committee, largely made up of Blacks, in August

1837. The committee was the primary instrument for moving slaves to freedom. In 1838, after the whites had burned an abolitionist convention hall, Purvis raised money for his committee from the public. In 1839 and 1840, he removed the whites from the committee and financed its work with Black resources.

The membership rolls of the Vigilant Committee demonstrate that Blacks of all classes and levels of education supported the liberation struggle. Those on the committee included Alexander Crummell, the Black Episcopalian founder of the National Negro Academy; Charles Gardiner, the Pastor of the First Presbyterian Church; Stephen Gloucester, Philadelphia editor of the *Colored American* and elder of Central Presbyterian Church; Peter Lester, a shoemaker; James Needham, treasurer of the Philadelphia Library Company; Reverend Payne; Dan Scott, pastor of Union Baptist Church; and Walter Proctor, pastor of Mother Bethel Church.

On the second committee, founded by Purvis, we find the names of Charles A. Bustill of the Robeson line, my ancestor Jean-Pierre Burr, a barber whose father was Aaron Burr and whose mother was a woman named Eugenie from Haiti; Jacob C. White, Jr.; and the head of the Institute for Colored Youth, Charles Reason. In 1838, a Female Vigilant Association was founded "to act in concert" and assist in the fund raising for Purvis's committee. Among its members were Elizabeth White and Hetty Reckless. In 1838, they raised funds through a public meeting and a fair held in December. In the early 1850s, Philadelphia women were well-known for their support of the fugitive slave movement.

My cousin, Miriam Burr Mitchell Cooper, recently showed me an account of our family's activities in the Underground Railroad written by her mother, Mabel Burr Cornish, in 1935. As a child, Cornish had listened to the stories told by her grandfather, John Emory Burr, the son of Jean-Pierre Burr and the grandson of Aaron Burr.

Jean-Pierre Burr ran a barber shop for whites only in the front room of his home at Fifth and Locust (then Prune) Streets. The house was full of hiding places—it contained an attic, a cave in the cellar, and a deep hole in the backyard, covered by a granite slab. Young John Emory was told to ignore any noises he heard in the cellar or attic, since the house was a station on the Underground Railroad, and slaves frequently hid there for a day or more.

Sometimes, John Emory told his granddaughter, overseers with bloodhounds would come to Jean-Pierre's barber shop in search of runaway slaves. Then, Cousin Mabel recalled, "Grandfather would call, 'Mother,' and she would come to the door and tell the men, 'Come and search, the house is yours.' They would find nothing and leave, having lost the scent, and the man would be safe until he could be taken away by Greatgrandfather at night."

Jean-Pierre Burr would lead the fugitive slave through side streets to the South Street bridge over the Delaware River. Burr, who was very fair, would pull his cap down low on his face in order to pass as a white man. If a nightwatchman along the way asked, "Who goes there?" Burr would reply, "Me with my man." The ruse usually worked. Burr and the slave would cross the bridge and meet Edwin N. Davis, who passed the fugitive along to a man Cousin Mabel called Highland Garrett—who must have been either Henry Highland Garnet or Thomas Garrett—and thence to Lucretia Mott.

William Still, along with Robert Purvis, was the head of the Underground Railroad during most of the decade before the Civil War. We recall that he had aided in the "rescue" of his own brother and that recognition of the "cruel separation" brought about by the slavers led him to write *The Underground Railroad*. Still's book tells powerful stories of terror and suffering in slavery, and of the slaves' relentless desire to be free. Of his personal bravery, we have already written. Let it be added that there is evidence that he, along with other Black Philadelphians, helped plan the raid on Harpers Ferry.

Antislavery activity took other forms as well. When the *Amistad*, the slave ship captured by Cinque and his fellow African warriors, was brought to Philadelphia in 1840, Black people from the Presbyterian church at Eleventh Street below Market solicited funds for them in the street. When more money was needed, they held meetings and raised the funds despite the "howlings of southern newspapers and their northern allies." The same men and women who worked on the Vigilant Committee went out and raised their voices in support of the African prince, Cinque.

Starting in the 1840s, some Philadelphia Blacks boycotted the celebration of the Fourth of July and created their own holiday, August 1, the date of the emancipation of the slaves in the West Indies. Charlotte Forten, James Forten's granddaughter, made the case against the Fourth of July: "The celebration of this day! What a mockery it is. My soul sickens of it." A report to the Banneker Institute in 1858 stated that the August 1 celebration "keeps before the minds of the American people *their* duty to the millions of slaves upon the Southern plantations and coming right in the wake of the 4th of July gives abolitionists a fine opportunity to espouse the hollow-headedness of American Liberty and Christianity and to offset the buncombe speeches made upon our own national anniversary."

Feelings of racial solidarity and unity in the opposition to slavery ran high in Black Philadelphia in the years before the Civil War. After the Harpers Ferry raid, on the eve of John Brown's execution, some Philadelphia Blacks tried to hire a hall to eulogize him. A Black custodian was somehow involved in the decision that denied them the hall and they passed a resolution condemning him: "Resolved that any Black man who will not stand up for his rights, particularly in the great struggle, shows a spirit unworthy of the notice of honorable men." And in 1861, the president of the Banneker Institute, proclaimed "the necessity of attention to our position as a people in this country and recommend the propriety of arming the Institute for defence." His recommendation was not accepted, but a motion to censure him for it lost.

In addition to their opposition to slavery in the South, Blacks in Philadelphia had to struggle for their own rights. In 1838, a new Pennsylvania state constitution for the first time specifically reserved the right to vote to white males, thus formalizing a situation in which no Philadelphia Black had ever been known to vote. The Black Philadelphians protested loudly that they were not slaves and would not be denied their rights. In one document—probably written by Robert Purvis— a familiar moral suasionist argument appeared. Improvements in the condition of Black people, it said, depended on what changes could be wrought in the white man's "heart."

Direct Self-Help: Fighting in the Union Army

With the start of the Civil War, Black self-help and protest activities centered on the Union armies. After their offer to fight at Gettysburg was spurned by the Union army, some Black Philadelphians went to Boston where the 54th Regiment, the first Black Northern outfit, was forming under Colonel Robert Gould Shaw, who later lost his life in the assault on Fort Wagner. For the most part, the Philadelphia men were in Company B of that regiment. Many, particularly the light-complexioned Charlestonians who had come to Philadelphia in the years just before the Civil War, joined white outfits. Others went into the Pennsylvania Black regiments that were finally formed at Camp William Penn, just outside of Phildelphia.

The 6th and 8th Pennsylvania Regiments are included in the list of the main Union combat units, the "three hundred fighting regiments." They fought everywhere. Black soldiers were in Maryland, North Carolina, west Florida, and the Rio Grande. The 8th Regiment lost 310 out of 575 men in Florida. The 6th Regiment was part of the Black phalanx sent in to take New Market Heights outside Petersburg, Virginia. A diary account of one company's action tells us that of 30 men who went forward in the attack, 15 were wounded and 12 killed. The regiment of 367 soldiers took 210 casualties. The next day, the Black Pennsylvanians repulsed a counterattack by the Rebels. General Benjamin Butler said afterward that the "colored troops by coolness, steadiness, and determined courage and dash have silenced every cavil of the doubters of their soldierly capacity and drawn tokens of admiration from the enemy." Butler told the troops to put Petersburg and New Market Heights on their regimental colors.

James Forten's son Robert, who had served with Purvis on the Vigilant Committee, left this country and went to London, where he prospered. A clipping from a Philadelphia paper tells us that he came home when he heard that the "Government had summoned the colored race to arms." When he got back to Philadelphia, he found that he could not be an officer since he was Black. Told that he was "vastly superior to his fellow soldiers," that "his habit and associations were strikingly dissimilar," and that he was too old to volunteer, he said that the first two points were good reasons why he should enter the army. "[My] country," he said, "asked her colored children to rally to her defense, and those of [us] who were blessed with education, should be foremost in answering the call." He enlisted in the 43rd Colored Troops where he was made sergeant-major and was detached for recruitment duty in Maryland. Exhausted from his work, he died shortly thereafter, leaving a wife and a "daughter [Charlotte], a teacher in the camp of the Freedmen at Port Royal." They buried him in a vault beneath St. Thomas Episcopal Church.

Intellectual Tradition

One of the legacies of the decades of self-help and protest in Black Philadelphia was the creation of an intellectual tradition. Central to that tradition was a belief in racial equality. Drawing both on their African cultural heritage and on American political and social ideals, Philadelphia Blacks developed a way of looking at the world that was uniquely theirs.

Philadelphia Blacks were aware of their African origins. Richard Allen once referred to Africa as "our mother country" and Absalom Jones called it the "nation from which [we] are descended." One Black Philadelphian, John H. Johnson, wrote a long history of Egypt declaring that its civilization had derived from sub-Saharan Africa—some hundred and fifty years before the *New York Times* published an article to the same effect. And the intellectual and political leaders of Black Philadelphia were grounded in the African-influenced prayers and music of their churches. Yet they struggled to claim their rights as Americans. The first Black convention, in 1817, rejected forced repatriation to Africa. The people's response, in 1838, to their disenfranchisement by the Pennsylvania state constitution was an eloquent plea for their rights as citizens. They never forgot the struggle to free the slaves of the South, but they also strove for the fullest possible rights of citizenship for themselves.

Philadelphia Blacks based their arguments on the same theory of "natural rights" that the American colonists had used to buttress their case against the British. "The Almighty having clothed us with the attributes of human nature, we are placed on an equality with the rest of mankind," Robert Purvis asserted in his discussion of the 1838 constitution. Given the presence among Philadelphia's Black leadership of French-educated refugees from Haiti, and the city's status as the entry point into the United States of French Enlightenment thought, it is almost certain that the ideas of the French Revolution also influenced Philadelphia Blacks. More than the American rebels, the French had spoken of the brotherhood of man. Surely Philadelphia's educated Blacks read Rousseau and other French thinkers.

In the South, Black community life was different. Slaves reinforced each other's sense of a shared culture, and in some states, like South Carolina, Blacks outnumbered whites. And, unlike Philadelphians, slaves had no rights. It's difficult to imagine Denmark Vesey, Gabriel Prosser, or Nat Turner making Robert Purvis's statement that "Our aim and end should be homogeneity with the American people—we being in fact Americans—with all the elements of character peculiar to the nature of this country." Slaves could think only of overthrowing the tyranny of the slaveholders. Philadelphia's free Blacks—literate and well-organized—had reason to believe that they could and should participate in the American system.

Like many other bourgeois nationalists, Philadelphia Blacks could think "Black" and "integrationist" at the same time.

Even James Forten, always portrayed as an integrationist, felt strongly that Blacks would "never become a people until they come out from amongst the white people." And while they built Black schools for their children in an effort to secure them the best possible education, they were in many respects still integrationists. The Philadelphia delegations to Black conventions frequently took integrationist stands. They even argued at one such meeting against a resolution declaring that Black people should control Black schools. And the sermons of the pastor of St. Thomas are the same as any other sermons in an Episcopal church.

Black Philadelphians were determinedly capitalists, and shared at least some of the American Dream of unbounded wealth. That is not surprising, for all around them were examples of self-made men. Forten, Allen, Still, Purvis, and a few others were wealthy even by today's standards. The wonder is that these early Philadelphians were not influenced by their wealth to be silent in the great struggle that was going on around them. As it was, they were radical in most matters that concerned Black people and conservative in regards to demanding fundamental changes in the structure of American society. But few Americans have ever engaged in such a sustained and protracted struggle for equality as those Black men and women in Philadelphia. The organizations they built and intellectual traditions they fostered give testimony to that effort.

Chapter 7

THE PHILADELPHIA OPPRESSION

I'm a rolling, I'm a rolling
I'm a rolling thro' an unfriendly world

Traditional Black Spiritual

In the three decades before the Civil War, white Philadelphians, spearheaded by newly arrived Irish immigrants, repeatedly destroyed the homes and institutions and physically assaulted the people of the Black community. These attacks dealt a harsh blow to Black Philadelphians' efforts to achieve a secure economic, social, and religious life.

Mob violence was common in America's rapidly growing cities during the 1830s and 1840s. The Irish, scorned as newcomers, were often the targets of attacks by earlier residents. But there was something special about racial violence in the Northern cities before the Civil War that set it apart from riots based on economic competition. At its root was a "fierce, and at least among the lower classes, an almost universal hatred of the Negro himself."

A historian who closely studied the Northern urban Black experience identified seven cities in which mobs "racially motivated ... almost always invaded black residential areas." These cities included Cincinnati, where whites drove more than one thousand Blacks out of the city in 1829, and New

York, where race riots in 1834 and 1839 culminated in 1863, when antidraft rioters "assaulted and lynched Negroes, wrecked their homes and places of business, and burned the Colored Orphan Asylum into a shamble of blackened ruins." In Chicago, in 1864, a mob of some four hundred Irishmen attacked a dozen Blacks because "it was degrading to them to see blacks working upon an equality with themselves, and more so, while their brothers were out of employment." But the worst anti-Black attacks took place in Pennsylvania.

Casual mistreatment of Blacks was common in the North. Blacks were "pushed from the sidewalk in Boston and Providence, stoned in Providence . . . and casually cuffed aside almost everywhere." Philadelphia was no exception. As early as 1809, a traveler noted that little children walking down the street casually called a Black man "nigger." Foreigners visiting Philadelphia were often struck by the intensity of the hatred which permeated white society from top to bottom.

Philadelphia, says one historian, was "the most anti-Negro city of the North and the most rigidly segregated metropolis above the Mason-Dixon line." William Wells Brown, famous for his escape from slavery in a box, wrote of Philadelphia: "Colorphobia is more rampant here than in the pro-slavery, Negro-hating city of New York." Frederick Douglass said the city was one of the "most disorderly and insecure" and that it was a "mean, contemptible and barbarous" place. Another contemporary observer said he felt "grave doubts in . . . mind whether the severest despotism, guided by justice, would not have been preferable to such republican license as then prevailed in the city of Penn."

Philadelphia's brand of hostility intensified as the century wore on. In the Pre–Civil War years, no white clergyman in the entire city spoke out against slavery except one who was a transplanted New England Unitarian. No publisher in the city would print *Uncle Tom's Cabin*. John Brown's body could not rest even for one night in the city; the mayor ordered the body sent on to New York. Finally the growing hostility erupted into violence.

The onslaught of white mobs upon the Black community

began in 1829. In August 1834, there were three days of upheaval. The rioters were usually young and Irish and angered by the competition of the Blacks for wages. They intended to drive the Blacks out of all the trades they had previously occupied: "Parties of white men have *insisted* that no Blacks shall be employed in certain departments of labor." But the mobs also destroyed the Masonic Lodge and attacked the homes of community leaders.

On the first night, Blacks attacked members of the Fairmount Engine Company and captured some of their equipment. The firemen formed ethnic clubs, and in many instances, ethnic gangs that assaulted Blacks. On the second night, a gang of white men attacked one of James Forten's sons. The whites then destroyed the African Presbyterian church and rampaged through the Black neighborhoods, sacking another church in the process. When the mob came upon a coffin in one house, they tossed the body into the street. In another house, they dashed the corpse of a dead baby upon the floor. After the burning of the second church, one hundred Black men barricaded themselves with weapons in a building close to where Mother Bethel Church is today. The mayor of the city, fearing war, somehow convinced the Blacks, and then the whites, to withdraw.

After further riots in 1835 and 1838 in which orphanages and churches were burned to the ground, in 1842 a mob destroyed the new African Hall, built by money donated by the Black philanthropist, Stephen Smith. It then destroyed the Presbyterian church once again. The mob spared no one, dragging old and young alike out of their homes and chasing them through the cobblestoned streets like "noxious animals." The whites "laid completely waste the Negro area from Fifth to Eighth Street near Lombard," and were stopped only by the militia. Thousands of Black political refugees streamed out of the city, trying to cross the river to Jersey and safety. There, they camped out in the swamps and many, afraid to go home, died. Some friendly farmers helped to feed them. During this riot, a band of Blacks led by an A.M.E. preacher fought the "thugs and pro-slavery firemen."

The last in this series of riots came in 1849 when Irish gangs with names like the "Blood Tubs" and "Stingers" attacked a hotel in the Black district because the Black owner had married a white woman: "Tearing up paving stones and bricks and also using guns, the Blacks defended themselves vigorously." Years later, Black men would be proud to have fought at that spot.

The terror had its impact on Black Philadelphians' education, work, recreation, and leisure. A measure of the effect of the violence is the fact that the white population of Philadelphia grew from 230,000 to 369,000 in the decade between 1840 and 1850. During that same period, the Black population remained at 18,000. The mobs, as was the case in other cities, had felt that they could "literally" force the Blacks out, and to some extent they succeeded. Some observers at the time believed that the lack of growth of the Black population was attributable to the terror.

Why did the whites hate us so much? One possibility is that before the Civil War, Philadelphia was still under the control of the old "commercial and financial elite" who had close banking, commercial, and social ties with slaveholders. "Many of the first families . . . established bonds of intermarriage with the South." This elite set an anti-Black tone in the city. Although the city's Quakers were antislavery, they did not necessarily favor equality for Philadelphia Blacks. Said one Black leader: "They will give us good advice . . . they will aid in giving us a partial education—but never in a Quaker school, beside their own children. Whatever they do for us savors of pity and is done at arm's length." A Friend's antislavery journal asked that the cause of antislavery be separated from the question of the general prejudice toward Blacks.

The Irish-Black relationship formed a "communal pathology." The Irish, said a nineteenth-century observer, "hate the Negroes, not merely because they compete with them in labor, but because they are near to them in social rank. Therefore, the Irish favor slavery in the South, and for the same reason the laboring class of whites support it—it gratifies their pride by the existence of a class below them." A historian of the riots claims that the Irish vented their anger on Blacks when their unrealistic expectations about life in America were dashed.

The Philadelphia Black community, the largest in the North in 1830, was highly visible and seemed to become a lightning rod for white wrath. While most Blacks, as we have indicated, were poor, there were Black cabinetmakers, blacksmiths, painters, and weavers. They were disliked because of their "efficient industry and their successful competition with white laborers." The wealthy and successful Blacks, no matter how small their numbers in relation to the general population, were active in public life. Whites of various classes resented their success: "Among upper-class whites, there was some annoyance over the rumor that ... James Forten was ambitious ... and ... coveted to wed his daughter to a whiter species at some sacrifice to his fortune." Sometimes the mobs aimed their attentions directly at affluent Blacks—Purvis, for instance, in the 1842 riot.

In addition, there were general white complaints about the Black community, particularly the conduct of ex-slaves: "When [the slaves] arrive, they almost generally abandon themselves to all manner of debauchery and dissipation to the general annoyance of many of our citizens." One historian concludes: "The great mass of the negroes of Pennsylvania were generally described as indolent, thoughtless, prodigal, and thriftless, though at the same time, cheerful and good-humored; fond of gaiety, music and dancing and devoted to showiness and dress...." Then, as now, we made up a disproportionate number of the prison population. In 1837, one-third of the jail occupants were Blacks, although their proportion in the general population was only ten percent.

Another possible cause of the white discontent might have been the large number of interracial marriages and liaisons in the early years of the century. An observer noted that these numbered in the hundreds and "there are thousands of Black children by them [white women] at present. One race riot, as we mentioned, seems to have been touched off by an interracial marriage.

The Struggle for the Vote

The physical onslaught upon our people was accompanied by an attack upon their legal rights. In 1822, James Forten marched his white employees to the polls to vote for a Federalist candidate, but did not himself attempt to vote. The state constitution of 1838 specifically denied Blacks the right to vote, and until 1870, no Black man could vote in Pennsylvania. The Blacks protested during those years, but did not secure the ballot until the passage of the Fifteenth Amendment. The agitation against the constitution of 1838 was led by educator O. V. Catto; Jonathan C. Gibbs, a Dartmouth graduate; and J. J. Wright, the first Black lawyer to be admitted to the Pennsylvania bar. At one meeting, Wright, who was later active in the South Carolina Reconstruction, said that he was simply asking the whites to act as if they believed the Declaration of Independence.

O. V. Catto, martyred in this struggle, looms large in the Civil War and post–Civil War history of Black Philadelphia. We recall that this South Carolina–born son of a scholarly Presbyterian minister had led Philadelphia's Blacks in their abortive effort to volunteer for combat at the Battle of Gettysburg. He later became the vice-principal of the Institute for Colored Youth, was active in the Banneker Institute, and was the captain of the Pythian Ball Club. He was recognized as a star baseball player throughout the Black Northeast, and he led his team to an undefeated season in 1867, which made him a near hero among the Black people of the community, rich and poor.

Catto, known as a stylish dresser, also was a bachelor who wooed women with poems like:

> And if, perchance one pleasing ray
> Of true poetic fervor beams
> Along my unambitious way
> Thyself hath been the inspiring theme.

By 1867, Catto had become engaged to a fellow ICY graduate and teacher, Caroline LeCount. The name "LeCount" is listed in my mother's family Bible.

Catto and LeCount struggled together for the rights of the Black community. In the fall of 1870, after the passage of the Fifteenth Amendment, Blacks voted for the first time in Pennsylvania's history. Catto was Philadelphia's acknowledged leader in organizing the Black vote. In the aftermath of one mass meeting, scattered shots were fired at some Blacks and Catto received threatening letters. The potential for violence was so great that marines were called in to insure peace at the polls where Blacks and whites stood in separate lines to cast their ballots. In one ward, Blacks had to wait until all the whites had voted before voting themselves.

The next year, there were no federal troops to protect the Black right to vote. Catto, by now considered "the pride of his race in this city, . . . being the ablest and best educated among the colored men," had spent the summer of 1871 in Washington, but by the time of the election, he was at his job of vice-principal at the ICY. The prospect of a large Black vote had the city in an uproar because the Democrats—corrupt and heavily supported by the Irish—stood to lose power to the Black-supported Republicans.

On the night before the election, "the spirit of mobocracy filled the air," and, in the wake of a murder of a Black man, Catto spent the early evening at a cigar store, a popular gathering place for the Pythians and Banneker Institute members. When he left, Catto chose a dangerous route, refusing to "stultify my manhood by going home in a roundabout way." Arriving safely, he found that a white had grabbed the hat off the head of one of the occupants of the boardinghouse where he lived. So Catto went around the corner into "one of the worst places" in the white section and retrieved the man's hat for him.

On election day, Catto went to school, but when fighting between Black and white voters broke out in his district, he sent the students home early. A colleague warned him that it would be dangerous to vote, but he said he was going to vote anyhow. In the street, some white ruffians harassed him, and he decided to ask the mayor's office for assistance. On the way there, more whites threatened him, so he bought a pistol but no cartridges, because he had some at home. As he turned onto South Street, an Irishman named Frank Kelly—he lived forty feet away from Catto, so he must have known what he was doing—called out to him, and shot him as a woman shouted, "Oh, Mr. Catto, look at that man!" Wounded, and perhaps pistol-whipped by Kelly, Catto staggered behind a trolley car for shelter. But the killer came around the other side of the moving trolley car and shot him several more times. He fell dead right in front of a police station.

Kelly fled—one account says he walked—to a corner tavern where he was caught by a local constable who turned him over to two policemen, stating that he had just killed a man. After the constable left the tavern, he heard noise, and the words "get away quick." Reentering the tavern, he saw the two policemen leaving through the back door. Kelly escaped to Chicago, where he was apprehended in 1877 and brought back for a trial, but he was later released.

O. V. Catto's fiancée, Caroline LeCount—who never married—identified his body. When the Black people of the city, who had been battling the whites all day, heard the news, sorrow so engulfed them that according to one account "strong men wept like children." Another Black was killed that day, and many whites and Blacks suffered injury. There are signs that the police and the whites were cooperating. One police lieutenant named Haggerty had instructed his officers to stop the Blacks from voting. A magistrate placed him under $10,000 bail. And a warrant was issued for a police officer who'd allegedly shot a Black man in the back. But in the end, no white was ever punished for any of these acts.

They gave O. V. the biggest funeral since James Forten's. Representatives from the Banneker Institute, the Pythian Ball Club, the State National Guard, and his fellow vestrymen from St. Thomas were among the pallbearers. As the contingent from the Institute for Colored Youth marched by, "many of the teachers and scholars [were] weeping bitterly." They mourned Catto for two weeks. The Quaker board of managers of the ICY said nothing. At a ceremony in his memory, a Black speaker asked, "Could it have been because of his erudition and eloquence that his life was taken?" Everybody in the audience replied, "Yes."

Blacks Denied Right to Ride on Streetcars

Streetcars had come to Philadelphia in the late 1850s. Blacks were not permitted to ride on most lines except out in the open with the conductor. Numerous shameful incidents occurred. Black Union soldiers were tossed off the cars when they tried to sit down. When two women going to visit wounded soldiers refused to get out of their seats, the conductor locked the doors of the trolley and brought the women back to the trolley depot where they covered one of them with whitewash. One bitter cold day, a conductor stopped the car, opened all the windows, and put all the passengers on a following car after a Black woman with her baby tried to ride on the inside. Robert Smalls, a Black South Carolinian who had been cited by Congress for his capture of a Confederate gunboat, was told by a trolley conductor: "Company regulations, we don't allow niggers to ride." The Reverend William J. Alston, rector of St. Thomas Church, wanted to ride one night because his child was sick. Pointing at the "deathly appearance" of the child in his arms, he hailed a car. Even though it was occupied by only a driver and conductor, they would not let him and his child ride.

The mayor of Philadelphia said that he would not let his own family ride on a trolley car with Blacks and that the police would enforce the policy of segregation. Sometimes the police did, and sometimes they permitted thugs to enforce the ugly practice. One white legislator protested: "Philadelphia stands disgraced before the world. . . . I arraign Philadelphia, her newspapers, her corporations, her judges, her lawyers, her churches, and her citizens and pronounce them hostile to the execution of justice between man and man. History will be just to Philadelphia and the fact will be recorded to her everlasting discredit that she left her weak, her poor and her defenseless citizens to be trodden by the wealthy, the wicked, and the strong."

Led by William Still and O. V. Catto, and aided by the passage of the Fourteenth Amendment and strong support from national Radical Republicans, Black Philadelphians finally broke down this barrier in 1867, with an act of the state legislature. O. V. Catto's fiancée, Caroline LeCount, was the first to test the new law. When she was refused entry to the trolley car at Ninth and Lombard streets—a block from where O. V. was later assassinated—with the words, "We don't allow niggers to ride," she sued, and the conductor was arrested and fined one hundred dollars.

Oppression, violence, and segregation continued on into the twentieth century. A few examples will suffice. In the early 1900s, near the University of Pennsylvania, a crowd of "about one hundred little white boys from six to about fourteen years of age" forced a trolley car to a halt by pulling the electric rod off its wire. Then they entered the car and beat the Black riders, including six women, with sticks, crying, "Kill the nigger! Lynch 'em. Hit that nigger." There was a major race riot in July 1918, when a Black probation officer's movement into a white neighborhood caused a violent reaction. Racial fighting broke out in South Philadelphia and West Philadelphia, and Blacks and Irish cops had at each other with a vengeance. The last major interracial riot took place in 1944, when whites protested a plan to hire Black motormen for the trolley cars.

Police brutality was a problem from the very beginning. The police force was heavily Irish and prejudiced. Blacks began serving on the force around 1900, and by World War I, there were two to three hundred Black policemen on a force of four thousand. At that time, according to a Black policeman, "a white man wouldn't take the job, and that was a good job for a colored man." Even so, there was segregation in the station house—where the policemen slept, Blacks were restricted to certain areas, and no Blacks were allowed to patrol in police cars or on motorcycles.

The beating of Blacks in the station houses was common.

Detective Firman Hopkins, one of the first Blacks to hold that rank on the force, recalled, "One day they brought a colored man in there, and, oh, they made a regular monkey out of him. Put him on the turntable and made him jump. At the time, detectives wore masks so they wouldn't be recognized. Well, this Negro started jumping. 'Jump,' they said, 'Jump!' I told him 'Don't you jump. Don't you move for nobody. Stand right there!' The whole place got quiet. I told the captain, and he said they meant no harm. I told him they didn't respect me if they didn't respect the colored prisoners."

Conflict between Blacks and the white policemen occurred daily. Thus, in August 1904, when a Black assaulted a white man, police from the Fifteenth and Locust station responded with so much force that it precipitated a riot in which four Black men were beaten and three policemen lost their uniforms. In 1915, a policeman, considered one of the toughest in the city, was attacked by some Blacks and left with a fractured skull after he used excessive force in arresting a Black woman.

By the time this century began, Black people had been cut off from real participation in Philadelphia's political, economic, or social structure. The Philadelphia that DuBois surveyed at the turn of the century was a Jim Crow town in which two separate societies were developing. Blacks were excluded from many activities, and were really not welcome at restaurants and theaters. By the time of my youth, the 1930s, Blacks had to sue to gain entry to Horn & Hardardt cafeterias. We could not sit in the white sections of movies. The school system was segregated so that Blacks could not teach in white schools. And Blacks lived with more crowding than any other ethnic group in the city. But most important, the Industrial Revolution, which eventually absorbed other groups into the American economy, passed the Black people of Philadelphia by: "The number and kinds of jobs at which whites of all ethnic groups earned their livelihood were greater and more varied than those of Negroes, and the margin of difference increased sharply between 1850 and 1880. . . . The vast majority of Negro men and woman—three of four throughout the period—labored in unskilled capacities at the bottom of the occupational ladder."

One historian's conclusion about urban Blacks in this period more than applies to Philadelphia: "Nothing—not the fact that one was an American, or a Philadelphian, or a property holder, or a father, or a barber, or a Methodist, or a voter, or a Mason—was one-third so significant as the fact that one was black in a society that legally, socially, and politically viewed Negroes as innately inferior and undesirable as occupiers of urban space."

Part II
SOUTH CAROLINA

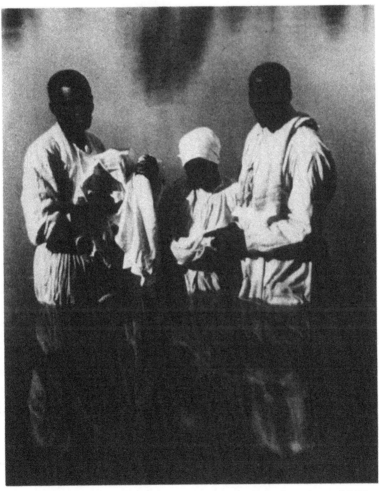

"Take me to the water"—a South Carolina baptism, 1930s
(Doris Ulmann, Schomburg Center for
Research in Black Culture, New York Public Library)

Chapter 8

SOUTH CAROLINA
BEFORE THE CIVIL WAR

'Cause their troubles were hard
Yes their troubles were hard, Lord, Lord
Oh, their troubles were hard
Yes indeed, their troubles were hard

Traditional Black Spiritual

The poet Dudley Randall describes, in "Southern Road," a journey South:

And where the earth is scarlet as a scar
Friezed by the bleeding lash that fell (O fell)
Upon my fathers' flesh. O far, far, far
And deep my blood has drenched it. None can bar
My birthright to the loveliness bestowed
Upon this country haughty as a star
And I set forth upon the southern road.

This darkness and these mountains loom a spell
Of peak-roofed town where yearning steeples soar
And the holy holy chanting of a bell
Shakes human incense on the throbbing air

Where bonfires blaze and quivering bodies char.
Whose is the hair that crisped, and fiercely glowed?
I know it; and my entrails melt like tar
And I set forth upon the southern road.

The aim of this book is to examine the influences that made
the modern Black Philadelphian. Since most of our ancestors
were Southern, our lives are tightly connected with slavery
and Reconstruction. Our grandparents were actors in the events,
great and small, that took place there. To know them, we
must walk that Southern road.

Many Black Philadelphians' roots are in South Carolina
and many of them are from Abbeville and Greenwood counties. Before the turn of the century, both were called Abbeville
County. When describing what happened before 1898, we will
refer to the territory as Abbeville County; after 1898, as Abbeville-Greenwood. We will focus first on South Carolina before
the Civil War and through the Reconstruction. We will then
analyze Black education and Black religion in South Carolina
generally, and in Abbeville County in particular. Finally, we
will look more closely at Abbeville County, examining the
terror visited upon Black people, the life of the Black community, and the migration of many of its members to Philadelphia in 1917–18. There they joined with "old Philadelphians"
and other Southerners to become the Black Philadelphians of
today.

In South Carolina our African forebears seem closer. There
are a number of reasons for this. One is that there were many
more Africans in South Carolina than in Northern states like
Pennsylvania. An informal estimate is that fully forty percent
of the slaves brought into the United States between 1700 and
1775 entered through Charleston, although the first Africans
to arrive there came via Barbados. And indeed Blacks were a
majority in the state of South Carolina for a hundred years
after 1820.

Because there were so many Blacks in the state, their influence on customs, folkways, and patterns of speech were

much stronger than in the North. In effect, South Carolina's traditions are part Black, part white, and heavily influenced also by Native American cultures. South Carolina was a racially mixed society. Black men married white women; Cherokee Indians both enslaved Blacks and married them; and white slavers frequently raped Black women. Sometimes, whites lived openly with their Black mistresses and children. An authoritative post–Civil War analysis declared that the "enunciation of mulattoes, attempted by the census of 1860 and 1870, was unsatisfactory and in the census of 1880 none was attempted." Apparently it was impossible to count South Carolina's mulattoes. The study concluded that: "Even now they are no longer negroes. One third has a large infusion of white blood, another third have less." Mulatto society was so intricate in its racial delineations that even today a casual look at South Carolina whites frequently reveals Black traits—the walk of the women or the "peach" complexions of their skins.

Unlike slaves in Philadelphia, who were mostly house servants living by ones or twos in individual white households, South Carolina Africans tended to live in larger groups. Many of the plantations on which the Africans worked were small establishments, with no more than ten slaves. This was especially true in the up-country and Piedmont regions. But on the larger plantations where the staple crops of rice and indigo—sources of the wealth of the South Carolina "aristocrats"—were grown, the slave population was larger.

Our people were captured from several west African countries, including Angola, Gambia, Senegal, and Sierra Leone, and groups from the same place were dispersed by sale to diverse locations throughout the South. But even if Africans who found themselves on the same plantation did not hail from the same village or speak the same tongue, they shared a common culture. And on the larger plantations, they were able to maintain it.

Nineteenth-century observers were particularly aware of the survival of forms of African culture in South Carolina.

Traveling to the Sea Islands, near now-fashionable Hilton Head, in the years just after the Civil War, Charlotte Forten was struck by the beauty of "Roll Jordan Roll" and of another song that ended with the words "No man can hinder me." She loved the African singing and feared that it would someday be supplanted by the white music, which was "poor" in comparison. Teaching in the schools of the Sea Islands, she noticed the "peculiar swaying motion" that affected both the old and the young when they sang. Although the granddaughter of James Forten was not completely one with the people of the islands, their "magical words" sang in her soul and never had she felt so "truly grateful to God":

> I wonder where
> my mudder gone, Sing
> oh Graveyard!
>   Graveyard ought to
> know he
>   Sing Jerusalem
> Oh carry my mudder in
>   de graveyard
>   Sing
> Oh grass grow in de
>   graveyard
>   Sing
> Lay my body in de graveyard
>   Sing

A white visitor to the Sea Islands at about the same time described an occasion when: "One of the men began a religious chant in a high-pitched voice, while the others joined in a sort of continuous accompaniment of four or five words ending with a cry mournful enough to have been the expression of great pain. . . . They had found their way back to Africa through their songs. . . . In a moment I was with them in the home of the race." But we need not rely on hundred-year-old sources. Go down to South Carolina today, near where Charlotte Forten worked, and you will see and hear the continued life of the African tradition.

I sat one Sunday in a church near Ruffin, South Carolina. The church lay deep in the woods and was reached by a boggy road. There was no organ, no piano. Finally the preacher, who had lived in Philadelphia, arrived. Suddenly the room—small as the proverbial one-room schoolhouse, the furniture covered in white for the communion service—resounded with the bass voice of an African-looking deacon singing "Must Jesus Bear the Cross Alone, and All the World Go Free." The feet of the worshippers began to pound and shuffle on the floor like a drum accompanying the voices. They soared down through the South Carolina mud back to Africa and became as clear as the sounds of the nearby river Broad, up which the slaves had been transported to work the earth of the state.

Then, the deacon moved into "There's Not a Friend Like the Lowly Jesus," which tells us that Jesus was poor and neglected and that if you trust him, he will guide you through any danger. Indeed, there's not a friend like the Lowly Jesus, no not one, no not one. The African emphasis comes at the end of each verse, when it is made clear by hand clap and slow foot pat that "not one" friend has the power of Jesus.

Later that afternoon, I arrived at a church not far from where Charlotte Forten had taught, and I was invited to attend another service. Soon after I entered the church, I knew I was home. For there in the choir was singing a woman with the face of my long-dead Aunt Oni, and there, wearing the white uniform of an usher, was another aunt long departed to glory. And the swaying that Charlotte Forten had seen, the rich and wild music of Africa, the drums made up of hand claps and feet pounding, attested to the survival of African culture here. The visiting preacher, a young Black Marine Corps chaplain from nearby Parris Island, said what was in my heart: that he felt like David who, when he was in the desert, had cried out, oh, how he would like to have just a little sip of water from his childhood home in Bethelem. All of us in that church had a sip of that water brought from Africa, sweeter by far than any water to be found in the land of our birth.

Slavery in South Carolina

The life of our people in South Carolina, especially the slaves on large plantations, was unspeakably hard. The cultivation of rice was killing labor "with people perpetually at work, often ankle-deep in mud, with their bare heads exposed to the fierce rays of the sun." After the rice was harvested, the men pounded it with mortars "to separate it from a hard stiff hull" and "this generally carries of[f] great numbers every winter." The slaves were also ravaged by the respiratory diseases caused by the alternate flooding and draining of the muddy fields where the rice was cultivated. At the end of the week, the overseer would check to see that a quota had been filled and, one slave said, "If you ain' do what he say do, he put de Nigger dog on you en he run you all night till he find you. No matter wh' you hide, he find you and hold you till de overseer get done. Bit you up if de get reach of you. When de overseer come, he carry you to de stable and whip you." Slaves were frequently punished. An observer of the pre–Civil War South Carolina scene noted that "hardly a Negro but bears the mark of punishment in large scars on his back and sides." In 1712, a law on runaway slaves had a scale of punishments ranging from slitting the nose to cutting off one foot. Whipping was common.

Some Black South Carolinians remembered, "Oh, my Lord, dey would cut them so hard till day just slash de flesh right off dem. Yes, mam, dey call dat thing dey been whip dem wid de cat o' nine tail." Another said that the slaves would run away to the woods "en perish to death dere 'fore dey would come out to take a whippin'."

An especially cruel punishment was the separation of a slave from his or her family by sale. The Africans in South Carolina had a song:

> De nigger trader got he
> Oh, hollow
> De speculator bought me
> Oh, hollow

I'm sold for silver dollars
Oh
Boys, go catch de pony
Oh
Bring him round de corner
Oh
I'm going away to Georgia
Oh
Boys, good-bye forever
Oh
Boys, good-bye forever
Oh

One historian believes that the threat of sale was the keystone of the slave system in South Carolina.

Urban Slaves and Free Blacks

South Carolina was also the home of an important group of free Blacks. They seemed to have fallen into two categories: those who fell between the cracks of slavery, in various locations around South Carolina, and free Black Charlestonians.

Typical of the first group is Bishop Henry M. Turner of the A.M.E. Church who was born in Newbury Courthouse, South Carolina, up in the Piedmont district, of a father whose own mother was a white German. Turner's maternal grandfather, an African king, had by some quirk of British law been declared free, so Turner's mother was free as well. He grew up laboring first in a cotton field and then as an apprentice to a blacksmith in Abbeville. Some other free Black men in the up-country were well-to-do and owned slaves.

A distinct group of free Blacks arose in Charleston; Bishop Payne, Morris Brown, Robert Purvis, and O. V. Catto's father were among its members. In 1790, Charleston's population consisted of eight thousand free whites, eight thousand slaves, and six hundred free Blacks. These included the children of Black women freed by slavers, and artisans who purchased their own freedom with money earned from hiring themselves out. "Hiring out" was an unusual feature of slavery in the cities. The slave owner profited from the rental of the slave's skills, but so, often, did the slave himself. They were masons, painters, bakers, and wharf builders and those who controlled such trades as shoemaking and carpentry. Some members of this group even became slave owners.

These free Black Charlestonians developed a strong sense of color and status. A member of their club, the Brown Society, betrayed the Denmark Vesey uprising and received as a reward "$1,000 and exemption from taxation for the rest of his life." A historian of the group has concluded that the "upper-caste free Negro served as a custodian of the system."

Free Black Charlestonians seem to have had particularly close connections with Philadelphia and frequently sent their children there to be educated at the ICY. Many of the group migrated to Philadelphia in the late 1850s as the South readied for war and tightened controls on the movement and occupations of free Blacks. T. K. Sasportas, the scion of a Black slaveholding family, attended the ICY, joined the 54th Massachusetts, fought through the war, and became a leader of the Charleston Black community during Reconstruction. Other descendants of the free Charlestonians provided the nucleus of the Black teachers of the freedmen in South Carolina. But some light-complexioned free South Carolinians brought their color prejudice with them to the North, creating discord and divisiveness in the Black community.

Religion

The Christianizing of the African captives presented a more serious dilemma to the large-scale slaveholders of South Carolina, where Blacks were close to a majority, than it did to the slavers of the North. Some whites in South Carolina had a "very genuine fear that Christian slaves would demand inevitably political, social, and religious equality." Others, like slave owner Charles C. Pinckney, argued that religion would help to pacify the always rebellious Africans. Moreover, said Pinckney, if the Blacks remained without religion, their immoral conduct would subvert the moral values of the white slave owners. This viewpoint seems to have won out. For beginning in 1800, there was an upsurge of mission work among the slaves.

Sometimes Blacks and whites worshipped together in pre–Civil War South Carolina. During the period of the Great Awakening—a time of intense religiosity and frequent revivals—in the 1740s, slaves, free Blacks, free whites, and Native Americans preached to each other. They sometimes worshipped together and sometimes separately. In the Episcopal church, the church of the Establishment, especially in the low-lying areas of the state, Blacks and whites worshipped together, but certain "seats were always reserved for house servants." A foreign observer saw both Blacks and whites worshipping together in a Charleston Episcopal church before the Civil War.

Eventually there was a move toward separation. Sometimes it was inspired by white fear of Black religion. In Spartanburg County "before the [separate] building was erected, Loss Goode, a Negro who was inspired to preach, went about the communities, preaching to both white and black people at their homes. . . . He was so imbued with the African traditions that many of the ignorant class of white people thought that he possessed supernatural powers and were so afraid of him that they would not let him come into their homes." In 1782, at one church, the whites had "knocked out the side of the church so as to run a shed alongside it for the blacks to worship." But in some churches, a Black deacon with power over the Black portion of the population was appointed. Such preachers sometimes had several congregations and were allowed to travel in the exercise of their ministry. Left is one such charge that "Brother Negroe Tom should exercise his gift of singing, praying, and exhortation to the extreme bounds of Tinker Creek, Fair Forest, Union, Friendship Head, Cedar, Shool, Newhope churches."

As it turned out, Charles Pinckney was wrong; religion

did not really pacify the Black people of South Carolina. Up near Long Cane Creek in Abbeville County, for example, a slave hired as a carpenter was overheard saying to the kitchen slaves that "God was working for their deliverance. He was working by secret means and would deliver them from their bondage sure as the children of Israel were delivered from the Egyptian bondage. There was no doubt that it would be soon, that they ought to pray for it, and their prayers would go up to God and be answered." The slaveholder, overhearing this seditious talk, had the man sentenced to thirty-nine lashes of the whip and removed "beyond the limits of this state never to return."

The churches established among the slaves—the first Black Baptist church in the United States was organized between 1773 and 1775 at Silver Bluffs, South Carolina—became important institutions. Frequently they monitored conduct, and, in many cases, they served as courts, particularly when one slave had a grievance against another. Sometimes they served the purpose of the owners, excommunicating Blacks for such acts as running away, or "impudence to masters." On the other hand, there were cases of Black people taking masters to church meetings to complain about mistreatment.

The whites, by establishing churches, created a unifying force among the Africans. White Methodists by 1860 had established a network of chapels with 26 stations responsible for 330 plantations. Forty-three white Methodist missionaries had, by that time, ministered to 9,000 African members of the church, 2,000 probationary members, and 6,000 African children in Sunday school. The whites had set up a structure that after the war became the base for the African Methodist Episcopal Church in South Carolina. As it developed, the missionaries could not impart the Gospel without educating the Africans. One missionary reported that the children "could answer every question in the Catechism prepared by the Missionary Secretary, could repeat the Lord's Prayer, Commandments, Creeds, and a number of hymns. The children were generally interested, behaved well and learned fast." In this way, too, the missionaries built for the free future.

By 1860, of some 400,000 African slaves in South Carolina, 80,000 were regular church members. Almost half of the 5,000 Presbyterians in the state in 1859 were Black. In the following year, the Episcopal church baptized a total of 491 whites and 1,100 Blacks. Surprisingly, Black members of the Episcopal church were almost equal in number to the whites. In the up-country, the same numerical parity could be found in the Methodist church. It seems possible that those of our people who were brought into the church and exposed in slavery to religious training developed certain skills that would, after the Civil War, place them in positions of leadership of and advantage over those who had not been churched.

From Resistance to Freedom

Difficult though it was, some South Carolina slaves mounted an active struggle against bondage. At the time of the Revolutionary War, thousands of them entered the British armed forces on the promise of freedom. When Charleston fell to the Americans in 1780, many Africans fled with the British rather than be returned to the slavers. In a more personal form of resistance, slaves sometimes poisoned or otherwise murdered their masters.

Despite the odds against it, armed insurrections occasionally occurred. There were attempts to burn Charleston in 1720 and 1730 in order to make the "Negroes of every Plantation ... their own Masters." There were other attempts in 1724 and 1741. Marauding war parties of Africans and Indians attacked some plantations. Armed bands of runaways lived in the countryside. In addition, three major rebellions were planned. The Stono uprising in 1739 resulted in twenty-one white and twenty-two Black deaths. The Camden uprising, set for July 4, 1816, was betrayed. Denmark Vesey's 1822 rebellion failed for the same reason. Thirty-five Africans were executed in the aftermath of that aborted uprising.

South Carolina before the Civil War was a state run on terror. Yet the Black population resisted insofar as it was able and managed to create a community and a culture. Some slaves even learned to read and write despite the laws against it. The participation of our people in armed struggle for their liberation culminated in the formation by South Carolinians of the first Black regiment to serve in the Union army during the Civil War. And nothing is more symbolic of the link between Northern Blacks and Southern Blacks than the liberation of Charleston by the 54th Massachusetts Regiment, with its contingent of Black soldiers from Pennsylvania and New York. Many of these troops took their discharges in Charleston and stayed to lead Black South Carolinians in the period of Reconstruction, to which we now turn.

Chapter 9

THE RECONSTRUCTION
IN SOUTH CAROLINA

Missus an' Masser a-walkin' de street
Deir han's in deir pockets an' nothin' to eat
She'd better be home a-washin' up de dishes,
An' a-cleanin' up de old man's raggity britches
He'd better run 'long an' get out de hoes
An' clear out his own crooked weedy corn rows;
De Kingdom is come, [we] is free
Hain't no slaves in de Year Jubilee

From Negro Folk Rhymes
by THOMAS W. TALLEY

O Freedom, O Freedom
O Freedom over me
And before I'd be a slave
I'd be buried in my grave
Go home to my lord and be free

Traditional Black Spiritual

Reconstruction is a name applied to the period from 1865 to 1877 when it seemed, for a time, that democracy might come to the South. Black South Carolinians fought a valiant but losing battle to carve out for themselves the same political and social rights as white American men enjoyed. The battle was waged against white South Carolinians buttressed by the federal government's ambivalent policy toward the enforcement of rights for Blacks. By 1877, ambivalence had turned to active support of the white Southerners. In dozens of incidents before that year, it had become clear that the sympathy of Northern white troops who occupied the state after the Civil War lay with the whites of South Carolina, not with the Blacks whose rights they were sworn to protect.

Reconstruction was a time of great changes in American society. The Civil War had intensified the rate of industrial growth in the North, and this technological superiority ultimately brought the South to bay. The North was poised on the brink of the expansion that was to make America into an industrial giant. But before that could take place, the South had to be brought back into the Union, and made into a market for Northern goods. That was a complicated process, involving the creation of new relationships among ex-slaves and ex-masters.

In the years between 1865 and 1867, under the presidency of Andrew Johnson, a lenient and conciliatory policy toward the ex-Confederates resulted in their resumption of power in the South. An angry Congress, led by the so-called Radical Republicans, then passed the Reconstruction Act of 1867, which placed all of the former Confederate states, except Tennessee, under military rule until they adopted state constitutions that recognized the rights of ex-slaves and ratified the Fourteenth Amendment of the Constitution. Under the provisions of this act, Reconstruction governments, made up of Black Southern Republicans, some former Southern pro-Union sympathizers, and both white and Black Northerners—the so-called carpetbaggers—were established. The rule of these governments from 1867 to 1877, backed by federal troops, is known as Radical Reconstruction. It was a contest between the Radical Republicans, whose main supporters were the newly freed Blacks, and the Southern Democratic party, to which the overwhelming mass of white Southerners of all classes gave their allegiance.

Reconstructing the Reputation of Reconstruction

Only recently has the real history of the Reconstruction begun to be widely known. For almost one hundred years, the Reconstruction was depicted by historians as a disaster that was finally righted by the establishment of all-white governments in 1877. And the views of such historians filtered down to influence the popular consciousness. Consider, for example, my freshman-year high school history teacher. He had white hair, slouched, and always sneered when he spoke to me, the only Black student in the class. In his view, Black people must have enjoyed slavery, because if they had not, they would have fought to the death as the Plains Indians had. Opening a textbook whose illustrations depicted drunk and clowning Black legislators, he mockingly asked whether they could possibly have run a government. I knew that he was wrong, but was overwhelmed and intimidated when he cited "leading historians" at Columbia and Harvard to back his assertions.

But in the past quarter-century, there has been a shift in the historical evaluation of the period. Indeed, one major historian describes the Reconstruction as an "inexhaustible reservoir for black and white Americans alike of the people and incidents demonstrating the indestructibility of the human spirit." The great achievements of Blacks during the Reconstruction, he says, "wait to be rediscovered to chasten white arrogance and strengthen black pride." The next chapters will attempt to do just that.

The Reconstruction in South Carolina left a mixed legacy. Certainly, as the old-fashioned view held, many of the legislators were corrupt. But they left a "constitution written in excellent English and embodying some of the best legal principles of the age." Moreover, the Reconstruction government created the basic administrative structure of the state of South

Carolina and democratized the procedures by which many officials were elected.

The politics of Reconstruction can be briefly summarized before we examine in detail the violence that characterized the period. In September 1865, the Southern whites who still controlled the state government passed the so-called Black Codes, which severely limited the rights of Blacks. They denied Blacks the right to be artisans, mechanics, or shopkeepers, and forbade them to join the state militia or own firearms. These codes were reversed by the Civil Rights Act of 1866, and by the Fourteenth Amendment. By 1867, with federal assistance, the so-called radicals, the same coalition of whites and Blacks to which we earlier referred, had taken political control of the state and set about drafting a new constitution. That constitution remained in effect after South Carolina whites regained power and was the basis for the constitution of 1895. The Reconstruction constitution established "the principle of equality of all men before the law with the right of all citizens to attend public schools, supported by the state." Federal intervention in the affairs of the state was directly attributable to the illegality and brutality of the "Black Codes."

At the convention drafting the new constitution, seventy-six of the one hundred twenty-four delegates were Black. Between 1868 and 1878, the radical Republican government of South Carolina sent eight Blacks to the United States Congress, elected two Black lieutenant-governors, and installed a Black justice—J. J. Wright, a friend of O. V. Catto—on the state court. For six years after 1867, Blacks constituted a majority in the lower house of the state legislature, although they were never a majority of the upper house. The Reconstruction gave Black political leaders more scope and power than they would exercise for another century.

Educated Black Northerners were a major source of Black leadership in the South during Reconstruction. And many of them were from Philadelphia. After the Civil War Jonathan C. Gibbs, a Presbyterian minister in Philadelphia, became the secretary of state of Florida, where he slept in a room full of weapons. Jacob C. Ballard, a former member of the Banneker

Institute, also became a state official in Florida. Pliny Locke, the father of Alain Locke, taught in Tennessee from 1867 to 1868. John H. Smythe, a graduate of the ICY, was an assistant cashier of the Freedmen's Bank and a member of the Constitutional Convention in North Carolina. John Wesley Cromwell, a former slave who eventually graduated from the ICY, and was described as a person of "brains, activity and . . . culture" was a teacher in Virginia. T. J. Minton, another graduate of the ICY, became a lawyer in South Carolina. William Whipper, the son or nephew of the Black abolitionist William Whipper, fought in the Civil War, became a lawyer, a member of the South Carolina legislature, and a brigadier general—along with Henry Purvis, the son of Robert Purvis— in the South Carolina militia. Whipper married Frances E. Rollin, a female graduate of the ICY who was teaching in Charleston. Richard Gleaves "gravitated from Philadelphia to South Carolina and was elected lieutenant governor. He was a suave, mild-mannered man and had become well-known the country over because of Masonry and other secret-order affiliations." Stephen A. Swails, of Columbia, Pennsylvania, first lieutenant in the 54th Massachusetts Regiment, became a state senator in South Carolina and a major general in the South Carolina militia. Thaddeus K. Sasportas, a native Charlestonian who was educated at the ICY, was a teacher and politician in South Carolina during the Reconstruction. Richard Greener, the Philadelphia-born Black dean of the South Carolina University Law School, had been the principal of the male department of ICY—succeeding the slain O. V. Catto— immediately before coming to South Carolina.

I often wonder what would have happened if my high school history teacher had told our class—which included future judges, district attorneys, surgeons, and business leaders of Philadelphia—the truth about the Black legislators of post–Civil War South Carolina. The first of them to be seated was Congressman Joe Rainey, whose grandson, a student at our school some years ago, broke the city record for the hundred-yard dash, and is now a promising Black politician in Philadelphia. The congressman was born of slave parents, and never attended a school in his life, but educated himself. Rainey felt so strongly about the dignity of his office and about integrated public accommodations that "he once refused to leave the dining room of a hotel . . . until he, a congressman, was forcibly ejected."

Robert Smalls, born a slave, moved to Charleston, where he became a sailor and rose to the level of pilot, in all but title, of a Confederate ship. In 1862, when white Confederate crew members went ashore, Smalls and other Black seamen sailed that boat under the menacing guns of the fort that guarded the harbor and delivered it to the Union fleet. Afterward, he was engaged as a federal pilot, fought in several naval battles, and piloted a Union ship in the attack on Fort Sumter. In December 1863, when a Union captain lost his nerve under heavy Confederate fire, Robert Smalls took command of the ship and sailed her out of range of the guns. For this act he was promoted to the rank of captain and commander of the ship until the end of the war. He was afterward elected to Congress, representing the Blacks of the coastal region of South Carolina, where he served with honor until 1887.

And there was Robert Elliot of South Carolina, generally considered to be one of the ablest men in Congress and probably the prototype for the hero of Howard Fast's novel, *Freedom Road*. After the assassination of a Black state legislator, Elliot said: "We have suffered much, and may suffer more. Let us not be driven from our positions by any threats." As assistant adjutant general of South Carolina, Elliot was chiefly responsible for the creation of Black militia units in the face of Ku Klux Klan violence in the late 1860s.

But towering over his other accomplishments were his oratorical skills and his leadership of the Black delegation in Congress. He fought tenaciously for the enactment of the Civil Rights Act of 1875, arguing that every citizen of the United States, Black or white, "is always and everywhere entitled to the equal protection of the laws." Almost eighty years passed before that position was recognized by the Supreme Court in the case of *Brown* v. *Board of Education*. On another occasion, when a white speaker in Congress said that there was not "one gentlemen on this floor who can honestly say he really believes that the colored man is his equal," another Black South Carolina congressman interrupted him to say, "I can." The Virginian replied, "Of course you can, but I am speaking to the white men of this House." The next day Elliot took the floor, but refused to address the remarks: "Let him [the speaker] feel that a Negro was not only too magnanimous to smite him in his weakness, but was even charitable enough to grant him the mercy of silence."

The Reconstruction in South Carolina was ended in 1876 by the Hamburg Massacre—in which Black militia men were murdered—and by the subsequent election of Wade Hampton, said by some to have been the prototype of Rhett Butler, as governor. That is the political history. But most discussions about politics during Reconstruction obscure the military struggle for power that took place in South Carolina. It was an unequal struggle between experienced Confederate veterans, sometimes led by ex-generals, and ill-armed Black guerrilla bands, composed almost entirely of men who had yesterday been slaves. The white South Carolinians also won the war of the Reconstruction because they were more ruthless than our people, and desperate to retain their social and economic privileges.

From the beginning, whites practiced random terror, boldly in the upstate counties where their numbers were even with ours, and timidly in the lowland areas where there was an overwhelming Black majority. One white historian of South Carolina claims that some South Carolinians would just as soon shoot a Black man as look at him. Once a white man asked a newly freed slave to whom he belonged. When the Black man said nobody owned him, the white man took out his knife and cut the Black man to pieces for his impudence. In Columbia, a white police chief who shot a "young freedman" while arresting him on a minor charge was absolved of any crime. A Black woman protesting the case wrote: "God knows what we will do. We are not allowed to have arms; if a white man strikes us, and we attempt to defend ourselves, we are carried to the Provost Court, and fined ten or twenty dollars. It is hard I tell you. . . . God knows it is worse than slavery. The Negro code is in full force here with both Yankees and rebels."

But we were not passive victims of this violence. Throughout South Carolina in 1866 and 1867, we formed ourselves into self-defense units, usually outgrowths of the Masons, the so-called Union Leagues, associations in support of the Radical Republicans, or of the official state militia. In 1868, after the assassinations of several major politicians in Abbeville County, a statewide militia, which became the backbone of Black resistance to the white South Carolinians, was organized. A state of war existed between these units and the Southern whites until 1877. Some of our units were never defeated in battle.

Some Black Military Leaders

The names of these Black captains seldom appear in textbooks that tell of Reconstruction history. Their names were June Mobley, Jim Williams (Rainey), Doc Adams, Ned Tennant, Jim Wilkes, and Simon Coker. They were soldiers who drilled with fixed bayonets and beating drums. In addition, they frequently "occupied the entire roadway—needlessly incommoded and naturally irritated the white people for whose benefit their offensive movements were plainly intended."

Outbreaks of violence between whites and Blacks were endemic. Thus, in Camden, the white marshal of the town had to take refuge from the militia after he attempted to arrest one of their number. But in January 1871, an encounter there between the militia and the whites resulted in the lynching of thirteen Black men. In Chester County, the leader of the Black militia was Captain Jim Wilkes. In the winter of 1870–71, his house was assaulted by some three hundred men of the Ku Klux Klan. They were driven off by a band of fifty-five Blacks. Seemingly surprised at the resistance, the Klan "didn't do nothing but run their horses for life."

When the tension ran high between the militia and the Klan, the state government, fearing a race war, attempted to

108

disarm us. Many of the Black captains laid down their guns whenever such requests were made. But Captain Jim Williams (changed from his slave name of James Rainey) of York County would have none of this. He was known as a "bold and aggressive fellow, unquestionably a hater of the white race and evidently bent on mischief." When asked by the government to disarm, he said that "the other captains were cowards, who gave up their guns." He said that the government had promised him forty acres and a mule and "they hadn't given it to him, and he said that if war had to take place that he would have a whole plantation." He wanted a fair fight with the whites, "to go into the old field and fight it out."

They came for him while he slept in the night of March 7, 1871. Sixty members of the Ku Klux Klan "hung him to a tree. They then departed as quietly as they had come." Our lack of depth of leadership told, for afterward his band was in confusion. Indeed, "for two days, they threatened to kill all the white men in the vicinity and might have done so had they found a leader." The federal government sent in U.S. troops to protect the whites in the aftermath of the lynching. Soon after, Williams's men turned in their arms.

The whites never did conquer Captain Ned Tennant of Edgefield County, though he was tricked a few times into laying down his weapons. Whites like to say that Tennant was the "first of his race to stand up to large bodies of rifle companies." The Klan and the so-called rifle clubs tried to kill him one night in September 1874, the same way they had killed Jim Williams. They fired into his house, but Tennant escaped with his family. The countryside resounded with the thumping of the once-banned African drums and three hundred armed Black men showed up to aid Tennant. He led his men into town where they stood down at least a thousand whites under the command of ex-Confederate General M. C. Butler. Tennant said that he did not like the idea of people shooting into his house at night: "Holding out one hand full of cartridges, he declared his intention to kill and to burn." Then the whites pulled a trick that they used repeatedly on the Indians—"they got an agreement to disband both forces." Once

Tennant's men had gone home, the whites denied having agreed to anything. Tennant was then arrested on riot charges and his company was forced to turn in its arms to waiting U.S. troops.

Captain Tennant had no taste for treachery, so in January 1875, he took his guns back. And on a January night, somebody burned down General Butler's house with his family barely escaping. The general naturally blamed Tennant and sent a posse after him with a warrant. Tennant ambushed them. His men set up roadblocks and "challenged travellers as they passed," while Tennant hid in the swamps until captured a week later. Tennant's actions caused such a fear of a race war that the white governor forced the Black militia companies in Edgefield County to give up their arms. In May 1875, one of Tennant's lieutenants, "a leading man" in this Edgefield war, was shot in the back while "escaping" from prison. In October 1876, a band, probably from Tennant's command, went out and ambushed a group of six whites. "There was intense excitement and there were threats of retaliation," but nothing happened and the band was settled finally on a "piece of state land within a mile of the spot where the ambush took place."

Captain Doc Adams, the leader of the Black militia in Hamburg, seems to have drawn the wrath stirred up in General Butler's breast by the actions of Ned Tennant. In July 1876, the Hamburg riot took place. General Butler said afterward that it was time these Black militia units were taught a lesson. An incident was provoked and a militia unit of sixty men armed with Remington rifles was beseiged in the armory of this little village just across the river from Savannah, Georgia. They fought well until the ex-Confederates stormed the armory with an artillery piece. Doc Adams refused to surrender, and most of his soldiers escaped. But a number were taken prisoner by the armed whites who now numbered in the hundreds. A Black first lieutenant of the militia was shot dead while talking to General Butler. Then the white "rifle clubs" chose some prisoners—either "the meanest characters" from among the militia company or "the most prominent Negro leaders," depending on your point of view—and ordered them to run so that the guards could shoot them and say they were escaping. It was done before "the eyes of their wives and children." Afterward, the rest of the Blacks were told to run, and the "rifle clubs" shot at random into their backs.

The End of the Armed Conflict

Our people in other parts of South Carolina, particularly where they held a large majority, retaliated. During the campaign of 1876 that brought Wade Hampton to power, South Carolina was aflame with skirmishes between the Blacks and the whites. At Ellenton, in September, a militia company under the command of Captain Simon Coker from Barnwell County reenforced the Blacks in that town and fought white forces commanded by ex-Confederate generals. Coker's men wounded the sheriff, killed one white, and wounded three others. Again, the U.S. infantry intervened and succeeded in getting both sides to retire. In the aftermath, Simon Coker, "an unusually bright mulatto, leader of the Republican party" of Barnwell County, was captured by "Captain" Nat Butler, the brother of General Butler at Hamburg. We are told by an unsympathetic Southern writer that Coker "died with unusual courage"—that is, for a Black man. When Butler solicited his last request, Coker asked him to take the key to his cotton house so that his rent could be paid and then said he wanted to pray. But "before the doomed man could finish his prayer, the order 'Make ready, men, aim, fire' was given and Simon Coker still in a kneeling position with pleas of forgiveness on his lips, passed from earth into eternity." Then, somebody shot a big hole in his head so he wouldn't come back. The murder of this representative of the state legislature of South Carolina and captain in the state militia took place before the eyes of federal troops. In the 1870 census, he was reported as having a five-year-old deaf-and-dumb boy and two daughters, ages four and two.

Calm eluded South Carolina. In Beaufort, where everybody

who was born there looks like Joe Frazier, our people almost killed a Black Democrat. A white posse was "resisted by a mob of armed Negroes and a fight ensued" in which one of the whites was killed and others wounded. Upstate, where the whites had military dominance, we still resisted. A militia band led by Captain Henry Daniels stopped a white Democrat as he was about to introduce a Black Democrat. Said Captain Daniels, "Colonel, I don't want to hurt you or cause any mischief, but the body of men I command are pledged that no man of our race shall speak on the Democratic side at our meetings." Daniels said that a white man could vote just like he wanted, ". . . but no damn Black man" had a right to vote for Wade Hampton.

And in Charleston, in September 1876, "Hamburg was strikingly reversed as whites here were terrorized by roving bands of rioting, looting Negroes." It was so bad that Wade Hampton cried when he heard of the cowardice of the whites. In one case, Black policemen sent to quell a riot instead joined the combat against the whites.

By 1877, it was all over as Wade Hampton became governor of the state upon the withdrawal of federal troops. Our people had fought well when given arms and leadership. Black women had refused to sleep with their men or wash their clothes if they did not join the militia. The churches had expelled men who would not fight. But superior weaponry and military leadership resulted in a coup d'etat whereby the old leaders of white South Carolina restored themselves to power. The Thirteenth, Fourteenth, and Fifteenth Amendments of the Constitution of the United States were reduced to meaningless words on paper when the Reconstruction in South Carolina was finished. Mao Tse-tung said that power comes from the barrel of a gun; white South Carolinians never doubted that.

Bishop Turner of the A.M.E. Church, ex-chaplain of the 1st South Carolina Regiment, deplored the white response to the Hamburg massacre: "Scores of newspapers come up with nickel apologies and thousands of pretended church members openly endorse the act. Still we talk about this being a Christian country. Did you ever read the history of the Dark Ages?

I have, and I have read of nothing being perpetrated during that long period of dissipation and cruelty, which surpassed [this] deed of horror." The bishop, who was born near Abbeville, said that he would rather live under a monarchy than in a "mobocracy" where the government countenanced terrorists. Martin Delany thought that the problem was that the whites would not submit to rule by Blacks.

Our resistance in Black-controlled territory was decisive in controlling white terrorism in South Carolina. Black Honky-Dory Clubs, secret organizations, plotted to eject physically the Democratic legislators from Edgefield and Lauren counties. In pictures of Philadelphia's Black community in 1920, you see stores named "Honky-Dory." Our South Carolina people brought the names of their heroes with them.

Chapter 10

THE BLACK CHURCH
IN SOUTH CAROLINA

I been 'buked and I been scorned
I been 'buked, I been scorned, children
I been 'buked and I been scorned
I been talked about sure as you're born

Well, ain't gonna lay my religion down
Ain't gonna lay my religion down, children
Ain't gonna lay my religion down
Ain't gonna lay my religion down

Traditional Black Spiritual

The history of Black Reconstruction and the history of the A.M.E. Church in South Carolina are tied together. Bishop Payne, who had left South Carolina, returned after the war to help rebuild the church, which had been proscibed after Denmark Vesey's attempted revolt. He was aided by R. H. Cain, who had been so instrumental in building the church in western Pennsylvania. Cain was the pastor of Charleston's Emmanuel Church, controller of a powerful journal, *The Missionary Recorder*, and a member of the state legislature. He was committed to land reform, was elected to Congress for two terms, and became, after Reconstruction, a bishop in the A.M.E. Church.

The organizational structure of the church was already in place by the time of Reconstruction; it had simply to build on the administrative apparatus. As one church leader said, Morris Brown had planted the seed of the church so deeply in South Carolina that nothing could uproot it. By the end of Reconstruction, the A.M.E. Church had 44,000 members and 1,000 ministers. In 1906, there were 79,000 A.M.E. Church members as opposed to 219,000 Baptists. But the statistics do not tell the full story. Twelve A.M.E. ministers served in the South Carolina legislature during Reconstruction, and their activities were paralleled by scores of A.M.E. ministers and lay leaders in the rural areas of South Carolina. So powerful was the church's organizational structure that "it is virtually a fact that the African Methodists moved their 30,000 members into the Republican Party as a solid phalanx."

The A.M.E. Church's Many Tasks

Finding, in 1865, "our race without education, and its means of unfolding, no schoolhouses, or even church edifices, belonging to them," the church bent to the primary tasks of educating the people and settling them upon their own land. Payne's insistence on the primacy of education was seen in almost every activity of the church. Committees focusing on education reported at every conference, emphasizing the link between freedom and literacy. Bishop Cain was downright eloquent on the matter: "The [minister] . . . must be an example to the believer . . . *Give yourself to reading.* You must study arts, science, literature." He went on to say that no nation could rise to greatness except on a bedrock of knowledge.

The church created a network of Sunday schools that often served as literacy centers for adults as well as children. In addition, parochial schools were attached to many churches.

The A.M.E. organizers were told to establish schools "whereas our people are destitute of day schools," and the ministers themselves were told to run these schools, if qualified, or, if not, to find qualified teachers. Recognizing that "disease and disorder" were prevalent among the freemen, the church recommended that physical education, the "basis of which is cleanliness, good wholesome food, pure air, and exercise" be taught as well as reading.

On the level of secondary and higher education, the church was also active. In 1871, the South Carolina Conference of the Church raised three thousand dollars as part of an endowment campaign for Wilberforce University. With reluctance, because of the "roving bands of outlaws who infest[ed] that section of the state," the church created Payne Institute in Cokesbury, South Carolina, on a site with 142 acres and the "best orchards about the town." The school soon moved to Columbia, where it took its present name, Allen University.

The church actively pursued a policy of establishing churches surrounded by Black settlers with clear title to the land. One report on the churches in Abbeville County noted that a church with twenty-five homesteading families had its "deeds made out properly."

Some Preachers Who Would Die for Their Faith

The magnitude of the A.M.E. Church's organizational achievement can be understood by focusing on the building of the Church in Abbeville County. The first A.M.E. preacher in Greenwood was Bouey Roye from New York City, who arrived in late 1867. He was in the last stages of consumption and so sick that no one could understand him: "He had lost his lungs completely. He could say nothing intelligible." But he pulled himself up to the pulpit and, waving his arms "by a hard struggle and painful effort informed us that he was an African Methodist preacher, sent up there for the purpose of organizing the African Methodist Church." He died shortly thereafter and the Black people of Greenwood organized a small society of keep the faith alive.

Roye's successor was the Reverend James T. Baker, born in Columbia, South Carolina, in 1832. He was a member of the white Methodist church in Columbia before the Civil War and was a protégé of Bishop Turner. When Turner left South Carolina, he told Baker, "You are to take charge of my class and don't be afraid . . . God will not let them kill you. If he has sent you to do his work, he will not let you die." Baker was converted to the A.M.E. Church right after the Civil War and was posted to Greenwood in 1867. He must have repeated the words of Bishop Turner when he was met by a General Gillam, who said that he could preach but that he'd better look out if he was a Black Radical. Another white told him he should leave town.

But Baker was ready to die for his beliefs, and he went on to church, "a big old wooden storehouse in old Greenwood." That afternoon, to intimidate him, fifty whites came to the church. But Baker went out to all the churches to which the Blacks belonged, urging them to join the African Church. He met opposition from the white clergy, who told the Blacks that the "African preacher has come down here with a new God and a new Bible." While some white churches had welcomed the establishment of independent Black churches, many preferred to maintain pre–Civil War arrangements, whereby Blacks worshipped under white supervision, either segregated in white churches, or in congregations supervised by a white-appointed deacon. As the A.M.E. Church became identified with Radical Republicanism in the late 1860s, whites became particularly antagonistic toward it: "When it turns the church into a political club . . . it should be rebuked."

Baker went to a hill near the white church and prayed, sang, and preached to those Blacks who would come. Their fear increased as a deacon of the white church came to stare. But Baker told the people that Jesus was there and no harm would come to them, and they stayed and became converted. Baker also went into gin houses and into the countryside, steadily converting the Blacks to African Methodism. He founded "Green Pond Church which is now Pine Grove. Next the Brick House Church and Wardlaw's Stand; here is where the guns were seen, but God was with us and we were successful."

From 1868 to 1871, Baker was in nearby Lexington County; he summarized his experiences as "Hard Times in This County." Back in Abbeville County by 1871, he built church after church and established Sunday school conventions. The church had enough members to invite Bishop Turner to preach to large camp meetings some four miles outside of Abbeville. Baker also organized the people to purchase their own homestead lots and founded the first Agricultural Society among the Black people of Abbeville Courthouse. Baker maintained his courage throughout his life. In the 1880s, when the whites were attempting to drive out all Black secret organizations, Baker hosted a speaker from the Colored Alliance at Abbeville, a "secret ritualistic organization" that aimed at improving the economic conditions of Black farmers and agricultural laborers.

Also active in the formation of the Abbeville County A.M.E. Church was the Reverend A. Weston, who arrived there in 1869 "because," as he said, "there was no other one to send." By then the county was ablaze with armed struggle. In the town where whites had just assassinated the major Black political leader in the state, Weston recalled: "We [he and a colleague] excited wonder and surprise. We went on like poor wayfaring men, with our lives in our hands, not knowing but that it would be the last day of our existence. So on and on we went." Weston too took Black people out of other churches: "Reverend Frank Brown came to me from nine miles above Abbeville Courthouse from the C.M.E. Church with 1,600 members." The Colored Methodist Episcopal [C.M.E.] Church was an independent Black church sanctioned by the Southern white Methodists, and because of this association early "suffered from the suspicions of Negroes," which it later overcame. By 1869, Weston had put up the frame for the A.M.E. Church in Abbeville Courthouse and had bought and paid for the "lot and church at Greenwood, South Carolina." From this base, the church spread up to Anderson, Greenville, and other towns in the Piedmont district. Of Weston, a fellow fighter from those early days, said, "Amid all the danger that surrounded him, he stood up like a hero."

Danger always hovered around the early leaders of the A.M.E. Church. Said one: "Often when we went out to preach we had guards out watching for us. During the greater part of our time, we dared not walk the highway to preach and organize our churches. . . . I always went to sleep with one eye open. I only held my meetings in the daytime; and I always left the neighborhood at night. In this way we made up our church."

When the Reverend Wade Perrin—a state legislator, who shows up in the 1870 census living next door to my great-great-grandfather—was killed, he was memorialized thus: "Wade Perrin fell by the assassin's bullet, a martyr to manhood and principle. He was a faithful and energetic minister of the Gospel of the African M.E. Church, and while we mourn his loss, we mourn not as those who have no hope, for we believe he was enabled to challenge death for his sting and the grave for its victory." The sacrifices created a strong sense of A.M.E. unity: "We love this Church. There are some of us who know what it cost to build this Church in this State because of our rough experience. We know what we have suffered and endured. I tell you that there are men in this Church, who are so devoted to its principles that they would lay their heads, if necessary, upon the block for the Church. God Bless the Church. God bless the brethren. God give us strength for all time to come." Thus were the A.M.E. churches of Abbeville County, South Carolina—including Pine Grove, later sacked in the race war of 1898—built.

The lives of these pioneers sometimes had light moments. One preacher, a fair-complexioned veteran of a Black South Carolina regiment, remembered how the people of the countryside had first regarded him. Someone asked, "Is this the African preacher? Well, this is the first redheaded African I ever did see." Another reminisced: "I used to do some things that would not now be tolerated. On one occasion, I married some twenty-five couples at the same time, with one ceremony. The way I did it, I just formed them in a line, with the men on one side and the women on the other, and I went up the aisle and performed one ceremony for all present. Then Weston signed the certificates. He told me to do the marrying and he would sign the certificates."

By 1874, the church in the Abbeville district had 7500 members organized into forty-two churches with one hundred odd preachers in assorted categories and twenty-three hundred children in Sunday school. On a statewide level, the church had similarly taken root. And it had formed links with churches in other states. The South Carolina Conference of the church organized the North Carolina, Georgia, and Florida districts of the church. By the late 1800s, the Southern branch of Richard Allen's church was firmly established.

The growth of the A.M.E. Church was paralleled by the creation of a network of Baptist churches throughout the state from 1875 to 1885, and by the rise of the A.M.E. Zion, Northern Methodist, Colored Methodist Episcopal, and to a lesser degree, the establishment of Episcopal and Presbyterian congregations unaffiliated with the white churches of their denominations. Of these, the Baptists were the most important, since they outnumbered the A.M.E. by almost two to one at the close of the century. Because the Baptist church was not centrally organized, less documentation on its early years is available. But it appears that white Baptists did not oppose the creation of Black churches as strongly as the members of some other denominations. Some authorities attribute this to the tradition of local autonomy in that church; the local Baptist church only had to approve the separation from their church of Blacks who had already been holding prayer meetings with a Black exhorter. Moreover, Baptist services were less rigid than some other denominations and they were less concerned with formal educational or training requirements for ministers.

We do know that much of the work of organizing Black Baptists was done by the Reverend E. M. Brawley, who had been born free in Charleston in 1851. At the age of ten he was sent to Philadelphia where he attended the ICY and studied under Professor Basset. Surely, he and O. V. Catto knew one another since Catto taught there in those days. By 1875, Brawley was a Baptist minister, and during the next eight years he put together five hundred fifty Baptist churches in South Carolina, with some three hundred fifty preachers, and nearly one hundred thousand members into a statewide convention that later became part of the National Baptist Convention.

Alexander Bettis was the driving force behind the creation of Baptist churches in the Piedmont region. An extraordinary man, Bettis preached to his fellow slaves on a plantation in Edgefield County and joined a white Baptist church before the Civil War. After the war, he was ordained—though not by the Edgefield white Baptists—and began an impressive career organizing more than forty churches and building an industrial school. The churches organized by Bettis did not join Brawley's association at first, but eventually most did.

The establishment of the Black church in South Carolina makes us understand the closeness of the ties between Northern Blacks and Southern Blacks, and between mulatto and Black. Weston could have passed for white, as could have many other prominent A.M.E. ministers. Instead of making personal escapes from oppression, they chose to serve their people. They had little money, but enormous faith, courage, and dedication. That sufficed to build structures that would permit Black people to survive in a state where the future seemed as grim as the past.

Chapter 11

BLACK EDUCATION
IN SOUTH CAROLINA

My work is hard and sometimes the way seems dark and I think nothing will be accomplished, but . . . there is no fun in doing easy things.

Black woman educator in South Carolina, 1890s

Educating the freed Blacks was the first mass effort in modern history to raise people to the level of skill necessary to compete in an industrialized society. The Russian, Chinese, and Cuban literacy campaigns, more recent examples, were backed by their governments. Certainly, the post–Civil War Freedmen's Bureau, by its expenditures on school buildings and supplies, was of great help between the end of the Civil War and 1870, but the attempt to raise Black people's level of literacy was made in the face of strong opposition from the white-controlled states in which most of us lived. The opposition was both official, in the form of minimal spending for Black education, and unofficial, in the form of burning down Black schools. But our people, with some white assistance, raised themselves. "Oh, child," sighed my Greenville aunt, an eighty-five-year-old former rural teacher, "you don't know what hard times they were." She referred not only to the lack of proper equipment, buildings, and money, but to the need for patience, humility, and toughness in reaching children scarred by the experience of slavery.

Not all the children were beautiful: some carried knives and razors. Others cursed their teachers. Some sat speechless, their minds focused on the image of a man burning at a stake, or hanging from some tall pine. Our people were poor and often had neither shelter, clothing, nor food. Hard praying and untiring effort were the main levers used to overcome these difficulties. They were successful; those Black teachers "reduced illiteracy among their people from 78.5 percent in 1880 to 64 percent in 1890, and still further to 52.8 percent in 1900." Let us now look at the schools where this work was, against such odds, accomplished.

Educating the Freedmen

One of the first of them was Seneca Institute, which according to Lewis K. McMillan's account of Black education in South Carolina was a "crude, humble, general country school" whose dormitories housed "robust, corn-fed girls from the back country hills of rural Blue Ridge South Carolina and Georgia." The Baptists and Methodists of Oconee County got together and agreed to a common site for this "college," which was really a high school. The "eight acres of choice location in the town of Seneca was bought and paid for by unlettered Negro Baptists of this county." The founder of the school, the Reverend J. J. Stark, was summoned by the people of the town, who had been waiting for him until he finished Morehouse College. At the time of Stark's arrival, there was only one high school graduate in the county, but Stark had the support of "hundreds and hundreds" of the poor Black people in that area who looked to that "humble" place as their high school.

Stark was followed by a great Black educator, Gordon Blaine Hancock, later dean of Virginia Union University, who injected the "zeal for learning" into the school. In Hancock's last year at Seneca there were thirteen "county boys and girls in the graduating class, all of whom, excepting one girl, went on to Morehouse, Morris, and Benedict Colleges and completed their college work." Hancock stressed Black pride, "self-help and Christian character." Receiving little assistance from the whites of the town, he believed that Blacks must sustain their own institutions. He became increasingly militant until eventually "word came that he would be lynched" and he had to leave on the night train to Columbia. He was my daddy's college dean.

"These wrecks were never honest to goodness buildings," McMillan tells us, "but they were all a forsaken poverty-stricken people had." The Bettis School in Edgefield County was fifteen miles from nowhere and could only be reached by a sandy road that led through "continuous stretches of monotonous, poor, sandy, land, dwarf oaklings and stringy short-leaf pine saplings." Its founder and president from 1881 to 1895 was Alexander Bettis, "who could not write his name." Apparently, Bettis and some other preachers were talking about dividing up the money in the churches' treasuries "for the purpose of enabling them to go to school." Said Bettis, "All of you who favor establishing a school with this money instead of wasting it on us preachers who are already on the verge of the grave, I want you to meet me tomorrow at Pleasant Grove Church." They did, and with the local families pitching in and cutting down the trees, they founded the school in 1881. And everytime that Bettis spotted a talented child, he would send him or her on to the Schofield School or Atlanta University.

Another school, Voorhees, was established with two hundred dollars in contributions from sixty-one churches with names like Willow Swamp, Bushy Pond, and Allen Chapel. None of them could contribute more than eight dollars. But with their money Elizabeth Wright, a graduate of Tuskegee Institute, who had seen her earlier efforts thwarted by white arsonists, built a school for their children. In a letter to Booker T. Washington, this young woman wrote, "My work is hard and sometimes the way seems dark and I think nothing will be accomplished, but . . . there is no fun in doing easy things."

Colleges were also established in South Carolina. Claflin and Benedict colleges were founded by Northern missionaries, but Allen University at Columbia was Payne Institute under a new name, and Morris College was started as an ideological split-off from Benedict.

Benedict College specialized in the education of "adults." Its first student was a man sixty-five years old. The college was satisfied to impart literacy to its students and then have these students return home to teach others. It also prepared ministers for the Baptist church; returning to the countryside, they "spoke a literary language to the multitudes of back-woodsmen." Of these ministers, McMillan says, "many of them were proud men. Many of them wore the fine old jim-swinger [Prince Albert] and the stately black derby." These cadres, in turn, "first organized small units, then larger and larger units until already five years after Benedict had begun her works the Negro Baptists set up their State Convention."

Founded by Northern white Methodists, Claflin University performed the same kind of work as Benedict and was an oasis of white and Black social equality. It heavily influenced Black education in the Orangeburg area and was a place where "every man who went away . . . even [after] a year's work there had learned to use the hammer and saw." Students in the first years at Claflin were ungraded because of the "mass adult education to which [the college] was devoted."

Claflin had an enormous effect on its students' later lives. McMillan's own father was a case in point: "He, a youth of 19, spent one year at Claflin. . . . At his death he had accumulated a substantial library in history, biography, agriculture, and religion. Claflin started him off. . . . [T]his is true of tens of thousands of Negro men and women. . . ." My aunt and her sister—the ones who taught Josh White and Peg Leg Bates and Jesse Jackson and founded recreation centers in Greenville—were graduates of Claflin around 1910. And the father of Philadelphia's first Black congressman, Robert C. Nix, graduated from Claflin at age thirty-five. Nelson Cornelius Nix went on to become a dean and head of the Department of Mathematics at South Carolina State College. His native talent was such that he did postgraduate work at the University of Chicago in Hebrew and mathematics. He was also a source of inspiration to Benjamin Mays.

These schools accomplished what they did with almost no support from the state. As late as 1918, South Carolina had only one public high school for Blacks, Howard High School of Columbia. In 1910, the state spent $10.00 on each white child and $1.44 for each Black child. That year, there were only seventy-one Black students in college classes in all of South Carolina. These inequalities were greatest in those counties with the highest concentrations of Blacks. A governor expressed the official attitude when he proclaimed: "I am opposed to white people's taxes being used to educate Negroes. I am a friend to the Negro race. This is proved by the regard in which the Negroes of my home county hold me. . . . In my opinion, when the people of this country began to try to educate the Negro they made a serious and grave mistake; and I fear the worst result is yet to come. So why continue?"

Education in Abbeville County

In Abbeville County most elementary education took place in small country schools. The Reverend J. J. Stark has left us a picture of a school outside of Greenwood, in the 1880s: "There was no ceiling of any kind. The floor was of rough, unmatched, unsized random width boards. The seats were of slabs with auger holes boared [sic] through them in which were inserted sawed off saplings for legs. These schools were ungraded. Spelling, geography, reading, grammar, history, and arithmetic made up the course of study. The length of the school year was from three to four months running a little over half in the winter with a short summer session. The teachers were faithful, but were not prepared to advance the pupils beyond the subjects named above." An old report tells us that there were "Free schools for colored people . . . supported by the colored people at Cokesbury, Turkey

Creek, Greenwood, and Due West." Many such schools were scattered throughout the county.

The center of Black education in Abbeville County was the Brewer Academy, which served as the high school for students from the surrounding countryside. In 1872, the Black people of Greenwood asked the American Missionary Association (AMA) of the Congregational Church for permission to move a school for Black children into a vacant building owned by the AMA. The AMA sent a teacher, J. D. Backenstose, to Greenwood; this the Black community found "gratifying." Backenstose was "very much pleased with the school building and grounds"—members of the community had just painted the schoolhouse—although he had no furniture except for a few "backless benches." The school was cold in the winter because it had no stove, and Backenstose worried that his students would have to stay home.

Tuition fees soon became an issue at Brewer. Upon his arrival, Backenstose had told students that the school would be free, but the authorities in the AMA's New York headquarters later urged him to institute fees, although Backenstose knew that the people could "hardly afford to pay as much as a dollar a month." A student—so bright that Backenstose had made him an aide—stirred up ill feeling by "telling people that the object of the AMA is to make money out of the people." The next spring Backenstose mourned the "loss of six of my brightest students this month. Their money gave out and they were obliged to return to their home and labor."

But by February 1876, Backenstose could say that "I have labored hard to build up this institution and it is just now beginning to be appreciated. I love the work with all my heart and am willing to remain in it for a trifling compensation." The school was often short of funds, but help always seemed to arrive just when it was needed. By 1880, Brewer Academy's influence radiated throughout the countryside, and its students included many youths who were teaching at the elementary levels. In 1916, the academy had ten white teachers and one Black and operated on a yearly budget of five thousand dollars, two-thirds of which came from the AMA, and the

127

remainder from tuition. A book on notable Black men of South Carolina, published in 1920, lists numerous graduates of the Brewer Academy, including the Reverend J. J. Stark, the founder of Seneca Academy and Morris College.

There were other Black-initiated schools in the county. In 1886, the Reverend Emory Williams from Washington, D.C., and his wife established the Ferguson Academy in Abbeville with some financial assistance from a New Jersey Presbyterian minister. By 1891, the school had been renamed the Harbison Academy, and financial responsibility had been assumed by the Board of Missions of the Presbyterian church. Reverend Williams had by that time resigned to open his own "Afro-American" school and church. He was replaced by another Black minister whose wife taught there and "regularly turned over to the institution her own salary in order that hers and her husband's work might bear fruit." The minister, a Reverend Thomas A. Amos, was forced to resign in 1906 because he "committed the unpardonable sin of taking an active part in a local political campaign." The school completely shut down for four months, and just before it was to reopen, the girls' dormitory burned down, but at the time the Presbyterians were not sure that it was malicious. Three years later, an incendiary bomb destroyed the boys' dormitory, killing three students and leaving three others injured. Since the victims were young, the fire was denounced by leading citizens of Abbeville and the state, and rewards were offered for information on the perpetrator, but nothing came of it. The school was moved to Irmo, South Carolina, away from Abbeville.

White teachers in South Carolina's Black schools did not have an easy time of it. In 1869, one of them wrote, "I reached Abbeville the 6th of April and felt like I was in the land of my most enraged enemies." He asked his correspondent to "hold me in remembrance if my Life should be taken from me." But some of these teachers succeeded. For example, Martha Schofield of Philadelphia created a fine school for Black children in the midst of the bloody wars in Edgefield County.

The whites in Abbeville County had public and private

schools of which they could be proud. In 1915, there were six thousand Black and three thousand white students in Abbeville County. The county authorized expenditures of $35,000 for the three thousand white students and $7,600 for the six thousand Black students. In that same year the average white student went to school for 128 days compared to 71 days for the Black students. The average salary of a white teacher was $340 as opposed to $83 for a Black teacher. In Greenwood County, in 1910, $13 per student in teacher's salary was allowed for the whites and $1.25 for the Blacks.

So it is no surprise that by 1910, the Black illiteracy rate in Greenwood County was thirty-five percent while among the white population it was six percent. All the efforts of the Black educators and of the white missionaries could not wipe out that deficit. But the fact that in such schools, with so little state support, sixty-five out of one hundred Black people in Abbeville County learned to read, is a tribute both to the dedication of the teachers and to their students' desire for education.

Chapter 12

THE OPPRESSION
IN ABBEVILLE COUNTY,
PART ONE

Thou shalt not be afraid for the terror by night; nor for the arrow that flieth by day; nor for the pestilence that walketh in darkness; nor for the destruction that wasteth at noon-day.

Psalm 91:5–6

The terror visited upon the Black people of Abbeville County after the Civil War marked them and their descendants. In his autobiography, Benjamin Mays claimed that in Greenwood County "most Negroes grinned, cringed, and kowtowed in the presence of white people. Those who could not take such subservience left for the city as soon as they could." I know that's true, because my grandfather from Greenwood would not raise his eyes to white people. Even though I'd been born in Philadelphia, I, as a six year old was drilled to say, "Yes sir, no sir, how do you do, sir," and nothing more, to white people. My mother's old Philadelphia family of St. Thomas Church and the Banneker Institute could not abide those words of Black Southern survival.

Mays continued: "Negroes lived under constant pressures and tensions all the time in my community. They knew they were not free. They knew that if attacked they dare not strike back—if they wanted to live." Like any people surrounded by a more powerful enemy, they knew that they endangered the entire community by acting violently against whites, and that made retaliation virtually taboo.

Abbeville County

The territory that was known for most of its existence as Abbeville County embraced today's Greenwood and Abbeville counties and parts of McCormick, Saluda, and Edgefield counties. In the early days of South Carolina, the region was known as the up-country or the Ninety-Six district. In 1897, it was divided into the present-day Abbeville and Greenwood counties.

Before the American Revolution, there were vast brakes of cane and hundreds of buffalo in the up-country. An early settler said that "a man can stand in his door and kill more game than would be sufficient to support two families." The early white settlers raised horses and cattle and crops of oats, wheat, and cotton ginned by slaves. Of one plantation, named White Hall, an early observer said, "This is one of the finest . . . in South Carolina, abounding with fine Rich Red Loamy land, famous for Raising Corn, Hemp, Flax, Cotton, Rice, Cattle, Hogs, Fruits of all sorts and great plenty. . . . In the year Sixty-six [the] peach orchard yielded near three thousand bushel baskets, which proved of great use to the poor young inhabitants of that part of the province. The woods here consist of fine white and black oak, ash, maple, hickory, birch, and many lofty pines." Another local historian recalled that in the nineteenth century the Hard Labor Creek was a "fine stream for bathing and fishing." A place called Granny Ponds was famous for its blue catfish and "the stream was well-stocked with cats, perches, suckers, pike, and other fish. . . . Many a time in the summer when crops were laid by, shouts of victory arose as large fish, a slippery eel or a great turtle were entangled and brought to land." This same writer summarized the white view of the place: "Dear old Hard Labor, the place of innocent recreation. Dear old Abbeville, the home of neighborly, kind, industrious people."

The Cherokee nation owned the land where Abbeville County stood. Their main trading path ran down from the Piedmont to Charleston, meandering along rivers with bell-tone names like Congaree, Keowee, Kiawah, Santee, and Wando. The white men came up the same path, dragging their slaves behind them. In the mid-1750s, the whites, by the usual trade of beads, persuaded the Cherokees to cede to them practically all of the territory that is now the up-country of South Carolina, and white settlers came pouring in. Among them was Patrick Calhoun, who settled his family just across Long Cane Creek in Cherokee territory in 1758. In the conflict that followed, the Indians killed forty settlers and forced the rest to flee. Shortly thereafter the Indians leveled thirty-six houses near the Hard Labor section and slaughtered the cattle and burned the food stores.

Patrick Calhoun founded "Calhoun's Rangers" and engaged the Cherokees in protracted warfare. They were finally crushed in 1776 when a combined force of North and South Carolina militia destroyed their villages and laid waste their land: "The boys and men of Edgefield and Abbeville were in this expedition which crossed over the mountains and joined the army from North Carolina in breaking the backbone of their Indian enemies in that quarter." The way had been paved for the expansion of slavery in the up-country, and Patrick Calhoun is believed to have been the first slaveholder there. John C. Calhoun, Patrick's fourth son, became its great apologist.

Diversity marked the white population of Abbeville County. One town, where a member of the Calhoun family helped settle 212 Huguenots on some thirty thousand acres of land, was called New Bordeaux. Their intention was to raise silkworms and grapes for wine, but failing in these endeavors, they turned to cotton and slaves instead. In 1767, some Palentinate Germans settled in the area. The name "Strum," as in Strom Thurmond, comes from these people. Other hamlets had such names as Scuffletown or Trickem.

Most of the inhabitants of Abbeville County were Scotch-Irish and many of them were Presbyterians. The German refugees were Lutheran. But as elsewhere in South Carolina, there were many Baptist churches, and they were likely to include both Blacks and whites in their membership. One church had fifty-seven charter members "of whom 11 were slaves and 6 free persons of color." And in one graveyard is a tombstone with an inscription in Arabic, French, and Latin.

The white families of the region included William B. Dorn, who owned "public mills and bridges, large plantations, many slaves with many horses and cattle." A Dr. Hearst who "married Ann Chiles" was kind, helpful to his neighbors, and a model farmer, one of the first in the region to use fertilizer. The good doctor was an elder in the Presbyterian church where he "aided in private ways in turning the minds of the young by conversation towards the religious life," and was also a trustee of Due West College. And he owned "a number of slaves at his home and a larger number in Southern Georgia." The white people of the county had names such as Widemann, Calhoun, Presly, Chiles, Cothran, Perrin, Talbert, and Bradley. These slave-owning families intermarried, and had large families—seven or eight children were common, and some families had as many as twenty-four.

Some of these families accumulated fortunes. One lived in a mansion with "14 rooms, decorated with hand carved wood work"; another house had twenty-two fireplaces. A well-known family lived on a two thousand four hundred acre estate, large enough to contain its own general store, and owned additional plantations in Louisiana. One Abbeville County resident parlayed seventy-five slaves and eighteen hundred acres of land into investments in banks, cotton mills, and railroads "worth considerably more than one million dollars" when he died in 1852. His offspring later owned department stores in Greenwood.

Education was important in this culture. At the school

where John C. Calhoun was educated, the headmaster sent the students "into the forests for study period. There, the wild woods of the Savannah resounded with echoes of Homer, Virgil, Cicero, and Horace." Some families sent their sons to Harvard and Vanderbilt to become engineers, professors, and diplomats, and to the University of Pennsylvania Medical School to study medicine.

These white slave-owning families supported each other through hard times and fought together through the Civil War. No white family in the county seems to have been spared, and some lost as many as seven or eight sons on battlefields at Antietam, Fredericksburg, and Petersburg. Five men from one street in Abbeville became colonels in the Confederate army. All five were killed in action. Many of those who returned after the war were maimed. And in addition to these personal losses, the Civil War shattered the slave system of Abbeville County. Certainly, the sorrow and anger portrayed in *Gone with the Wind* accurately depicts the way most Abbeville whites felt about the Civil War. Almost thirteen thousand white South Carolinians out of fifty-five thousand in combat were killed in action—twenty-three percent of its "arms-bearing" population, compared to a ten percent average Confederate loss.

In the years immediately after the war, Abbeville County's white ruling class attempted to recoup economically and to regain civil control. In 1866, a local newspaper called for a white-run legislature; otherwise "the blacks would have absolute control of the state government; the whites would be annihilated with all the horrors of the Jamaican Revolution." The local militia was headed by a former Confederate colonel. But in 1868, the slaveholders' political power was eroded as Radical Republicans—both white and Black—took control of the state government. The Black Codes were repealed and Reconstruction began. This meant that the white men who had represented Abbeville County in the legislature were replaced by men who had been their slaves. It also meant that whites were placed under what they experienced to be the military rule of Washington, and—possibly more important—

that taxation as a means of redistributing land was imposed at a level far higher than the ex-slaveholders had ever known. Their livelihoods were at stake. Nor were Blacks, who wielded more power in South Carolina than in any other state, reticent about placing their own people as judges, constables, tax assessors, and county commissioners. It was a complete rout for the whites, for whom it was "unthinkable" to be ruled by "alien whites and native Blacks." Nor were they reassured by the strong organization of Black people. The Union Leagues, secret organizations of Black Radical Republicans, reached down into every county. They were directed on the state level by a council, whose executives in 1870 included the Black Philadelphians, Henry Purvis, Robert's son, and R. H. Gleaves, an influential Black Mason. The Union Leagues became special targets of Ku Klux Klan violence. And Blacks, once enfranchised under the Reconstruction, really did vote. In 1868, some sixty-seven thousand out of eighty-four thousand Blacks voted "to ratify the new constitution." And they outnumbered the whites. Only about half of the eligible white voters cast their ballots in that contest, and only half of these voted against the Republicans and the new Constitution.

The Terror Begins

The Abbeville County whites reacted with violence. A federal army officer reported that between April and September 1868, he knew of four Blacks killed—two definitely by whites and one possibly—and of five Blacks wounded by whites. He said the assaults of whites on Blacks were so numerous that he had lost count of them. His report of October 27, 1868, contains page after page of reported house burnings, murders, and other acts of violence of whites against Blacks.

One of the instigators of the violence was D. Wyatt Aiken, the son of an Irish immigrant who had come to Fairfield County, South Carolina, with nothing. He opened a "small store in Winnsboro in 1805, and as this business prospered, so did his other ventures into farming, cotton ginning, and the like. At his death, the estate was valued at $192,000 including Winns-boro property, plantations, and Negro slaves." D. Wyatt, an Episcopalian who, before the Civil War, sometimes went to church three times on a Sunday, was a man of intense and almost mystical feelings.

Before the war, Aiken owned a large plantation outside of Winnsboro which he "farmed" scientifically, using slave labor. He described one small experiment: "I used simply a rafter level of twelve feet span, made by my own Negro carpen-ter. . . . In using the level, I take with me into the field a small boy with a hoe." On the eve of the war, Aiken owned thirty-six Blacks and seven hundred and fifty acres of land in Winns-boro and an additional fourteen hundred acres elsewhere.

D. Wyatt rose to the rank of colonel in the Confederate army, and was wounded in action. Discharged, he returned home where he was elected, along with other former slave-holders from the district, to the state legislature, where he served until the Radical Reconstruction of 1868. Times grew hard and, according to his biographer, his well-treated ex-slaves cried as they left him to seek employment elsewhere. Aiken's fortunes recovered and soon he was running his farm again, first with hired hands, then sharecroppers. Aiken hated lib-erated Black people. He traveled around the countryside in-citing whites to rise against the "Negro" who sought "to oppress" the white people. He also told whites that they should "show the world and the Negro" that white people really knew how to work. He was an enlightened champion of the white small farmer.

A state investigating committee later charged Aiken with the responsibility "for all the murders committed in Abbeville County immediately before and after the [election of 1868]." Admittedly partisan, the committee charged that Aiken "in-cited the white people to commit acts of violence upon colored people which would not have been done had it not been for such speeches." During the summer of 1868 Aiken made a speech in which he declared that "before the white man should be ruled by niggers, they would kill the last one of them. They wanted the nigger to understand that it was a white man's government and that they intended to kill every leading radical, and would not leave one on the face of the earth."

The Assassination of a Black Leader

Aiken was most directly implicated in the murder of B. F. Randolph, a Black Methodist minister, graduate of Oberlin College, head of the state Union League, and chaplain of a Black South Carolina regiment during the Civil War. Like Richard Greener, Charlotte Forten, William Whipper, and J. J. Wright, he had come South to help raise his people. Portraits show a fine figure of a man with a strong, sensitive face. A member of the state legislature, he had said in a debate on the new constitution that "the object . . . is to get rid of those two little words race and color. We are laying the foundation of a new structure here and the time has come when we shall have to meet things squarely and we must meet them now or never. The day is coming when we must decide whether the two races shall live together or not." They killed him six months later.

In October 1868, Randolph was upstate encouraging our people to vote in the coming election. D. Wyatt Aiken had said that if Randolph came up that way the whites should give him "a piece of land, four feet by six." At one train station Aiken accosted Randolph and reportedly said that he was signing his death warrant and would never see Columbia again. Randolph replied that they would have to kill him to shut him up. Either on that occasion or during a speech that day, Randolph, a "mulatto," said that he was proud of the Black blood in his veins.

Three men were then hired by Fletcher Hodges, a member of a large, old Abbeville County family, to kill Randolph. One of the assassins was "the leader of a band of desperate men" who killed Black men almost for sport. He convinced two companions that they would be recognized as *"patriots"* if they killed the Black troublemaker who was "stirring up the worst passions of the freed men." The killers thought they "were doing their country the highest service."

Hodges told the white people in the town of Hodges Depot, where Randolph was scheduled to arrive, that when the train's whistle sounded they should go down to the depot if they wanted to see the "nigger" Randolph killed. When the train pulled in, John Brooks, probably the brother of the man who caned Senator Sumner, pointed Randolph out to the killers. The three men "shot him and he was killed dead." Fletcher Hodges told the dying Randolph, "You said yesterday that Negro blood ran in your veins, and you were proud of it; Now God damn you, it is running on the ground."

A Black man, Aaron Mitchell, who was standing so close that "the blood at the time [Randolph] was shot blew out of his nose into my face," told Hodges that "there are more men that got blood in them than him." When Hodges threatened him, Mitchell replied, "You may start my blood in the same stream, it makes no difference to me." Whites would not permit Mitchell to retrieve Randolph's personal possessions, or to carry the body away for burial. That night, the rifle clubs and the KKK debated whether to cut the body up, throw it to the dogs, or "box him up and express him to Governor Scott as a present."

Guns at Polling Stations

Violence flared all about Abbeville County both before and after the murder of Randolph. It was spearheaded by the KKK, led by J. G. Boozer and many other prominent local white citizens. The violence was random and sudden. A Black woman reported that a man had "stole her son Samuel about 15 years old first of the year and took him off into Georgia." In another case, a white punched a Black man simply because he was rumored to be a Republican. Once a Black found a coffin-shaped paper slipped under his door at night. White outlaws roamed the district unmolested: "Briscoe and Curtis are in this county doing a great deal of mischief and say they will kill the Guffin [white Republicans] boys before they leave. They . . . was laying around town all last week. They are allowed to go all over the county and no one attempts to arrest them. They are generally with a crowd of 80–100 men I am told." By 1868, a federal officer was requesting additional troops to pacify this "very disloyal" county.

In August 1868, a man later testified "they took me out of my house and went and took my brother-in-law also. My wife was screaming and they threatened her life. [One] kicked one of the little children. . . . They laid me down on the ground, after stripping me as naked as when I came into the world and struck me five times with a strap." The man escaped and stayed out in the woods all night, but his brother-in-law died from the beating. Nor were white sympathizers of the Blacks immune; James Martin, a white radical, was assassinated by the same band that killed Randolph in October 1868.

The violence peaked during the election of 1868. Hutson Lomax, a mulatto who had been elected to the school commission, had, in his capacity of commissioner of elections, argued that a colored man should be appointed as a poll watcher at each of the polling stations. He was overruled by his two fellow white commissioners, one of whom told Lomax that if other whites even heard of the idea he would be dead before the week was out. Lomax said, "I didn't think it anything but right . . . just to appoint one colored man . . . as colored men had a right to vote as well as white men." An unfriendly observer complained that Lomax had been a good slave during the war, but that "he has apparently come to the conclusion that 'all men are born free and equal.' "

A few days later Sam Hodges, a relative of Fletcher Hodges, told Lomax that if he did not desert the Republican party and become a Democrat, he would be "killed world without end." Hodges added, striking the table for emphasis, that although a band of armed Black men guarded Lomax's home every night, they would kill him in the daytime when his guards were not about. It is probable that Alfred Ellison, the grandfather of novelist Ralph Ellison, was among that band since Lomax was the president of the Union League to which he belonged.

The night before the election a KKK leader told a meeting that they were not "going to allow a Negro Republican to cast a vote." If the Blacks insisted on trying, the Klan would "force them back . . . fight them, kill them, shoot them." At Greenwood precinct the next day, four hundred unarmed Blacks were driven from the polls by armed whites.

At Calhoun Mills, the whites kept up a running fire on the polling booth; at the Bordeaux polls, one hundred fifty unarmed Blacks were forced "to return home without voting"; at Bradley's Mill, our people were told that to vote was "to be killed"; at White Hall, at least two Blacks were killed when a band of whites, led by Dr. Moses Taggert, fired between fifty and a hundred shots into a crowd of "entirely unarmed" Blacks. One survivor of the massacre stated that Dr. Taggert personally fired at him. As the people fled, the doctor, after whom Taggert Avenue in Greenwood is named, is said to have taunted them, "Come back, you shall have the chance to vote."

A state investigating committee concluded that during that election campaign the "system of intimidation in the County of Abbeville was perfect." A federal officer on the scene declared that the withdrawal of troops would mean that Blacks who voted Republican would be "killed off. Many have deserted their houses and all live in fear and trembling." The election results reflected the violence. At Greenwood itself the vote was 255 Democratic, 0 Republican; at Cokesbury, 190 Democratic, 80 Republican; at Bradley's Mill, 145 Democratic, 64 Republican; and at Bordeaux, 103 Democratic, 0 Republican. The wonder is that so many of our people presumably cast their ballots despite the guns and the threats that they would be tossed out of their homes on the plantations. We have no way of knowing how many whites were among the Republican voters, but they were probably few in number.

After all the murders—at least twenty in 1868—the leading Republican figure in the county wrote that he would like to create a Black militia unit, but "that . . . it will have a ruinous affect [sic] on the farms as the hands are leaving their work and coming in here in gangs." The state vacillated on the new issue of a Black militia. And the white farmers who had done all the killing argued that the organization of a Black militia—if there had to be one—should be put off until after the crops were in. Some of the white leaders declared that they would vouch for order in the county if the Black militia unit was not formed. The idea of arming the Blacks gave them a good scare. The Republican official said: "No garrison that has ever been hear [sic] had done one half the good that the mere threat of a militia company has done." After the killing of one Black man, an officer reported that "I found there exists a strong disposition on the part of the freedmen in this neighborhood to take matters into their own hands." The Blacks were eager to organize and "determined to use all their exertions" to stop the violence being visited upon them. Indeed, on July 17, 1868, a group of armed Black men stood down a force of whites who had come for "commencing a war on the radicals."

By August 1869, Blacks were officially armed by the state and the weapons placed in a local bank. But by February 1871, whites were killing again. This time the victim was Henry Nash, a Black county commissioner who had testified about Aiken's remark that he "would kill the last of them." Nash was killed by two young men who had previously been accused of grabbing a woman by her breasts, pulling her about by them, and threatening her life with a knife. The murderers "shot the colored man [Nash] and walked up and caught him by the hair and shot him three times in the back and once in the neck and once in the face." Both were from well-to-do and respected families in Abbeville County. So by 1871, Randolph was dead, Wade Perrin was dead—although killed in Laurens County—and Nash was dead. The family of another Black legislator, Everidge Cain, had been run out of the county by "pressure from other citizens."

Bravery Amid the Terror

Black leaders braved economic reprisals and death to tell the story of the election of 1876 to federal authorities. Beverly

Vance, for example, was a constable and the leader of the Black community in Cokesbury, close to where B. F. Randolph had been murdered. The night before the election, Vance had "to have a bodyguard around me the whole night. We were expecting them. They had sworn they would kill me." On election day, Vance said that the whites had taken one Black man and "pulled him up to the polls, and he had a republican ticket in his hands and [a white] put his hands against his knees and tried to make him walk, tried to drag him to the polls and they carried him to the polls." They finally pulled the Republican ballot out of his hand and forced him to place a Democrat ballot in the box. The week after the election, according to Vance, the whites "beat five or six men. They broke two bottles over one man's head, cut five gashes in his head, and the trial justice was standing right there looking at them." When asked to intervene, the justice told the Blacks, "You must get out of the way."

Vance had himself been the object of an economic boycott for five months: "No one was to give me any work in order to perish me out." The person who had sold him his land called in the note early, causing Vance to lose both the land and the downpayment. After the election, the whites came around to his house, called him a "son of a bitch, cursing and abusing me to everything they could think of." They uprooted the flowers in his neighbor's yard, broke down the latch on his gate, and fired bullets into his door. Said Vance, "The bullets are in the door now."

Most of the men testifying at the federal hearing after the election were duly elected or appointed federal and state officials. Their crime was leading Black people to claim their legal rights as citizens—and supporting the Republican party. Beverly Vance said, "[I'd] always taught the colored people in my part of the county to stick to the Republican party, and to stick to a solid ticket . . . and not to scratch their ticket for no man." One Black witness at the hearing declared that all the beatings had been "on account" of their political opinions.

Lewis C. Waller, Black deputy U.S. marshal, recounted that a week before the election he was ambushed and wounded in the shoulder on the road between Abbeville and Green-wood. Waller recalled that after the shooting a member of a white family said to him "it was a damned pity but what the ball hadn't gone through [his] head instead of [his] shoulder." On election day when he went to vote, armed whites told this government official that it "was best" to leave. Waller resisted, but when the whites drew their pistols, he "took across the woods to Abbeville Courthouse and voted. That is about thirteen miles from there and [he] walked every bit of the way."

A most violent place in the county on election day was near the White Hall precinct and its central figure was a U.S. marshal and schoolteacher, A. M. Heard. He joined the A.M.E. Church in 1879 and moved to Philadelphia in 1888. Years later Heard, a great African Methodist bishop, was responsible for much of the growth of the A.M.E. Church in Africa and in the North, especially in the city of Philadelphia. Born a slave, Heard was a plow boy in Elberton, Georgia, right across the river from Abbeville County. He was early impressed by a Black preacher: "He was the first colored man I had ever seen who was well educated, and who could use the King's English readily, accurately, and convincingly. . . . I determined from that night to be a Man and to fill an important place in life's arena." Heard was also influenced by Bishop Turner, who had been raised in Abbeville County, and showed Heard "pictures and historical facts . . . presented of the race in past ages, and of the men in the present."

Before the election, Heard had received threatening notes that would say, "The Edgefield Fellows have their eyes on you, and you know the name of the Edgefield boys is awful." One week before the election Heard sent his wife to Georgia, and he moved into a neighbor's house. On his way to school one morning around that time his children came running up to him, warning him to turn back because about thirty gunmen had come looking for him. Heard had the normal fear of any man, but he realized that "if I left there they wouldn't get any republican votes at all in that township, as they considered me their leader, and they were trying to run me off, so I thought I would stay there even if they killed me."

On the day of the election, the people voted early despite massive intimidation by the whites: "We didn't pay much attention, just voted right through, and went on." When Heard went to vote around noon, he was stoned by a crowd of whites and struck in the face. A nearby federal lieutenant refused to protect him. When the whites drew pistols, he drew his own. Then, as Heard later recounted: "The colored people ran up and surrounded me, so that if they had shot at me, they would have shot at them instead of me, and by some means they didn't shoot." Another witness said "the colored people gathered him up and carried him off." Heard insisted that he voted—whether before or after the confrontation is unclear—but by then our people were frightened.

That night Heard demanded to be admitted to the counting of the ballots: "I didn't know if I had any right . . . to be there, but as I was a republican, I thought I would like to see it, but they refused me." Always a fighter, Heard, "a republican from principle and nothing else," instituted a suit against the Interstate Commerce Commission because of railroad segregation and won in 1887.

On August 22, 1876, white rifle clubs took over the town of Abbeville: "Many wore plumes on the sides of their hats which gave the effect of greater numbers." They were under the command of a Captain Perrin and "the order of the line of march" stretched for two miles through the town. D. Wyatt Aiken was there. Then on September 18, in an attempt to prevent a march scheduled by Republicans, the combined rifle clubs of Abbeville and Edgefield marched in red shirts. But our people were not intimidated. They marched anyhow.

Richard Greener, the first Black graduate of Harvard College, who had replaced the murdered O. V. Catto as vice-principal of the ICY, left a graphic description of the mood in Abbeville. At Hodges Depot, where Randolph had been murdered, the whites invaded Greener's railroad car and in Abbeville itself he saw thousands of Red Shirts: "They came galloping, halooing and shouting. They [were] good riders and a rough set of men. Probably they looked to me more ferocious than they really were, being accustomed to city life. Sometimes they were blessed with long beards and hair and apparently hadn't been shaved in a long while." Greener carried a pistol as, said he, did every other sensible Republican politician: "From the time I started until I arrived home, I never felt certain whether I was going to get back alive or not."

The 1876 election's stakes had been high. And the results showed that the former slaveholders had won the battle to preserve their way of life. But the terror didn't cease.

D. Wyatt Aiken eventually became a long-term congressman and later organized the Grange movement in South Carolina. The D. Wyatt Aiken Grange in present-day Greenwood County was named after him. His son, Wyatt Aiken (1863–1923), likewise became a congressman from Greenwood, serving from 1903 to 1917. And until World War II, whites celebrated the anniversary of "Big Tuesday."

Chapter 13

THE OPPRESSION
IN ABBEVILLE COUNTY,
PART TWO

There is a Balm in Gilead
To make the wounded whole
There is a Balm in Gilead
To heal the sin-sick soul

Sometimes I feel discouraged
And think my work's in vain
But then the Holy Spirit
Revives my soul again

There is a Balm in Gilead
To make the wounded whole
There is a Balm in Gilead
To heal the sin-sick soul

Traditional Black Spiritual

Patrick Bradley, a man of "property and influence," was descended from a Pat Bradley who had come into the Long Cane Section around 1784. He had been elected to the rank of general in the state militia in 1842, but at the start of the Civil War the Confederate army made him a captain. Bradley, who served in the state legislature along with D. Wyatt Aiken, was "a leading figure in efforts to have a railroad from Greenwood to Augusta and was president of the railroad company. When it was formed, after the line was built, he became a vice-president and one of his privileges was a railroad stop in front of his home in southwest Greenwood County. The village which grew up around the railroad stop was named Bradley for him." Among the supporters of the railroad was General M. C. Butler, the leader of the Hamburg Massacre, who thought "it ought to be built in order that the young men who could not marry at home might have a chance to go abroad." Other large plantation owners welcomed the railroad as an improvement over "hauling cotton over steep hills and boggy roads to Augusta."

So down along the Savannah River runs a railroad, built through the swamp and bogs. It's so hot down there during the summer that you feel faint even as you gaze along the tracks. It's rarely used now that highways lace the area together. One hundred twenty-eight men, mostly Black, although some few whites may have been among them, died putting down that roadbed.

Stockade No. 5

Those who ran South Carolina after the Civil War needed to make our people stay put so that production on the farms could be assured. So they passed vagrancy laws so loose that any Black man who could not account for his work and home could be thrown in jail. It kept people off the streets and production steady on the farms. Hughsey Childs, who spent his youth in Greenwood, remembers: "It was a good while before I could get a job. But I had to get up every morning and do like I had one. Because there they would lock you up for vagrancy. The only way they didn't lock you up, you couldn't go out of your house. . . . Of course, you could go to church on Sundays, but during the week you had to stay in the house if you didn't have a job." But not everyone was willing to stay inside, and the question arose as to how to use the resulting convicts. The solution was to lease out anyone serving a term up to ninety days to a county chain gang or to a corporation. It was called the convict-lease system and General Bradley was one of its first beneficiaries.

How did 128 of the 285 prisoners in "stockade no. 5," Greenwood and Augusta Railroad, Edgefield County, South Carolina, happen to die in 1879? One convict in shackles was shot because the warden said he had been planning a revolt. But it was mostly sickness that killed the men. Doctors who examined the convicts found "with the exception of nine . . . all [were] infected with scurvy and with an eruption that was evidently caused by the vermin on their person." They noted that "the inspiration and re-inspiration of an atmosphere polluted with emanations from so many bodies, together with the effluvia arising from the accommodation of urine and feces in the vessels used in the quarters at night, . . . poisoned the blood and lowered the vital forces to such an extent that the system could offer no resistance to diseased impressions."

What the doctors meant was that sixty to seventy-five men were packed at night into a room twenty feet by thirty feet. One bucket held their excrement, and another, next to it, was for drinking water. When some of the men—their strength drained by the ninety-eight-degree heat and eighty percent humidity—got sick, they could not control their bowels, and fouled the drinking water. Some of them became "emaciated, anemic, depressed, covered with dirt, unable to sit up" or turn over in their beds. Among the convicts were "ten or twelve boys, some of them under fourteen years of age," one boy an epileptic and another with hands "so badly burned that he could not hold a tool to work with."

As I pondered these deaths, I wondered what songs they sang in the stockade at night. For surely they did sing. Was it, "There's no danger in God's water, no danger in God's water" or did they think, as they lay in their own fouled trousers on pallets stacked against the wall, that the "sweet chariot" was coming, and that in the morning it would "carry" them home. Or sing out "Oh, Lord, oh, my Lord! Oh, my good Lord! Keep me from sinking down." Perhaps some crazy sense of African humor and defiance caused them to shout out:

Don't care where you bury my body
Don't care where you bury my body
O my little soul's going to shine

Maybe, in their mind's eyes, they saw their girl friends, eyes sparkling, starched white dresses rustling on Black skin, as they left the church on a Sunday morning, all ready for courting time. And so they sang, "In the evening when the sun go down, I lay my head down and lonesome cry."

I believe I know what held them together. I have observed it on the faces of old scrub ladies who can barely walk up to the church altar on a Sunday morning, but who smile through their pain and glory at the miracle that God has given them another day to live—"One more day's journey, and I'm so glad." And my own soul has taken on power as I've watched a bald man, with a razor-scarred face, limping on a work-injured knee, rhythmically clap his hands together and sing in a voice that cannot be imprisoned or chained that "the rocks and the mountains shall all flee away, and you shall have a new hiding place that day."

The commandant of stockade no. 5 was J. J. Cahill, who worried that that "priceless legacy"—his good name—would be sullied. He said, "If those charges be true, then I would be a monster unfit to die. God only knows how the sickness, suffering and death among the convicts has lacerated my feelings, and how earnestly I have toiled to ameliorate it. [God] at least will do me justice, even if my fellow men should fail to mete it out." He was removed from his post by the railroad, but never punished. General Bradley, on the other hand was concerned only with money. Even after an official investigation had begun and authorities had ordered him to return sick convicts to a central penitentiary, Bradley attempted to keep them. He said, "I am trying hard to do my part in building up the waste places of our country." Bradley blamed conditions in the camp on the "careless and indifferent" attitudes of the prisoners toward their "own persons." He also declared that "there may have been cruelty practiced in my absence, but if so it has been carefully kept from me."

Forty prisoners escaped, probably because the stockades were in "the heart of the territory where Ned Tennant and his notorious Negro militia had their headquarters." Cahill feared that the "colored people of the neighborhood were threatening to make up a military company of their own race to attack the guard and release the convicts."

The convict-leasing system was in effect until at least 1901, but the practice never really ended. Indeed, by 1914, even "lifers could be put to work on a county chain gang": "I asked the judge, 'What could be my crime?' / He said, 'Nine years on the Greenwood-Augusta Line.' "

A Race War over the Ballot

Phoenix is about eight miles south of Greenwood, near Cuffytown Creek, in an area bounded by Pine Grove A.M.E. Church and the Black Damascus Baptist Church. The village, gone from today's map, is memorialized by Phoenix Road, which leads the traveler from Greenwood to Phoenix. Close by the Black churches was the Watson Store, the polling place in 1898, the last time that Blacks in South Carolina, with some scattered exceptions, attempted to vote until the mid-1950s.

The Phoenix riot was a direct outcome of an attempt by Blacks—led by a white Republican family, the Tolberts—to test the validity of the 1895 South Carolina constitution. The new constitution disenfranchised Blacks, who accounted for sixty-six percent of the population of Greenwood County. I have reconstructed the facts of this race war, which took place between November 8 and 10, 1898, both from written sources and from the oral traditions passed down in the Black community.

At Phoenix on November 8, as some Blacks led by Tom Tolbert prepared to vote, a local "ne'er-do-well" attempted to stop them. Blows were exchanged, shots broke out, and the interfering white was killed and Tom Tolbert wounded. The Black people, expecting trouble, had buried their arms nearby. In the melee after the guns had gone off, doubt and fear beset them, and they debated about whether or not to fight back. In the end they did, agreeing with Charles White that "we can shoot as long as them white folks can." It is reported that our women stood and shouted at some of the men who were retreating "to go back and shoot the white folk."

The wounded Tom Tolbert was escorted by Black men to his family homestead, near Verdery, about nine miles northeast of Phoenix. Later that day a lynch mob, led by a schoolteacher's son, the son-in-law of Dr. Taggert, who had led the mob in 1868, came to Tolbert's home intent on murdering the wounded man. After some debate, the mob decided to spare Tom Tolbert, but as they left the house they declared that "every Republican shall leave this land. No colored people shall live on their land." Outside, John R. Tolbert, a decorated former Confederate colonel and the patriarch of the Tolbert family, rode up in a carriage. They fired at him and he, badly wounded, was carried away on his bolting horse. Tolbert was saved from further pursuit by a band of armed Black men, who "closed behind the clattering buggy." The "white mob did not pursue believing that the Negroes were part of a kind of underground militia the Tolberts were rumoured to have trained."

That night one posse of night riders headed out toward Rehobeth Church, close by the Black churches, and was ambushed by our guerrillas. Three of the whites were wounded. A onetime member of Damascus Church tells the story: "They was coming right down this road right in front of Pine Grove Church and those colored men got together and got barbed wire and stretched it across the road and at night they couldn't see it. And then they came riding on those horses and got tied up in this barbed wire. And the ones that got away said, 'Noo, we ain't going back there! See now, they got tied up in the barbed wire. That was something and then when the colored folks started shooting, they didn't have much to shoot with, but what they had, they shot."

This resistance infuriated the whites, who got word to Edgefield, Saluda, Columbia, and Abbeville that the Blacks were in armed revolt. Hundreds of armed white reenforcements poured into the embattled area with disastrous results for us. But many of our people never faltered. The next day twenty armed Black men reported to the Tolbert house and escorted the Tolberts onto a train to Columbia. Some Black people in Philadelphia still remember that their kin were part of the twenty.

The day after the election, Hughsey Childs remembers, the whites just "got together and was gonna kill as many Black folks as they could. . . . Just like you killed my father and I couldn't catch you, I'd try to get all your family, but this wasn't family, this was Black folks. They just got themselves together and rode out on horses into the fields and got every Black man they could and killed him for vengeance, that's what it was."

Some Atrocities

The mass lynching took place in front of Rehobeth Church, where the Tolberts had worshipped. That morning, a mob of whites, fearful, by their own accounts, of attacks by Black guerrillas and also afraid to assault the armed guard at the Tolberts', took out after anybody they could get. Twelve men were killed in front of the church that rainy Wednesday and Thursday. Eyewitness accounts tell us that "one Negro was dragged out in the road and 100 shots were fired into his body. At this time two [Black men] ran one way, two another, leaving three on a log who were immediately lynched." They were "riddled with bullets and buckshot probably 150 shots being fired" by about seventy-five men.

The next day the marauders caught Essex Harrison: "They just stabbed him in his feet, and then made him get up and walk and through the strength he had he tried to walk. They stabbed him all over his feet." Harrison, according to one report, "looked at his slayers. He said nothing. . . . The rifles rang forth, shot after shot went into him and Essex Harrison fell headlong on the pile of already dead Negroes." The whites went berserk with the bloodletting and shot the heart out of Essex Harrison so that they "almost endangered each other." The lore of Greenwood Blacks is that the child born to the man who stabbed Harrison's feet was born lame: "Just the way that Harrison wobbled, that's the way the man's son wobbled."

Some of our people were freed by the mob. They included David Latimer, whose daughter taught school near Phoenix and later came to Philadelphia. A man named William Harris also escaped the mob: "He asked them to let him pray. And when he said 'Amen,' the mob was gone. He talked to God so that they changed their hearts and rode away. . . . That man could pray better than any man I ever heard in my life."

Over the next few days, a reign of terror was loosed upon the Blacks of Abbeville-Greenwood County. The white riders shot and wounded a man riding in his wagon: "He was seen to fall and crawl off into the woods. Later when a party went to look for him, he could not be found." But another posse found an old woman named Eliza Goode who lived with an invalid daughter. They "fired either through the doorway or a crack in the wall" and shot her in the abdomen and killed her. They came into my Aunt Anna's house where her mother was holding a baby and rode their horses right on through the house. And Benjamin Mays's earliest memory was of this day when "a crowd of white men rode up on horseback with rifles on their shoulders. I was with my father when they rode up, and I remember starting to cry. They cursed my father, drew their guns and made him salute, made him take off his hat and bow down to them several times. Then they rode away. I was not yet five years old, but I have not forgotten them."

Most of the Black population of Greenwood and Abbeville counties melted away into the countryside. Hughsey Childs, now a resident of Philadelphia, but baptized at Damascus Baptist Church, who guides us through much of the county's

Black history, tells us: "See, when they used to have slaves and we had some caves there, you could get in there and nobody could ever find you. You know them big hills and when it rained sometimes the water would run in there. You could go down there and, man, they would never get you, all that you had to do is get in there. And then you see, the Southern white man is afraid of a Black man. They wouldn't want to have no one man come to kill a Black man. Come fifty or sixty. . . ."

During the Phoenix riot, as in the Reconstruction, "well-known and highly respected citizens" led the mob. How can we understand their savagery? We should remember that Abbeville whites came from a violent culture and were not averse to shooting each other. They used guns to settle arguments about property, women, or any other vexing matter. And in Abbeville-Greenwood County in 1898 some whites found a lot of things to be angry about.

The White Terror

Although white opposition to Black attempts to vote triggered the Phoenix riot, there had been conflict between the races in Abbeville-Greenwood for a number of years. Apparently some whites and Blacks had been burning each other's bales of cotton. In 1897, a prominent Black farmer had been shot in his home near Pine Grove.

A number of explanations emerge from the accounts of Blacks and whites alike. One is white resentment of the relative prosperity of the area's Black farmers: "You know, some of them had plantations. I mean if you had a plantation when I was a boy, you was big. . . . Pine Grove was a kind of outstanding church because it had a good many farming people. . . . People who were kind of in the upper bracket because they rented." Benjamin Mays's father was one of those prosperous renters.

Another recurrent theme is the white community's outrage at the Tolbert family's violation of the societal norms.

154

Tom Tolbert apparently preferred to rent his land to Black tenants "who would work hard and pay their way and try to do right over the shiftless white trash who are the curse of the southern community." Tolbert even went so far as to share his home with Blacks, "living all the year in one end of a house, consisting of two small rooms, with a family of Negroes in the other end." And Tolbert had met with Blacks at Pine Grove and Damascus churches, after the murder of the Black farmer in 1897, and urged them "to rise up and put a stop to it."

But Tolbert's deepest outrage, that one that cut closest to the bone of the Abbeville whites, was, as he said, "I do not believe in disenfranching, on account of their color, men, who because of property or education or established character as good citizens, should be allowed to vote." Whites believed— as one wrote in the *Greenwood Index*—that "it is an unwritten law that the white man must rule—a law firmly rooted in our natures. . . . Everything that pertains to citizenship, to property, and the pursuit of happiness must conform to this law." Some of them were willing to use any means necessary to enforce this "law." The potential power of Black suffrage was especially frightening to whites in a county where they were outnumbered.

Some whites felt—as one of them said in the local paper— they "had no apologies to make" for their violence against our people. They spoke openly about putting the fear of God into Blacks in the area, and counseled each other to "give to the most powerful enemy the severest blow." Other whites had mixed feelings. The same newspaper blamed Harrison's ugly murder on "fools in the crowd" and deplored the way lynchers, instead of attacking the armed Blacks who ambushed them, "rode about, picked up Negroes at random, and butchered them cruelly and in cold blood."

But even if some whites opposed it, the terror did not subside. Into the next year, white bands roamed the countryside "at night terrorizing and intimidating" Blacks. Certain farms were "posted" and our people forbidden to work them "on pain of death." The house of "a prosperous colored citizen of Cokesbury" was destroyed in a mysterious fire. Lynchings and random barbarisms continued in Abbeville-Greenwood County between 1900 and 1917. An incomplete list of victims would include Oliver Wideman and his wife, December 27, 1902; Allen Pendleton, September 17, 1905; Robert Davis, August 16, 1906; Willis Jackson, October 10, 1911. And an attempt was made to lynch Albert Tolbert.

Robert Davis of the Mount Moriah section was accused of molesting the adolescent daughter of a white farmer. The governor of the state came to intercede with the mob that gathered to lynch Davis and persuaded them to shoot Davis instead of burning him. So after the Reverend J. C. Goode, pastor of Mount Moriah, prayed over him, the mob fired "thousands of shots into Davis." Then they cut off his ears, fingers, and toes, and took him out and strung him up. Says Hughsey Childs, "I pass[ed] by there many a day and look[ed] at this tree." People from Mount Moriah Church came to Philadelphia a few years ago for a family reunion; as I listened to a distant cousin lead its choir in a beautiful rendition of "Take Me Back to the Place I Come From," I thought of that tree and Robert Davis.

Another Black Leader Is Lynched

Anthony Crawford was a wealthy and prosperous Black farmer who owned "427 acres of the prettiest cotton land in the county." Born in 1865, Crawford was the personification of Booker T. Washington's call to Black people to "cast down their buckets where they were." Crawford's stern face seemed a mixture of Indian and African heritage. He had twelve sons and four daughters, nine of whom were married and lived around him on the farm. So important was education to him that he built and financed a school on his land. Crawford was a religious man who was the secretary of Chappelle A.M.E. Church and its chief financial supporter. In addition, he had been the head of all Black Masons in the state. Clearly, he was not an ordinary Black man. Said to have been strong-willed, he declared that "the day a white man hits me is the day I die."

One day during the cotton-ginning season, Crawford went into a store in Abbeville Square to sell some bales of cotton. He got into an argument about the price to be paid and did some strong cussing. A mob soon formed and went after him, but the sheriff rescued him, put him in jail for a short time, then released him. Crawford headed back to the store determined to recover his bales of cotton. By this time, a large mob of Abbeville whites had formed to kill this Black who had been crazy enough to swear at a white man.

Crawford was as good as his word. When they came for him, he had a four-pound hammer in his hand and he crushed the skull of the leader of the mob. Then the ". . . citizens of Abbeville took Crawford into the road where everybody could get at him. Under their ministrations, the Negro regained consciousness, got on his feet, and fought his way for fifty feet up the road, before a knife plunged into his back again. While he was down bleeding, two hundred white men kicked him into unconsciousness." After forty-five minutes, the sheriff got the mob to stop beating the dying man.

There Is a Balm in Gilead

They took his crumpled body back to the jailhouse, where he regained consciousness long enough to tell the sheriff to give his bankbook to his son and to say "I thought I was a good citizen."

The mob swept on into the jailhouse, overwhelmed the sheriff, and seized Crawford. They put a rope around his neck and they dragged his body through the Black quarter of town, shouting, "Here is your leader, look at him." Crawford was dead when they got to the fairgrounds in Abbeville, but they "hanged Crawford to the solitary great pine that stands in the row of junipers at the gate" and then they "expended a couple of hundred cartridges in firing at his body." When the sun went down, the coroner pronounced Crawford dead, killed "by persons unknown."

That night, the murderers got drunk and wanted to go down and burn out the Crawford house, but they did not. People from the area say that it was a fortress that night. But the next day the whites passed a resolution that all of the Crawford family must vacate its land within two weeks. Then they shut down every Black establishment in Abbeville. One Black man, Gus Roman, refused to close his blacksmith shop and a white man, J. S. Perrin, helped him guard it. It may have been on this occasion that Alfred Ellison, the grandfather of Ralph Ellison, walked through the streets of Abbeville, hands behind his back, telling the whites, "If you're going to kill me, you'll have to kill me right here because I am not leaving. This is where I have my family, my farm, my friends; and I don't plan to leave."

When it was all over, one white commented, "I reckon the crowd wouldn't have been so bloodthirsty, only it's been three years since they had any fun with the niggers and it seems as if they just have to have a lynching every so often." A local newspaper commented that Crawford had been wealthier than most of the white farmers in the area and "property ownership always makes the Negro more assertive, more independent, and the poor whites can't stand that. There is an element of jealousy that enters wherever they see a 'nigger' forge ahead of them and they lay for a chance to get him."

The resolution on the expulsion of the Crawford family from the territory was rescinded afterward and an investigation of the murder was ordered by the state government. In this aftermath, our people simply brought their cotton to Abbeville, received their money, and went home "without spending a cent."

But practically every Black in Philadelphia, Greenwood, or Abbeville who was of an age to know, remembers that murder: "Child, they rode him up and down the roads so the little children could see him." Members of the family were scattered to the wind, some reportedly even changing their names to escape persecution. Even today we are still connected to that event in the most direct ways: the obituary of the grandfather of a member of Philadelphia's Mother Bethel Church says, "He was then sent by Bishop Coppin [Fanny Coppin's husband] to the Cedar Grove circuit where he served five years, during which time the horrible lynching . . . took place." Walter Clementine Crawford, Crawford's son, was the presiding elder of the Manhattan district of the A.M.E. Church as recently as 1948.

The Chain Gang

Of course, Greenwood had its chain gang. In South Carolina of 1916 there were 2,660 Blacks on the chain gang and 340 whites. The head of the chain gang in Greenwood was "Jim McCoy. I remember my mother went there many times and said, 'don't kill my son. Spare him.' "

There was one Black convict they didn't get to kill. His name was "Stonewall Jackson" Bouie, and his name is recorded in a book given to me by his family. His daughter tells the story, known to all Greenwood Blacks, of how he was falsely accused of a crime and went before a judge who sentenced him to time on the chain gang. Stonewall Jackson said to his mother, "Momma, don't you worry, not one day will I spend on that chain gang." On his twenty-first birthday, they moved him to the place of work. *Well, guess I'm gonna die with this hammer in my hand.* He raised the hammer above his head, brought it down, and died on the spot. So tight was his grasp that they were unable to remove the tool from his hand. They say that no man was put on the chain gang for a long time thereafter.

The Terror's Impact on the Black Community

In this atmosphere, the protection of our women and children was a major concern of the Blacks of the community: "White men used physical force to protect white

159

women. . . . Negro parents had to contrive other methods to protect their daughters, often without success." Hughsey Childs tells how as a young man he drove his three sisters to Sunday school: "I'd take my surrey, you know, with two seats. My sister would sit in front with me and my two sisters in the back. Well, I had this pistol strapped between my legs. And I get in the middle of the woods, and white boys, about 18 or 19 years old, they don't respect me. One of them would take the horses and stop them and the others would try to snatch my sisters right out before me. They didn't do it because I had a gun. And sometimes to let them know I had one, I'd shoot it before I got in the woods." And Benjamin Mays recalls: "Virtually all Negro parents tried in some way to protect their children from the ever-present menace of white violence. The meaning was unmistakably clear. It was dangerous to argue with a white person."

Some of our people were described—not surprisingly—as "cowed and helpless." in the face of the terror. Mays, who grew up in Greenwood County, says: "Among themselves, Negroes talked much about these tragedies. They were impotent to do anything about them. They did not mention them to whites." But Hughsey Childs insists that "those people had more nerve than we have. . . . See, they had the odds against them." Another local resident agrees: "They was fearless."

This terror did not confine itself to Abbeville-Greenwood. It reached up into Anderson County and into Greenville and down into little towns like Cheraw where Dizzy Gillespie was born. It entered into our music and became the whine of a Gillespie trumpet and the high-crying twang of Josh White's guitar and the thankful power with which a Baptist church choir in Philadelphia today sings:

> Blessed quietedness
> Blessed peacefulness
> Sweet assurance
> In my soul

In the stormy seas
Jesus rescued me
And the billows ceased to roar

Our people began to leave Abbeville County after the Phoenix riot. In 1898, while thousands of Italians, Jews, and Slavs were fleeing Europe for the United States, a local paper described another migration: "During the past week, three cars of Negroes have left Greenwood for lower Mississippi. These cars have carried away 45, 35, and 24 Negroes, respectively." But it still took several years before the community gathered itself together to go North. And it took several other developments—the arrival of the boll weevil that decimated the cotton fields, forcing people to abandon farming; the war that created jobs in industry in the North; and the availability of cheap railroad tickets—before the journey out of this blood-soaked land could really begin.

The Phoenix race war along with the Wilmington, North Carolina, riot of the same dates was a signal to the Black population of the South that the federal government would not defend the right of Black men to vote, even if it was taken from them by violence. A one-party system, propped up by the use of indiscriminate terror, was instituted in South Carolina and other Southern states under the code names of "federalism" and "states' rights." It was almost unchallengeable for the next half century.

But in the end, the Black community's will to survive and to live free rose out of the ashes of this Phoenix. Benjamin Mays, the mentor of Martin Luther King, came out of that inferno. Gordon Blaine Hancock, who always remembered Phoenix and the lynchings, became dean of Virginia Union University, a great inspirer of Black youth, and the founder of the Southern Regional Council. Lewis Alfred Ellison left Abbeville County for Oklahoma, where his son Ralph was born. My own family left Greenwood and moved to Bradley on the beginning of the long hegira to Philadelphia that eventually put this pen into my hands.

Chapter 14

ON THE EVE OF
THE MIGRATION

I'm so glad trouble don't last always
I'm so glad trouble don't last always
I'm so glad trouble don't last always
Singing Glory hallelujah
Trouble don't last always

Traditional Black Spiritual

On a church in Durham, North Carolina, an inscription reads: "Good trees do not grow with ease / The stronger wind, the stronger trees." The Black people of Abbeville-Greenwood managed to build institutions and raise and educate their children despite the violence directed against them and the economic system that kept them in poverty. Black families named Chiles, Moragne, Marshall, Ballard, Bradley, Hackett, Chappell, and Mays toiled to surmount adversity and provide a better life for their children—and they almost succeeded. As Benjamin Mays noted: "Despite poverty, however, Negro life was very stable. As a rule, men did not desert their families. There were not many illegitimate children in my community."

Despite the hardships of living in South Carolina, many former Abbeville residents have warm memories of rural life. Benjamin Mays recalls: "I loved the farm. To this day I enjoy seeing a beautiful crop of green corn growing in the wind, or a patch of growing cotton." A Philadelphia woman told me: "It used to be so nice. I used to have good times in Bradley. I can tell you I loved Bradley. It had a dozen stores and a post office. It had two different waiting rooms, colored and white. The train stopped there. Oh, it was good times." Hughsey Childs remembers: "We lived not too far from a creek and there were some good-sized fish in there and me and my brother went down—you know how you do—when you're going swimming, you make the water muddy and the fish come up to the top and you can pick em up. Mom fried the fish. She fried all the fish so beautiful. . . . I had two fish, and I think we also had corn and biscuits."

Farming Was Their Livelihood

Both races in South Carolina essentially had one means of livelihood, the cultivation of cotton. After the Reconstruction and before the Great Migration at issue was who was going to work the land, what incentives would be used, and who would direct the operation. This economic question was closely connected with the issue of political democracy, for two main directions of development were theoretically possible, as we consider it today, but never possible politically or ideologically at the time. The great plantations could have been broken up, the land confiscated, the owners compensated, and the former slaves given ownership of the land. Many Black people believed that land was owed them for their long servitude. As one said, "What's the use of giving us freedom if we can't stay where we were raised, and own our houses where we were born, and our little pieces of ground?" Such a movement would have broken the power of the Southern land-owning class and created, over time, independent Black farmers with the power to control their own destinies. Owning land would have permitted them to flourish and might have led to a democratic society in the South. The other outcome—the one that actually occurred—was the restoration of a system of Black servitude to whites in a different guise.

163

With few exceptions, our people in South Carolina did not receive land, and they became a landless proletariat with only their labor to sell. The whites who owned the land still needed Blacks to work it. But many former slaves had moved off the great plantations, frequently reassembling in small Black villages on the peripheries of the estates. In addition, freedom, to many ex-slaves, was the ability to move from one place to another, and they did. Their mobility was much remarked on by white observers.

It was to the advantage of the white landowners to fix Black labor in one place so that agricultural production could be assured. And it was to the Blacks' advantage to remain there in order to secure pay and food for their families. As one laborer said, "I ain't got no vittles for my wife and chillun; I ain't got a day's rations in my cabin." Whites and Blacks needed each other, and economic necessity became a prime determinant of the relationship between them.

The relationship between the freedmen and the whites varied from region to region in the South, but in South Carolina it was largely determined by cotton. Although rice continued to be grown until the turn of the century in the coastal areas, and fruits, meats, and other staples were raised for local consumption, South Carolina was the leading cotton-producing state. By the end of Reconstruction, slave labor had been replaced by a system of sharecropping, renting, tenant farming, and wage labor. Under the sharecropping system, the workers contracted their labor out to the landlord and in return were given land, shelter, rations, seed, tools, stock, and stock feed. At the end of the season, they received one-half to two-thirds of the crop they grew. Under another arrangement—usually called renting—laborers rented the land, supplied their own tools and seed, and paid rent with a share of the crop or cash. Tenant farming meant that workers tilled a certain portion of the landlord's fields under supervision. He supplied them with a house, rations, a separate plot for themselves, and a mule and plow to till it every other Saturday. At the end of the year, they also received cash wages. In effect, they shared the land with the landowner. Under the last arrangement, wage labor, workers received wages, shelter, and food in return for working the fields. This particular form of land usage was preferred by some landlords who occasionally paid the workers in worthless IOUs.

An elaborate network of liens, credits, and advances kept most of the Black tillers in perpetual indebtedness and dependency on local merchants. Stores advanced food and clothing, expecting to be paid at harvest time. An all-too-frequent outcome is told in the Blues phrase, "I get another day older and deeper in debt," or in Paul Robeson's lament in "Old Man River" that "I get weary and sick of trying."

The reliance on oral contracts between tenants and white landowners or merchants made it harder to escape from this cycle. A white man's word was always taken as truth when there was any dispute, and it was a crime for anyone to interfere with a laborer under contract to someone else. The contract system helped create peonage, fixing Black labor on the land. By the end of Reconstruction, cotton production was higher than during the pre–Civil War period. The basic contours of the economic system of South Carolina had been set.

Social Status in the County

Relationship to the land determined, in large part, social status in Abbeville-Greenwood. At the bottom were the sharecroppers, who made up close to half of the families. Next were the renters, and finally were those who owned their own land. About ten percent of the Blacks in the county fell into the last category with the rest of the population divided between sharecroppers and renters. A "sharecropper was in the low grass." Black people were frequently cheated, and there was not much they could do about it. Sometimes, they would conceal a few bales of cotton at home, and bring them in only after the white farmer declared that all expenses for the year had been paid. This tactic led to much strife. "Oh, man, they started ripping and roaring and tearing things up."

At the next level were the renters, who sometimes owned

their livestock and paid for the land with a number of bales of cotton at the end of the season. One old Abbeville-Greenwood resident I spoke with recalled that his father's rent was two bales of cotton; Benjamin Mays's father paid four bales of cotton for his forty-acre farm. In a good year, a renter might have ten to twelve bales of cotton left, and their sale would provide his livelihood for the coming year.

At the top of the economic and social pyramid were the landowners, among whom was Anthony Crawford. He was one of many Blacks, including the residents of Promised Land, who "owned their own lots and took pride in the fact that they had never had to work for white people." Some had obtained their land and their start in life through close relationships to former slave masters. Some were the mulatto offspring of the slavers, but they seemed to pride themselves on their independence: "None of us ever worked for white people, never. We had nothing to do with white people 'cause we had our own property and you know we were comfortable. Now . . . others had to live on white men's plantations. There was jealousy even among your own people with anybody that tried to have something and be somebody."

Differences of color and economic standing sometimes created friction in Abbeville-Greenwood. Some families "didn't like no dark persons. They didn't have nothing to do with you. Unless you were light, you couldn't do anything right, period." Segregation by color was often tacitly accepted in some of the Black churches: "You'd be surprised. There was a certain section of the church they'd sit in and you didn't sit with them neither. That was wrong, but that was carried on."

An even greater source of internal conflict was the presence in the community of the mulatto children of white landowners. Miscegenation did not end with the Civil War and the Black community was frequently unable to protect its women from the demands of white males. The Black community in its effort at self-protection did not tolerate the occasional open relationships between white men and Black women: "They called them 'bastards,' that's what the old folks called you back then." Hughsey Childs recalls: "[Whites] would never accept this white baby. When it was born it had to come live with us. But every chance he got, he was taught that he was better than us, because he was white and we was Black. He did that to keep you apart. . . . Anytime that we started something secret, tried to have something to improve ourselves, if we had a half white man in there, the white man knew it before we could get it off the ground."

Cohesion of Black Community

Despite these conflicts, the most important feature of the Black community life of Abbeville-Greenwood was its cohesiveness. There was an ethic of sharing, so that "if we had cows, what I mean, and you had none, then we would give you one of our cows. Same thing with pigs." The men who led the community "was strong. . . . They had some way of getting people together and making it work. They were so loyal. They didn't have nothing, but what they had, they helped you." Leaders "used to have secret meetings, like they used to have in slavery times," to discuss common action against the whites. The chief vehicle for community cooperation other than the church was the Masons, which merged our people in Greenwood-Abbeville into the larger Black community of South Carolina and provided a basis for affiliation once they arrived in the Northern cities. So did groups like the Bradley Burial Society, organized to help pool money for burial expenses.

Another factor making for cohesiveness was that practically everybody in the community seemed to be related, by blood or close marriage, and it was not uncommon for cousins to marry. The extent of this kinship network can only be realized when, at a family reunion, you look around and see that practically everyone in the room, from great-grandparents to great-grandchildren, share the same skin tone and facial features.

Life Centered About the Churches

The churches that connected the various Black communities of the county are better described as settlements. In most cases, a school was on the grounds of the church or close by. Benjamin Mays said that "Old Mount Zion was an important institution in my community. Negroes had nowhere to go but to church. . . . It was a place of worship and a social center as well." The A.M.E. Churches were connected by a circuit. Similarly, one minister would frequently pastor several Baptist churches. On the Sundays when service was not held at their community church, people would go to a neighboring church. All of this visiting made for a strong sense of community. Hughsey Childs reflects this: "Now you take Old Mount Zion. The Deans were big dogs in that church. Go by Mount Moriah, Deacon Davis, Tom Davis. Now they had trustees and services at the Methodist Church. See old man Bennie Williams. He used to sing in the choir." Indeed, a man or woman's membership in a community was signified by saying, "Mount Moriah," "Pine Grove," or "Mount Zion."

The churches frequently got together for singing contests, pitting one choir against the other: "I didn't realize that my father could sing until there was a singing convention in Greenwood and he was called on to sing a solo, and I was there and I was amazed. The chorus to the song was 'just as the sun went down.'—It was beautiful." They sang without music: "The choir now, they used to sing by notes and some of them would start it off, but they'd just keep on going. My father had a book, but he wouldn't be reading it. He'd be holding it up." And they used "to do a lot of shouting. Oh yes, they did. Up here, you just say you're joining the church, but down there they sang and prayed you through. You felt something, yes, you did." The songs would include "Amazing Grace," "What a Friend We Have in Jesus," and the center of the Black service, the "Old Ship of Zion."

The most important and joyous time of the year was the "revival," a term that covers all the festivities, religious and social, that occurred in August: "You see by the end of

July . . . Your crop was complete, your cotton, your corn, the potatoes—everything was in full bloom. You didn't have to work them anymore. You had only to wait till they ripen and then you start to harvest them. So a man would come to do revival."

In August, there were several services a day: "They had 11:00 preaching. When the service was over, we had benediction and then went out into the church yard and under those big oak trees they had tables and they was all set up. Every family that was a member of the church usually brought a basket. People that didn't have nothing, they could eat too. That was a fellowship. . . . After they had the dinner, they would go back about 2:30 and have a devotional service with the same minister. . . . The next morning we'd be back at church." The revival breathed great life into the community: "You could be a long way from the church and you'd hear the singing and see the people just putting on speed to get there. Them days I'll never forget." Baptism was held once a year, after the revival month was over. After the baptism service, the congregation welcomed the newcomers with a song:

> Everybody want to bid you welcome
> Welcome, welcome
> To the Promised Land.

There was some feeling of competitiveness between the Baptist churches and the A.M.E. churches: "Baptist folk wouldn't let you go to Methodist church and some Methodist people wouldn't let you go to a Baptist church. That's how come I stole the wife I married. She was a Methodist and her father didn't like no Baptist boy. He told me right to my face and I stole her. After we finally made up, he told me: 'Why didn't you ask for her?' I said, 'I already told you that I loved her and you told me to get out of your house.' He said: 'You're right, cause I wouldn't have let you marry her.' " Benjamin Mays explains the ingenious ways young people found to get around their parents' prejudices.

The churches were led by strong men. The pastor of Benjamin Mays's church, for example, was James Foster Marshall, born a "slave . . . [and] not permitted to go to school, but he accompanied the white children and heard them spell and read. He was at times a houseboy and thus had some advantages over the field hands." He became a minister and after some years of preaching attended college for two years. Reverend Marshall served the congregation at Mount Moriah, and Morris Chapel, the church founded on our family's plot, and spent thirty-five years at Old Mount Zion. In 1902, he founded a small industrial school.

Benjamin Mays considered Reverend Marshall "the best preacher in the world. He was eloquent. He could moan, and did. Almost invariably he made the people shout." Reverend Marshall was believed to have "special power with God. Even when he prayed for rain and it didn't come, they still believed he had influence with God. If he prayed for rain on the second Sunday in the month and it came the next day, it was obviously in answer to Marshall's prayer." For his pastoring of four churches, he received eight hundred dollars a year.

The content of Marshall's sermons was appropriate to the conditions of the people he served. He told them to be "honest and upright" and the sermons were attuned to helping them survive. He never, said Dr. Mays, made one comment about lynching, for had he done so he would have been lynched himself. Dr. Mays, who should know, says that our people in this county could not have endured without the strong emotional anchor provided by ministers such as Reverend Marshall. He and the other ministers provided sustaining grace amid the violence that hovered over the Black community of Abbeville-Greenwood. The schools were closely tied to the churches. Their names tell the history of the county: Hard Labor School; the White Hall School, where the election shooting took place; the Cedar Grove School, across from the home of General Bradley who used the convicts; and the Pine Grove School, attached to the church that was sacked during the Phoenix race war. Several teachers in these schools later moved to Philadelphia where they provided a link between Greenwood and the new city.

Baseball was a popular Saturday pastime and a league of teams centered around the churches played against one another. As in Philadelphia, the Saturday afternoon baseball games were also social occasions marked by courting and just plain visiting. Thus the people of Bradley came to know the people of Pine Grove and of Old Mount Zion and of Promised Land. The teacher at the Pine Grove School was Mary Latimer, the daughter of the man who had been released by the mob at the oak tree near Phoenix. Hughsey Childs remembers, "It was forty kids that went to school and she was the teacher for all forty of us."

The school at Cedar Grove was taught by Emily Baldwin Johnson, my great-aunt, who was born in 1885 and had been educated in Abbeville at the Harbison School, which the whites burned down in 1907. There was the legendary Sarah Gayle, who taught at Cedar Grove and White Hall and was considered to be among the most inspiring of teachers. She too came to Philadelphia in the migration.

Though the church gave cohesion to Black community life, a few all-Black settlements also existed. In the section called Promised Land, near Bradley, some Black families in 1870 created an enclave with its schools and churches where whites seldom ventured. There were other smaller enclaves, scattered about the two counties.

The tight bonds formed in the South were forged by love and a common effort to survive. They were weakened during the Great Migration northward, but to a surprising extent they persisted.

Chapter 15

GOING TO THE CITY

You'd better run, run, run-a-run
You'd better run, run, run-a-run
You'd better run to the city of refuge
You'd better run, run, run

Traditional Black Spiritual

A great theme in human history is the movement of people from the country to the city. We know that this change imposes enormous stress on the structure of rural communities, and later we will attempt to analyze the process. Here, we focus on the change as the participants viewed it and so, for the most part, we will let Black Abbeville-Greenwood speak for itself about the Great Migration northward at the beginning of World War I.

How They Moved to Philadelphia

Sometimes the first step in the migration was so tentative that the participant in the process did not realize he or she was taking it. Thus Hughsey Childs, a farmer who had just married, decided to move into the town of Greenwood where, despite several disastrous incidents with trays and dishes, he found a job as a waiter. The training he received was invaluable as he prepared to move to Philadelphia.

His older brother had already moved to the city, and wrote home urging the others to come along: "Now the next one that came here was my brother Lewis, and then John. Then my sister came up with her husband, Moses Goode." Visits home to Greenwood for the August revival also spread the news about the employment opportunities in the North and the relative freedom from terror. A summer visit to Philadelphia planted the seed in Childs's mind, and finally in 1921 he moved to Philadelphia too.

In another case, a woman from Bradley was in love with a young man who was tired of the degradation of life in the South, and she eloped with him to Philadelphia. In many instances, people went to a specific place or to a specific relative who was already settled in Philadelphia. Other migrants were actively recruited by big Philadelphia industrial plants in need of labor. They "come up in groups to steel mills like Midvale, Eddystone and Hog Island."

The home of the recruiter often became the center of the new community, since he sometimes rented out homes near him to the migrants. As one said, "They didn't know nothing about Germantown or South Philadelphia. They come right here to North Philadelphia. This was their ground." The territory to which most of the Greenwood refugees came was bounded by Girard Avenue on the south, Susquehanna Avenue on the north, and between Tenth Street on the east and Twelfth Street on the west.

Sometimes a refugee like Mr. Childs's brother, would "be intelligent" and rent out a house "on purpose to make money. He only had two children and they had such a large house that he rented rooms. See, people was glad just to get a room." Naturally, people from Greenwood were directed to such a house when they arrived in the city. Another person recalled that he first stayed in a house rented by his sister, in which three families from Greenwood, including the family of an A.M.E. minister, also lived.

The area in North Philadelphia where the Greenwood refugees settled was soon thickly populated with people with names like Bradley, Ballard, Hackett, Logan, Crawford, Gayles, and Tolbert. In time they began creating institutions to support themselves. One of the first was the store of George Bailey, Sr., who had been raised in Greenwood and came to Philadelphia, where he worked at the Campbell Soup Company: "Being a very ambitious man, he opened his first community market at 1422 North 10th Street, and expanded his business to 803 Oxford Street. By the year 1922, he was the second Negro member of the Frankford Grocers' Association." Bailey married a Greenwood woman, and his store became the communications center for many Greenwood Blacks. If you were looking for a place to stay, a job, or news of relatives, or if you wanted to send a package home, you went to the store. It was a particularly important place for those without a church affiliation.

A bar run by Roosevelt "Buddy" Peterson of Greenwood at Thirteenth and Oxford streets served as a social gathering place before Peterson, an astute businessman, who was a benefactor to many of the migrants, purchased the Chesterfield Hotel, which later became Father Divine's Philadelphia headquarters. People from Greenwood would "go on down to the Chesterfield, have a few drinks and go home." Initially, they had very little social contact with "Old Philadelphians," who generally seemed to be "condescending," and for the most part the transplanted Greenwooders hung out together, or with other people from the South.

A Greenwood Church Becomes Many Philadelphia Churches

The church was, of course, the center of the life of the newcomer to the city. Thus, in Philadelphia today one finds Morris Chapel Church, founded and named by five families who had played active roles in the life of Morris Chapel Church in Greenwood.

One night, several of the newly arrived Philadelphians

renting rooms in the home of Childs's brother "got to talking and started to have a prayer meeting. After that meeting, one said, 'Let's name a church after Morris Chapel in Greenwood.' " Eventually, they rented the first church building: "A horse stable. You went up the steps and on that second floor was something like a little hall where they used to store bales of hay. The first service in 1917 was held in that horse stable. The service was good and we had a nice little choir." Practically all the members in the early days were from Greenwood, and they sent for a pastor from home. By 1927, the church had moved to a new location in the 1200 block of North Tenth Street where they knocked down the walls between two row houses. After one more move, the church settled into its present location at Tenth Street and Lehigh Avenue in North Philadelphia. By the mid-twenties, people from Edgefield County, then Georgia, then Virginia, then Philadelphia joined the church, and it gradually became an urban rather than a transplanted rural institution. But its roots and its music were still heavily Southern Black.

During its formative years, the pastor of the church was Reverend Parrish, "a fine man who would come in the snow to see the sick even though he had arthritis and diabetes." So self-sacrificing was he that on a salary of $85.00 a week—until the late 1950s—he still paid his dues to the church. He willed his own home to his people and his church on his death.

Many of the original members of Morris Chapel Philadelphia broke away and formed the Calvary Baptist Church, and some of them then moved into the congregation of Bright Hope Baptist Church, the church of Philadelphia's only Black congressman at this writing. One reason was that "Bright Hope favored Morris Chapel in Greenwood. It was built just like Morris Chapel, only it was made out of stone. After they split, they didn't want to bother about no little church no more. They all went to Bright Hope because it was already established and a good-sized church." Another split took place after World War II when the Reverend James S. Hall of Greenville departed from Morris Chapel with a portion of the original membership and formed Triumph Baptist Church, which now

175

gathers its congregation from a formerly Jewish area now turned Black.

Morris Chapel was not the only church heavily dominated by Greenwood folk. Ebenezer Baptist Church at Tenth and Girard was pastored by a man who had formerly led the original Morris Chapel in Greenwood. A break-away from Ebenezer resulted in the formation of Mount Sinai Tabernacle Church, first located at Seventeenth and Ridge and now at Twenty-Eighth and Lehigh. Other churches formed from the original Ebenezer Church are Childs's Memorial Baptist Church and the Greater Ebenezer Baptist Church.

Space precludes detailing the internal politics that led to these changes, but we must understand that the churches were buffeted by the same economic and social forces that beset the Abbeville-Greenwood Philadelphians. People moved as they found jobs in different neighborhoods. The changing locations and names of the churches indicate population movements across Broad Street and into the huge area that is today known as North Philadelphia. Conflicts frequently arose as the founders of a church saw their power threatened by newcomers from other areas of South Carolina or the South. Hughsey Childs gives another reason for the frequent split: "They had been used to a different service at home. When we went home, we had different preaching than we had up here."

Greenwood's People Enter Other Churches

Just as Bright Hope, Morris Chapel, and Triumph drew large numbers of Greenwood refugees, so did Mother Bethel Church, founded by Richard Allen. The South Carolina Society of the Church—there are also Virginia and Georgia societies—is heavily populated with natives of the Abbeville-Greenwood region. Even today, people from Mother Bethel send money—sometimes as much as one hundred dollars—to Mount Sinai A.M.E. Church in Greenwood County as a contribution to the homecoming celebration. A list of the

Greenwood-Abbeville families who joined the church between 1917 and 1923 would include Cothranes, Chiles, Perrins, Holloways, and Bradleys, many of them directly from the town of Bradley.

Moreover, we find letters of transmittal to Mother Bethel from Weston Chapel A.M.E. Church in Greenwood, named after the same Weston who walked bravely through the guns at Hodges Depot. The letters, written in 1917, typically say that "we take pleasure in recommending her to any church she desires to come under the watchcare of or join. She leaves with our prayers and good wishes."

R. J. Williams, a graduate of the Institute for Colored Youth, was the pastor of Mother Bethel when the migrants arrived at the church. Bethel A.M.E. made a powerful effort to attract them and set up an information bureau to help the newcomers in finding homes and jobs. On the letterhead of the Information Bureau was a poem by Reverend Williams:

> Beloved, let this be your home
> Even if your stay is short
> To all I say, never roam
> Heaven loves a contrite heart
> Enter Bethel, enter now
> Let the spirit teach you how
> To the City of Brotherly Love you are welcome
> At Mother Bethel
> You will be at home.

In a pamphlet published by the church, Mother Bethel is described as the "home for the stranger, the pride of the connection." The same pamphlet tells the newcomers that things will be better for them and their children in the North. They will find "justice" and educational opportunities if they are prepared to work hard. Then followed some important advice: "When you go into a strange community, the first thing you should do is to find the church. . . . The church is the haven of safety. The tents of wickedness are on every hand." It was good advice to the newcomers. For the church was almost the only lifeline to which they could cling in the midst of the uprooting that had taken place in their lives.

The Baptist and A.M.E. churches were not the only recipients of the people from South Carolina. St. Augustine's Episcopal Church numbered many new members from among the migrants, and many of the Abbeville-Greenwood people joined churches that Arthur Huff Fauset, the great Philadelphia scholar and activist, has labeled "urban cults."

Two brothers of Mr. Childs joined the church of "Prophet Cherry, the Church of the Living God. He preached that they wouldn't never die and they lived like hermits. Met them one Saturday night. They told me: 'So sorry, brother, but you're going to hell.' I told them: 'We was all baptised in the pool down to Damascus Church in Greenwood, South Carolina. If God hadn't blessed you to gather here and meet this man [Cherry] and you died within the faith you confessed there, where would you have gone?' They said: 'To hell.' I said: 'Well, that's just where you're going.' "

The faith of Mr. Childs was shaken and that night he had a dream: "I went to sleep and in a dream a path appeared before my two feet. Looked like it was no wider than my hand and it was bright as the sun. I was looking in the distance; then as my sight focused, the path came down and when it got to my feet, both of my feet were in it, facing the sun. I woke up and said, "Thank you, Lord."

Prophet Cherry "was originally from the deep South, which he refers to as a place worse than hell." A completely self-educated man who read Yiddish and Hebrew, he believed, as had many other Southerners, in a Black Christ: "He will pull out a so-called picture of Jesus suddenly and scream to his followers: 'Who in hell is this? Nobody knows. They say it's Jesus, but it's a damn lie.' " He further said that Black people were the "original inhabitants of the Earth" and that God was Black. The walls of the church were decorated with swords, and the worshippers called each other "Brother and Sister." How reassuring it must have been for some of them after the persecution in the South to know that God was Black.

Strains of City Life

The move to the city was too much for some people. Sometimes community leaders never regained their lost status. One man who had been a prosperous farmer in the country was reduced to a trashman's job in Philadelphia: "He made some headway, and bought this home, but he turned out to be a rummy, a real rummy. And everybody was so amazed how he had let himself go like that, 'cause he was a strong man." A minister also took refuge from the strains of urban life in a bottle: "I went to the father and I said, 'Oh, oh, what happened? You came here from the South and you used to preach down there. You used to be a minister. Now, how did you let this happen to you?' He said, 'I am sick and scared because I must have an operation.' And I said, 'You have no more faith in yourself than that. You were a minister and you can't trust God.'" Many Abbeville-Greenwood refugees died of drunkenness. A Philadelphia resident remembers "you could see them lying on the streets, just like dogs lying in the shade. I used to shun them as a young man because I was ashamed."

Our people from Greenwood soon developed a reputation, deserved or not, for being violent. It had been customary for them to carry knives and guns in their rural environment. The habit got them into trouble in the city and led one judge, tired of sentencing Greenwood people to jail, to say that he was going down there to see what caused all this meanness. One of my cousins, remembering a time when police had picked up some fifteen or sixteen of them for loitering, told me, "It made you feel so bad, the judge would ask each man where he came from, and he would say 'Greenwood.' Made you feel so poorly." As another said, "If they [Greenwood people] figured that you were taking advantage of them, you'd have a fight on your hands."

The violence was sometimes, not surprisingly, directed against whites: "They come here with anger in their hearts against the white man in the South and they throwed it off on the white man in the North and that was wrong. They would say things in the North that they couldn't say in the

South. I went into this taproom with a boy from out around Mt. Moriah. And a white policeman was in this bar drinking. John and I walked in and he ordered me a beer and himself a beer. Now the officer was fixing to drink his beer and John just slapped it out of his hands and said to this white cop, 'What the hell are you doing in here?' "

Adjusting to City Life

Poor rural folk sometimes had trouble adapting to city life. Some had been "raised way back in the woods, had seen nothing but pigs, chickens, and cows," and were unprepared to meet new demands. As one observer said: "It was hard for them to get along. They simply didn't understand some things. You could say some things and they would not know what you were talking about. And that was pretty rough, because they'd sometimes take the wrong conception of it."

The way they lived—which made sense in South Carolina—took on a different meaning in the city. For example, in the country, it was acceptable "to wash your face and dump the water back out of the window. The people did the same thing here even though they had a bathroom. They'd wash and dump the water right out the window. I've seen them throw dishwater out of the front door till they learned better."

One family, feeling that outhouses were more sanitary than indoor toilet facilities, had one built in the backyard and "ranted and raved and resented it terrible" when health officials refused to permit it. There are likewise accounts of people who suffocated when they blew out the gas jets just like they would blow out a lantern down in the country. Sometimes people would sweep trash right out of the door and into the street because it was natural in the country to sweep a house clean and the dust outdoors.

Smaller tragedies beset some Abbeville-Greenwood people as they fell victim to city con artists. Childs remembers a time when "I looked under the bed to get my $16.00 pair of tan shoes, 'cause I had a suit to match it, [and] it was gone. Man,

I cried. I was nineteen years old and I cried like a baby. The picture was very good, but you know I didn't enjoy it 'cause all I could do was to sit there and think about those shoes."

The way was hard for the newcomers. Many worked hard only to have their savings wiped out by the Depression. Others died in the construction of such major public works as the Broad Street subway. They saw their children falling prey to drink, drugs, and sometimes getting killed in a crazy quarrel or locked away in the great big stone Philadelphia prisons.

The Greenwood Heritage

Abbeville-Greenwood's people probably make up a disproportionately large percentage of the North Philadelphia Black population. Considering the other South Carolinians who came to the area during the Great Migration, an observer might conclude that North Philadelphia is South Carolina all over again. Indeed, it would be almost impossible to walk on any street in North Philadelphia without encountering Abbeville-Greenwood folk.

The heritage they brought with them to Philadelphia helped to shape the urban culture at the same time that it was modified by city life. Tossed into the urban world, the Abbeville-Greenwood refugees fought hard to maintain their identity. That sense of Black identity was their first contribution to modern Black Philadelphia. Not having been part of any white culture, they were forced to rely on their African communal heritage. They brought with them a strong suspicion of white people and white ways. They developed a strong kinship network to support one another.

Our people also brought with them a strong pride in their ability to survive adversity. Their deaths in the pool halls and on the streets of Philadelphia indicate that this pride may sometimes have been misplaced, for in its way the city was as dangerous an adversary as the killers of Anthony Crawford. But finally they brought with them a deep and abiding sense of justice. They had had their property stolen, seen their daughters and sisters raped by the whites, seen a Black man lynched on the strength of a white girl's nod, and seen that life in a lawless place "was nasty, brutish, and short."

Dressed in loud country clothes and talking in down-home accents, slapping each other's backs with big hands, they personified the concept of "equality," the idea that a nation is judged on the way it treats its poor and downtrodden. And they brought with them the music and rhythm of Africa. It poured out of the bars at night and the churches on Sunday morning till it suffused the city. The Abbeville-Greenwood people joined with other South Carolinians, and in turn with Black Virginians and Marylanders, to form Black Philadelphia.

Chapter 16

THE GREAT MIGRATION

Sometimes I feel like a motherless child
Sometimes I feel like a motherless child
Sometimes I feel like a motherless child
A long way from home
A long way from home

Traditional Black Spiritual

By 1900, the process of modernization that changed the politics and economics of the United States was in full swing. Black Americans, pushed out of the South by political and economic oppression, were pulled into the North by the burning steel hearths of Pittsburgh, Weirton, Cleveland, Detroit, Trenton, and Philadelphia. Thus, the Black population shifted from states like Alabama, Georgia, Virginia, South Carolina, and Mississippi where they equaled or surpassed the white population, to states where Blacks were outnumbered. The shift from country to town made us a minority among the European whites flooding into the Northern cities. By 1910, our people accounted for only 2.4 percent of the total urban population. We therefore became a minority in both the North and the South, and the pattern of American politics for the next half century was set.

The Migration's Impact on Philadelphia

In the first decade of this century, Philadelphia had a total population of 1.5 million. Of this number, nearly seventy percent were whites who had been born in the United States, while only twenty-four percent were foreign born. Blacks made up six percent of the population; nearly two-thirds of them had been born in the South. These migrants came from the upper rather than the deep South. The Black population was centered in South Philadelphia in 1910, but in no political district were we a majority.

The refugees came in two waves, one in 1917–18, the other in 1922–23. Our numbers rose rapidly from 84,000 in 1910 to 134,000 in 1920 to 220,000 in 1930 and 250,000 in 1940. In comparison to the city's population, these numbers represented a rise from six percent in 1910 to eleven percent by 1930, and finally to thirteen percent of the total population of Philadelphia in 1940. By 1930, Philadelphia had a Black population equal to that of New York City. More important, the Black population of Philadelphia had nearly tripled between 1910 and 1930. At the same time, 63,000 Italians, 100,000 Russians—the majority Jewish—31,000 Poles, and diverse other European immigrants had recently arrived.

By 1930, almost seventy percent of the Blacks in Philadelphia had been born in the South. And while Virginia contributed the largest number of refugees—41,000 persons—28,000 came from South Carolina, 22,000 from Georgia, 18,000 from North Carolina, and 15,000 from Maryland. For the first time in its history, the Black community of Philadelphia contained many refugees from the racial oppression in the deep South states. Indeed, they made up almost half the total Black population of the city.

Most of the newcomers settled in what is now North Philadelphia. School registration statistics indicate that South Carolinians composed almost half of the migrants in certain North Philadelphia districts, closely followed by North Carolinians. On the other hand, in South Philadelphia in the early 1920s, the majority of students had been born in Philadelphia and many of the rest came from Virginia. Indeed, only one out of every ten children had even one parent born in Pennsylvania. We were a "tossed and driven" people.

Controversy remains about the causes for the migration of Southern Blacks into the cities of the North, and a study of Philadelphia reveals the complexity of the process. The major industries in the city, particularly the Pennsylvania Railroad, in the person of one Mr. Doughtery, actively recruited Blacks from the South. The Midvale Steel Plant, Atlantic Refining Company, Franklin Sugar Company, Keystone Paving Company, Eddystone Company, and Disston Company all actively searched out Black people from the South. "They were paying men to come down and get people to come up to Philadelphia to work," an informant told me. "A guy would come down and pay your transportation and you'd pay off your tickets when you got to work. Ten or twelve workers would come together and when they got to working and were established they'd send home for their families." In 1923, Anderson's Employment Agency of Richmond, Virginia, played a major role in recruiting Blacks to the North from the Carolinas and Georgia.

Between 1916 and 1919, when the war cut off the supply of unskilled workers from southern and eastern Europe, Black "hands" were hired to replace them. In addition, some hands were hired to break strikes, and this became a source of antagonism between white and Black workers. The magnitude of the recruitment effort can be seen from the near-frantic request for 257,000 Black workers from the South when the Federal Labor Exchange opened in August 1918. The industries in the Philadelphia area required 186,000 unskilled laborers.

Industry clearly encouraged the movement North. But unlike some historians who see the "pull" of jobs in the North as the mainspring of the migration, I am convinced that the oppression in the South was the major reason for leaving the region. Indeed, the most recent examination of the migration concluded: "Racial violence on the part of both Southern officials and the Ku Klux Klan became factors so important in out-migration that the effects on the Southern labor force were evident. . . . Both blacks and whites mentioned lynching as one of the most important causes of the out-migration of blacks from the South during World War I. . . ." The *Christian Recorder*, the A.M.E. Church journal, devoted the entire May 31, 1917, issue to the migration and published the results of a survey of Black leaders, both Southern and Northern, on the reason for the departure from the South. The answers were that people wanted "unrestricted freedom," legal rights, treatment as citizens, education for their children, and an end to humiliation. As one person said: "A Negro's home is not his castle: his family may be invaded, his daughter seduced, and even his life destroyed, and there is nothing to do but weep and pray." Black men who would not sell their property to whites "for a song, have waked up to find the savings of a lifetime in ashes. Every Negro knows this, though few will confess it except privately."

Correspondent after correspondent referred to the brutality of life in the South. The pastor of Mother Bethel Church wrote, "I believe it is the voice of Abraham's God, saying get thee out from among the people and go to a land that I shall afterward show thee." One expert on the migration cited the Anthony Crawford murder as a major cause for the exodus of Blacks from South Carolina. Black school principals in Philadelphia at that time used to be able to tell that something had happened in a particular section of the South by the concentration of refugees from a certain place.

Among the refugees, the men were mainly unskilled laborers, but a surprising number had been trained as painters, bricklayers, or cabinetmakers, and some were doctors, lawyers, and pharmacists. Emphasizing this point, Alexander Manly in the *Evening Ledger* of October 1, 1923, said the Black people represented in the migration were of the very best quality of the Southern Negro and that "the danger lies not in the character of the persons themselves, but in the strangeness of the atmosphere into which they are suddenly transplanted." His views were echoed by the most serious students of the migration, who concluded that the Southern Blacks were "steady, reliable, ambitious, and law-abiding." Indeed, a study of one sample group of immigrants found that sixty-five percent of them were church members, with sixty percent of the congregants belonging to the Baptist church and thirty percent to the A.M.E. Church. And sixty percent of the men in this group already belonged to such Black institutions as the Masons, Knights of Pythias, or the Odd Fellows when they arrived in Philadelphia from the South. In view of the reputation that some Southerners acquired for being violent and rowdy, these studies might have tended to overstate somewhat the "respectability" of the refugees.

Reaction to the Migration

White officials expressed concern about the migration. One official charged with housing the migrants asked his counterparts around the country for information on this migration. Why, asked he, were Blacks leaving the South and just how many more were heading for Philadelphia? He offered information on the Philadelphia migrants in exchange. Indeed, he had his hands full, for on some days, five to six hundred people arrived in those trains from Greenville, Greenwood, Charleston, Charlotte, and Richmond. By 1925, the City Club of Philadelphia was holding luncheon discussions about the migrants. The city's white elite recognized that they had a new problem.

The Black reaction to the migration varied from the warm welcome extended by Mother Bethel Church and the Reverend Albert Tindley, a Methodist minister who was perhaps the most important Black clergyman in the city, to resentment and hostility. Forrester Washington, head of the Armstrong Association, a precursor of the Philadelphia Urban League, said in 1917, that "both the native colored and white people of our community have a feeling that the southern man is more criminal than the northern which creates a very unpleasant attitude towards the newcomers." Sadie Pace Alexander, in a pioneering study of the migrants, noted that the Old Philadelphia Blacks resented the newcomers and "stood aloof from them." Another observer of the Old Philadelphians told this writer that some of them secretly hoped that the whites would recognize that they were different from the Southerners, and treat them accordingly. But a strong article in the A.M.E. journal emphasized that the duty of Northern Blacks was to give a "frank and open institutional reception to those fleeing from injustice and caste oppression." The *Christian Recorder*, the publication of Richard Allen's church, counseled its readers, quoting Deuteronomy 10:17–18, "Love ye therefore the strangers, for ye were strangers in the land of Egypt."

By 1925, the shape of modern Philadelphia was becoming clear, and some people knew the implications. One wrote to the *Public Ledger* on June 25, 1925, that North Philadelphia was becoming a "city within a city." The migrants, said the writer, were welcomed by the "hooch peddler, the wine-monger, the low-life movie, the low-type dancehall, the vicious kind of poolroom with its reprobates calling aloud to the young men and women." In North Philadelphia there was "no Y.M.C.A., recreation center, no public library, no municipal betterment center" and the Black churches were housed in "pitifully small and antiquated structures," unable really to help their congregations. The article continued: "a slum can be found strongly entrenched in this North Philadelphia neighborhood. Ignorance, dirt, overcrowding, disease, sloth, wine, drunkenness, corruption of youth all have their stranglehold."

> Everybody want to bid you welcome
> Welcome, welcome
> To the Promised Land.

Richard Allen
(*Library Company of Philadelphia*)

William Still
(*Library Company of Philadelphia*)

James Forten
(*Historical Society of Pennsylvania*)

Robert Purvis
(*Historical Society of Pennsylvania*)

Appeal to Men of Color
(*Library Company of Philadelphia*)

MEN OF COLOR, TO ARMS! NOW OR NEVER!

Harper's Weekly depicts "The Invasion of the North," 1863. Note scenes at bottom of page. (*Library Company of Philadelphia*)

O. V. Catto
(*Library Company of Philadelphia*)

Ebenezer Bassett
(*Schomburg Center for Research
in Black Culture, New York
Public Library*)

The Assault on Fort Wagner
by the Fifty-fourth
Massachusetts (Colored)
Regiment. Its ranks included
many Philadelphians and
New Yorkers. (*Schomburg
Center for Research in Black
Culture, New York Public
Library*)

Civil War soldiers
(*Schomburg Center for Research in Black Culture, New York Public Library*)

South Carolina leaders during Reconstruction (*Schomburg Center for Research in Black Culture, New York Public Library*)
Robert Smalls, *top*
B. F. Randolph, *center*
Congressman Joseph Rainey, *bottom*

Radical members of the South Carolina Legislature. Note especially
Randolph, Lomax, Wright, Cain, Martin, Rivers, Mobley, Nash, Swails,
Perrin, and Rainey. (*Library of Congress*)

South Carolina people
(*Schomburg Center for Research in Black
Culture, New York Public Library*)
Families on the move during Reconstruction, *top*
Freed slave children, *center*
School children, *bottom left*
Young woman, 1930s, *bottom right* (Doris Ulmann)

One More Day's Journey
(*Doris Ulmann, Schomburg Center for Research in Black Culture, New York Public Library*)

Pioneers of African Methodism in the upcountry of
South Carolina (*Proceedings of the Quarto-Centennial
Conference of the African Methodist Episcopal Church
of South Carolina, 1889*)

Reverend and Mrs. J. T. Baker, *top*
Mrs. Anna Brown, *bottom left*
Mrs. Winnie Simmons, *bottom right*

Maria Logan
(*Collection of Allen Ballard*)

Pictures from a family album

Jean-Pierre Burr
(*Collection of Miriam Burr
Mitchell Cooper*)

The Abbeville County
courthouse square, scene of
the Crawford lynching. Note
statue of John C. Calhoun.
(*Allen Ballard*)

Old country churches in Abbeville
County look like this. (*Allen Ballard*)

The Ugly Fishing Club
(*Collection of Dorothy Warrick Taylor*)

Among the members are William H. Warrick, seated with derby at right, and Andrew F. Stevens, philanthropist, next to him. Warrick was the father of Dr. William H. Warrick and of Meta Warrick Fuller, sculptor.

"The Migrants" by Ellen Powell Tiberino
(*Collection of Balch Institue of Ethnic Studies*)

Hughsey Childs
(*Donnie Roberts*)

Marian Anderson
(*Schomburg Center for Research in Black Culture, New York Public Library*)

Reverend Charles A. Tindley
(*Collection of Allen Ballard*)

In Sunday morning service
(*Donnie Roberts*)

North Philadelphia woman
Donnie Roberts)

Making a joyful noise unto the Lord
(*Donnie Roberts*)

Congressman Willliam Grey
(*Congressional Photo Services*)

Robert N. C. Nix, Jr., is assisted at his
installation as Chief Justice of the
Supreme Court of Pennsylvania by his
South Carolina-born father, Robert N. C.
Nix, Sr., the former Congressman. (*Brad
Bower, UPI*)

W. Wilson Goode,
Mayor of Philadelphia
(*Aaron Singleton*)

Part III
AFTER THE MIGRATION

A hot summer day in North Philadelphia, 1970s
(*Donnie Roberts*)

Chapter 17

NORTH MEETS SOUTH

The Southerners had their eye out for something. That was the great difference between them and the Old Philadelphians who depended on their rank, their tradition, and their pedigree, whereas these shrewd South Carolinians came here as if they knew there was something they could get and they went after it.

ARTHUR HUFF FAUSET

Like any child, I didn't understand much about what was happening to me during my first years. There was a mother, father, grandparents, uncles, and aunts, of all shades and varieties of language, culture, and color. None, however, were white. I was raised in the home of an uncle, a failed pharmacist turned successful numbers banker.

No child walks alone in this world, at least not any child who perseveres. I was surrounded, imperceptibly, by persons and institutions that contributed to my mastering the mechanisms for survival in the world around me. So, on Sunday mornings, it was away to an Episcopalian church where a litany of duty, work, and introspection was drilled into me. No sociologist was there to explain that a dynamic and powerful Black patriarch lay behind the force of the Black Episcopalian church in Philadelphia. That man, Archdeacon Phil-

191

lips, at the age of seventy, preached a funeral sermon to Philadelphia's Black jet-setters and told them he was going to live to be a hundred and preach many of their funerals if they didn't mend their ways. Both prophecies came true. Nor, as I looked around me at the church on Sundays, was I aware that I was being raised in a certain class and that many of the parishioners around me were Old Philadelphians sorely besieged and unhappy about the Black newcomers from the South in their midst.

Up the hill from my house stood the African Methodist Episcopal Church. To get there you had to walk past shacks whose yards were spotted with fetid puddles and garbage. The people who lived in those houses died from whooping cough, pneumonia, and tuberculosis. You could feel death as you walked by. The church on the top of the hill was, by the time of my birth in 1930, increasingly dominated by Southern migrants; among them was my paternal grandfather, John Ballard. I don't remember going into that church often, but I can dimly recall the smell and texture of the rough wooden benches and see my grandfather's head bent in prayer beside me. No word was ever said against that church, but it was a place to which I did not go. My parents—the father from the South, the mother from the North—were divorced. So too were the churches separated, the African from the Anglican.

Yet the music from the African Church was transmitted to me as directly as if I had sat in the pews every Sunday. I absorbed much of the music from the daily chants of the people as they tried to sing their way through the Depression. Women, returned from a day's work in a white house, sang as they ironed and patched their children's clothes. I can recall vividly the voice of Marie Price, a lady who lived across the street who seemed always to be ironing. She was a warm and loving woman—"How are you this morning, sugar?"—always resplendent on Sunday in her starched and spotless white church usher's dress. Then there was the singing of the "Southernnaires," a quartet whose music welded the community so tightly together on a Sunday morning that you could walk five blocks to church and never miss a song—because every house had its windows open and radio tuned to their singing. I also heard the music of the blind man who came down the street, his cane tapping, every Sunday. He sang only one song— "When I've gone the last mile of the way." We children always went outside to drop coins into the white porcelain cup he carried. It was chipped inside from the coins hitting its sides. "God bless you," he would say, scarcely missing a note of the tune, and continuing, "I will rest at the close of the day," meaning, as I knew even then, that the day would surely come—as it did before I was grown—when he would sing no more on Sundays.

On Sunday afternoons, I would sometimes run down to Mother Garry's. She was blue-black, solemn, and blind, an ex-slave who, I thought, had been placed in that block by God to remind us of whence we came. I would stare and listen, but avoid her because at the least provocation she would pinch. The grown-ups told us that we should never forget Mother Garry when we grew up.

Then would come Monday and off we'd go to the Hill School, full of Black teachers who didn't pinch, but instead used rulers. The school was headed by Nellie R. Bright, the stern and beautiful daughter of a Black Episcopal minister. Lord, was she stern. All of life was to be subordinated to learning. One day in 1980, as I watched them tear down the Hill School, I said to Nellie Bright—by then dead—"It's all right now, Miss Bright, I'm ready to take the test." She disliked two things: lack of personal discipline and disrespect for any human being, black, yellow, brown, or white, poor or rich. She was furious when, in the mid-thirties, health authorities tried to experiment on us with a new smallpox vaccine.

The curriculum included everything Nellie Bright could squeeze into it about the history of Africa and of Africans in America. Marian Anderson, by then on the threshold of fame, sang frequently at the school. Roland Hayes's voice would sometimes roll out over the auditorium. The students at Joseph E. Hill School were sent out into the street to make surveys of who was sick, destitute, or in need of heat. But still Nellie Bright could do nothing about the children who slipped away in the night, dead of malnutrition and disease.

It was all around the children growing up in those days. There was Jean Thomas, a beautiful fair-skinned child who was the May Queen one bright spring day at the Joseph E. Hill School. She looked so pretty, all dressed up in white, but she had tuberculosis, and not long after the May Queen ceremonies, we were told, "Stop, stop the rough-housing—she's weak." And she died. So did Leroy Jordan. He used to run all around the schoolyard, barely stammering out his words sometimes, but bright, articulate, and my friend. Then the damn cough came and he got weaker and weaker, until one day he too didn't come to school. His brothers too. I don't think anybody could tell us he had died. The "old Black Philadelphia" teachers couldn't get the words out of their mouths. Then there was Terry Johnson, barely clothed, practically never bathed—and he died in a shack made up of shipping boxes. Used to eat out of garbage cans. He would make good scooters out of grocery crates and old roller skates. And damned if behind the dirt on his face he wasn't one of the gentlest and kindest kids you ever wanted to meet. T.B. took him too, just like it did Mary, the smartest one in the class. Cut through us like a knife.

When the children died, they already knew the "Erl-Konig," Schubert's Death King who came to snatch children away from their parents. We heard Marian Anderson sing it on a record in the first grade—"My father, my father!" the child screamed, "I see the Death King." Sitting in the row ahead of me was a girl named Ramona. She came into the class when we were in the fourth grade, she stammered and I remember how she used to wrap her arms around herself and sometimes shiver. Her speech was heavily tinged with the South, and we used to call her "country" and tease her the way children do.

I believe I know now why she shivered. Her sister later told me: "My father had gathered all the crop. The barn was four hundred yards from the house. So they set a match to the barn and we lost everything. All the feed and the cattle was in the barn. All of our corn. All of our potatoes. Everything, including the livestock, the cows, the pigs. I can hear them now. . . . It is hard for me to accept whites today. . . . I don't want anybody to know this, but when I go to the South, I'm scared." That's probably why the girl in front of me stammered and shivered, and I am truly sorry that I called her "country."

That Hill School which taught both classical music and the "Negro National Anthem," formed Black children from Virginia, South Carolina, and Georgia into a community. To the teachers, the South, Black or white, and its ways were distinctly repugnant. Their aim was to root out every bit of Southernness in us so that we could survive in the cold and mechanistic world controlled by Northern industrialists. My role and place in that institution was dominated by two facts: that I came from a line of Old Black Philadelphians who had been free before the American Revolution, and that I contained in me the blood of South Carolina slaves. All of us in that school were part of a privileged class of Blacks. Not absolutely, because we did have the poor and wretched among us in great numbers; but relatively, because there was a leavening of lower-middle-class children whose families had lived in the city for two generations. The community and the school were partially protected from the storm that was breaking over the heads of my blood cousins from the South in the slums of North and South Philadelphia.

Just across the street from my house was another institution, a VFW post. Most of the men in it had fought in World War I. And there they gathered, like thousands of other Black veterans across the country, to drink, play cards, and just plain socialize. Theorists would dub that a latent function, but for us children the primary function of the VFW was the Memorial Day parade, when the post would march in blue uniforms with gold trim. To watch them snap from parade rest to attention and then, to the quick roll of drums, break sharply into columns of four was beautiful. My numbers banker uncle, a lieutenant in the war, headed the parade. Leon, a tough little man who was a good numbers runner, and kind to children, always carried the flag. Under the *Evening Bulletin* almanac, when I came home from school, I would find three pennies. He and my uncle were tight companions. Leon's face was Indian, his voice Southern—from Maryland, I think. Nobody was supposed to mess with him, and when Big Joe did, Leon blew him to pieces with a shotgun. It was just after we got home from school one day. They took Leon to the penitentiary and I never saw him again.

Diagonally across from the VFW post was a bar run by Italians. We coexisted easily with them at the time. The bar was loud, noisy, and physical, with razors or brass knuckles flashing on weekend nights. The customers liked to sing along with the jukebox. You would hear a line from a song—"I don't want nobody"—punctuated by a loud "Yeah" from the entire bar, followed by "Always hanging 'round" and another "Yeah," accompanied by the sound of seventy-five hands slamming down in unison. This continued until the jukebox was, in effect, accompanying the patrons.

There were "nice" families on the block, and families that were considered not so nice. But I cannot recall one where the parents set out to put their children on welfare or equip them with a third-grade reading level, or ensure that their grandchildren in 1984 would be heroin addicts. The children were "Son," "Billy," "Brownie," "Country," "Chiz," "Step," "Junie," and "Ernie." We used loud, guttural yells and grunts to communicate. I had not then, of course, heard Africans or West Indians use our native intonations.

We cared for one another. While the community revolved around my house—the uncle was the doctor, banker, welfare department, and offical ward leader—numerous mechanisms of socialization and communication existed. Pastors of all denominations aided the spiritually and physically sick and wounded. The usher boards of individual churches, continuing a practice developed in the South, formed neighborhood, then citywide self-help assemblages. Sunday school superintendents from various churches met at conventions where they exchanged methods of teaching the children their ABCs on Sunday morning. The Masons assimilated the brothers who came North from the Southern lodges. The center of the Black community, the A.M.E. Church, carefully assessed the changes and established new missions to meet the needs of the Southerners come North.

Within a radius of five blocks from my home, two Ys and two recreation centers for Black youth came into existence. The boys at the recreation center went about Africanizing basketball, baseball, and football. Gradually, they left the neighborhood and came back as members of the Harlem Rens, the precursors of the Globetrotters and the beginning of Black professional basketball. The Black professional baseball leagues took root—Roy Campanella, who played ball with my uncles, was our connection to them. Campy took a back seat to the legendary Oscar Charleston, a pudgy tanklike man with the moves of a jaguar who visited often in our home. When Joe Louis won, the entire neighborhood, adults and children, poured into the streets chanting, "Hot diggety dog and dynamite, Joe Louis done won the fight," exulting in this proof of our physical superiority to the white man, if given a fair chance, which was rare.

But the Depression ground us down. My grandfather lost five houses in Philadelphia while trying, successfully, to put his eight children through college. Other people lost more. They lost their children to alcohol. Veterans wandered the streets in rags, while some children went hungry so long that the bones showed through their skin. World War II changed the community. The young men, instead of going into the Civilian Conservation Corps, ended up in the army. A lot of them went to Bougainville with the 93rd Black Infantry Division. The rest of the community melted away into three-shift defense plants. Walking around Philadelphia, the streets seemed empty.

Let us look in a bit more detail at the way the Northern and Southern traditions merged, drawing from my experiences, and those of people whom I interviewed over the years. It would tax our space to analyze this process in every aspect of Black life in Philadelphia, but we will examine color conflict, education, leadership, politics, music and sports, and the self-help tradition.

Class and Color

The Old Philadelphia families, by and large, reacted to the 1917–23 migration with shock and disbelief, fearing thatthey would lose all the gains they thought they had made in integrating themselves into the Philadelphia community. The reader is asked to imagine the feelings of a man who has built up a catering business worth one hundred thousand dollars, sent his children to Harvard, given generously to Black causes, and then finds himself lumped together with the refugees from Greenwood, South Carolina. He must have felt as threatened as a white family that woke one morning to see the house next door occupied by Blacks. The reaction of both the Old Philadelphians and the whites are wrong, but both reflect the racially oppressive history of America.

Old Philadelphians tried to assert their superiority by discriminating against migrants whose color might be darker than theirs. One Southerner told me that a "color caste system" existed and that "it was petty and vicious. . . . Well, if you hadn't been here two generations and even if you had, if you were dark-skinned and from the other side of the tracks, then you just didn't belong. . . ." Said another: "It was one of the most vicious discriminatory systems that ever existed."

The Old Philadelphians' color prejudices sometimes found an echo in the Black Southerners' ideas about color and class. Indeed, until recently, it was not unknown for families to boast of their "aristocratic" white blood. One woman explained that her mother did "not have anything against Black people," but rebelled when her son wanted to marry a dark-skinned woman: "She was too black for my mother." The woman's mother "had belonged to the Black aristocracy of the South—people who'd never lived in rented property and never seen their womenfolk work for whites. The majority of them were the teachers and preachers and the like." The woman spoke to me about the "unconscious arrogance" that she regretted in herself, and said that, in retrospect, "I hold this against my mother." Nevertheless, even the Black aristocracy of the South was not good enough for the Old Philadelphians. This woman never became part of the Philadelphia "broad stream. You see, Philadelphia society was snobbish."

Color prejudice could also be seen in a number of the Black community's institutions. Ralph Jones, a former newspaper editor, describes the "color caste" of the South Philadelphia Ys: "The so-called better families would send their sons to the 'Y' and their daughters to the Y.W.C.A. . . . That was their social thing. Only thing that broke it down was the athletic competition. You would date girls and take them to basketball games and you got to know the Old Philadelphians socially. . . . You'd be invited to the dances. If you were acquainted with a team member, and didn't belong to the light set, then you didn't get invited to these dances, and when you knew one of the light-skinned girls, and they invited you as a guest, you didn't go. It was vicious. I mean those social clubs were crushing."

Separation by color also appeared in the Black churches. Sometimes, as we have seen, it had its origins in the South. A minister tells how his father, pastoring in Virginia, "one morning just got up and told them, row by row, 'now you move on that side, and you move on that side,' mixing Black people with the light people. Eastern Shore of Maryland was famous for that, and they still are. I know some people in this city who belong to my church because I'm my daddy's son and they hold me very close because of what my father did." Ralph Jones repeated to me his father's account of the time the color line at the First African Church at Sixteenth and Christian was broken: "He and two of his friends went there one Sunday and they were lighter than he was and the usher tried to send him to the balcony. And he told me all three of them turned around and walked out."

The preoccupation with color and class existed at all levels of Black Philadelphia society. Thus, a woman tells of a club in early twentieth-century Philadelphia, made up of working men who called themselves the "Yellow Daffodils" because "every man was yellow." One of the members died young at a time when "it was awful cold. People didn't have no coal, no heat. His wife had no money, one child and one still unborn. When he was buried, the club came to the house to see her and they brought a great big wreath of yellow daffodils. The girl was hungry and they brought this big wreath of yellow daffodils instead of bringing her milk or bread or giving her some money. It was so cold when they got there that two of the flowers were frozen."

Some Black Philadelphians discriminated against others on the basis of place of origin and length of residence in the city as well as color. Thus the Marylanders who made up the bulk of the membership of the great Reverend Albert Tindley's church, according to Jones, "resented a lot of 'dumb' Blacks from the South coming up here. They were from Maryland, Delaware, and Virginia Eastern Shore. We discriminated against those people from the Deep South coming up here to ruin things for 'us.' And what did 'us' have? We did have a brick house and a job, that's all."

But there were some Blacks of Old Philadelphia stock who refused to categorize people by color or wealth, and who helped our people from the South. One was Arthur Huff Fauset, the son of Redmond Fauset, an A.M.E. minister and member of the Banneker Institute, who spoke with me before his death in 1983. Dr. Fauset, a school principal and the political conscience during the 1930s of the Black Philadelphia community, never relented in his fight to improve the conditions under which Black Southerners lived. A trained anthropologist, with a Ph.D. from the University of Pennsylvania, Fauset explained that his own family traced its descent from Blacks who were free in 1750. From the time of his youth, he was aware of the social class known as "Old Philadelphia," but he was always critical of it. He confessed himself still "at a loss to understand what it is those people thought they were representing. If you take the X family, it was even in the way they walked. There was something about the way they carried themselves. And the way they spoke. It was a peremptory manner, rather amusing to see because sometimes they were very slow on the pick up. . . . I called them simply 'Black Quakers' because they dressed so plainly, pretending that nothing mattered to them while all the time their noses were up in the air and they wouldn't do anything with the masses of the people. The masses were people that you walked on, but did not walk with."

Yet the presence of this elite made for a creative tension in the Philadelphia community and, according to Fauset, this class had a "catalytic effect" on such people as Alain Locke, grandson of the first teacher at the ICY and son of an ICY graduate who had taught in Tennessee during the Reconstruction. Locke "came up in Philadelphia and had to operate against the attitude of the people who were themselves part of this Old Philadelphia situation." Locke loved Philadelphia "because he knew everybody," but "his constant cry was 'get away from the city; get away from the city.' He meant 'get away' from this deadening situation here in Philadelphia, whose people are satisfied to make a pretense . . . standing out there in butler's clothes on Delancy Street."

In time, distinctions of class and color faded. As one woman told me, "The light people found there were more Black people than light, so they said, 'Let's all get together.' They found out they couldn't rule the Black people." Such leaders as Fauset and Joe Rainey (grandson of the South Carolina Reconstruction congressman) formed a leadership that helped to convince some Old Philadelphians that their future lay in the advancement of the masses of Black people. Of course, the main reason for the eventual acceptance of our Southern migrants into the Black Philadelphia community was their own achievements.

The pervasiveness of the class and color code led to bitter resentments, which, to some extent, linger today. I suspect that the discrimination struck hardest at the aspiring children of the immigrants—those who have been born in the South and were teen-agers during the twenties and thirties were made to feel color differences most strongly. But antagonistic feelings against the Old Philadelphians cemented the new immigrants together. The Old Philadelphians gave them both role models and authority figures against which to rebel. Eventually, the resentment led to—usually successful—attempts to outdo the Old Philadelphians in the fields of business and education. Thus, a typical response was: "Those Old Philadelphians. They couldn't snub me in the first place. I made my own society. I made it through preparation and some of the things I was exposed to at high school. . . . When I came home from college, I made my own social order through the church, my college fraternity, and business connections."

Another successful person said: "We really washed out the supposed intellectual superiority of the Northern Negroes, just washed them away. And I can see the waves coming in now; I can see myself in that wave; I can see my brother in that wave; and our kids and my sister's kids. . . . All our brainy kids grew out of the field Negroes." Said another: "The Old Philadelphians were not intellectuals. They were caterers, barbers, butlers, cooks. They worked for these rich white people. They didn't have to worry about making it. All they had to do was keep the house clean. But the others, they had to make it. And they became more versatile, smarter, more competitive, tougher. . . . They were dark and brown and could not lay claim to the kind of life that these people had here."

The Southerners' response to the Old Philadelphians was a subject that elicited a great deal of comment from Arthur Fauset. The Southerners, Fauset said, "had their eye out for something and that was the great difference between them and the Old Philadelphians who depended on their rank, their tradition, and their pedigree, whereas these shrewd South Carolinians and Southerners came here as if they knew there was something they could get and they went after it, like Eugene Rhodes [E. Washington Rhodes, editor of the *Philadelphia Tribune*] and Nix [Robert N. C., congressman from Philadelphia, 1957–76]. There was a vacancy there and the Southerners filled it.

"Their English was horrible and there is no question that we would laugh at them with their verbs preceding subjects and so forth. . . . Well, while we sat back and laughed at the crudities, these people took over the important places. . . . Now the people who had lived here all their lives realized they had literally given away the city to people who were not nearly as competent as they were. . . . Take Rhodes, for example. Imagine a fellow like him coming to Philadelphia and taking up a great deal of the Black political power. Yet that's exactly what he did. . . . Crude filthy language he would use, and he didn't hesitate to use it even in front of women, which was a bit rare here for people with culture."

Fauset concludes that the migrants "did a good thing. It was better to have people like Nix, Rhodes, and Joe Rainey raising a storm, because every time they raised a storm that got us somewhere. That's how we moved ahead. It was much better to have that than to have those Old Philadelphians doing nothing because they were so busy being Old Philadelphians."

In a period of twenty years, the city changed from a place where the "afternoon tea was a prevalent and popular social gathering" and where "any dancing that departed too far from the waltz, quadrille, or square dance was frowned upon" to a Black city where the music and life-style of the American South would become dominant. South Philadelphia, the center of the Old Philadelphians' settlement, was itself changing in the 1920s and 1930s as South Street, the main thoroughfare became "lined on each side with an unbroken row of storefronts stretching block after block, filled with garish hats, dresses, or suits, sometimes all three in one window or conglomerations of knick-knacks and red meats." The description continues: "Part of the sidewalk space [was] occupied by stands piled with vegetables. Restaurants, beer gardens, pan shops, jewelery stores, and an intermittent voodoo den, in the windows of which the herb doctor display[ed] his fantastic roots, concoctions, and weird symbols, with sometimes a live snake undulating its coils in the midst." Uptown, on the other side of William Penn's statue, North Philadelphia, the home of Fat Albert, began to take shape with the "blare from the honky-tonks just as loud as in South Philadelphia." But the shabbiness that marked much of South Philadelphia's buildings had not yet overtaken North Philadelphia. That would come later.

All of these changes took place in a Black community that prided itself on being the home of the first Black Rhodes scholar, having more "Negro caterers than any city in America," having had the first Black public schools in the country, and being the residence of four A.M.E. bishops, including A. M. Heard, and two A.M.E. Zion bishops.

Black Leadership in Philadelphia

Black leaders have a hard road to travel. Whites attempt to coopt them and, failing that, destroy them, physically or by other means. Most Black leaders are well aware of the plight of the Black masses, and often they hear an ancestral voice urging them to be about the work of completing the liberation of their people. But the natural desire for tranquillity can sometimes mute that voice from the past. And sometimes leaders, conflicted and torn, must shut it out all together.

W.E.B. DuBois in 1899 tells us that the Black leadership of Old Philadelphia had, by that time—for whatever reason—opted for the latter course. Said DuBois, "so hard has been the lives of the better class of Negroes that they fear to fall if now they stoop to lend a hand to their fellows." The young scholar upbraided the Philadelphia upper class, arguing that their only reason for existence was the work of "lifting the rabble." DuBois must have been seeing what another observer had noted was the tendency of some Old Philadelphians—constantly referring to their ancestors—to be like "potatoes. The best part of them was buried under ground."

In light of today's evidence, DuBois was undoubtedly too harsh on the Old Philadelphians. The work of Alain Locke (1886–1954) shows that something more profound was at work in the creation of the modern Philadelphia Black community. Some Old Philadelphians merited DuBois' scorn, but many did not.

The most distinctive trait of Philadelphia's Black leadership was that it represented a mixture of the old and the new.

There was no sudden shift of leadership from Old to New Philadelphia. Indeed, the new Southern leaders frequently married into Old Philadelphia families. The changes showed up most quickly in the political sphere where aggressiveness and ambition could be translated into political power.

The intellectual leadership of the community was vested in the Old Philadelphia families. They tended to be the teachers who had both the leisure time and the training necessary to assume that position. It was natural that their major interest would be Black culture and self-help since the Philadelphia tradition drew from the African heritage. It was thus possible for Arthur Fauset to say that the Old Philadelphians publicly disavowed Marcus Garvey, the 1920s leader of the Back to Africa movement, but privately applauded him. Garvey catered too much to the masses for their tastes, but they shared much of his ideology.

Many Black community leaders had substantial formal education. Often, politicians of the 1930s earned their credentials as the first of their race to break academic barriers. To finish Temple or the University of Pennsylvania was no mean feat in the twenties. Receiving a degree from Harvard or Yale, as did Pennsylvania-born politician Austin Norris and the famous jurist Raymond Pace Alexander, was almost impossible. The community, moreover, placed a premium on high-level literacy. Many of the medical doctors and ministers published articles or books and listed this fact prominently in their biographies.

On one program in 1921, you could find Arthur Fauset lecturing on "What Were the Primordial Causes of the Negroes' Fall?", Raymond Pace Alexander speaking on "Will the Negro Be Able to Retrieve His Past?", and A.M.E. minister R. R. Wright of Georgia talking on the topic "Will the So-Called Nordic and Negroid Races Clash Before the Latter Comes into Its Own?" In 1933, Alexander, the politician Hobson Reynolds of North Carolina, and Reverend Wright cooperated in a Black fund-raising drive. A measure of the prestige and integrity of the leadership was Marian Anderson's decision that year to cancel six European concerts in order to come home and promote a community effort at self-improvement. She said she was proud to "inaugurate such a movement on behalf of Negro accomplishment."

Black leadership in Philadelphia, then, was both well-trained and literate. However, these leaders lacked power over the allocation of the resources that most directly affected the lives of Black people. Yet within the confines established by the ground rules of capitalism and racial oppression, they helped shape Black Philadelphia.

Politics in Modern Black Philadelphia

Politics, according to one theorist, determines who gets what in a society. It's concerned with how the wealth produced by the people of a society is distributed. There's no mystery about whether a group is successful politically or not: you know that the Italians in Philadelphia have been as soon as you cross the bridge over the Delaware from Camden— many of the names of the toll collectors are Italian. On other levels, politics decides who is going to become a millionaire and who is going to commute to the mansion from the city and wash the laundry, nurse the babies, and scrub the floors. Politics is also evident in the way in which the police treat the children of the community. By any and all of these measures, the political achievements of Black Philadelphians have been limited in scope.

To make such an assessment of the efforts of our politicians in Philadelphia is not to mock them. Their position reflected the general economic level of the Black population in the city. A realistic appraisal of their situation reveals that the Black masses they were supposed to represent were poor, uneducated, and divided. They were not yet ready to unite behind Black leaders.

Black political leaders did not have many options. To remain in power, a leader had to achieve something. The main provider of suitable achievements was the corrupt white political machine, which did not require Black votes to maintain its power. Moreover, the Irish, and then the Italian politicians represented constituencies that were bitterly anti-Black. That enmity was of long standing, as we know from our examination of nineteenth-century racial divisions in Philadelphia. Further, those Blacks who became political leaders were, for the most part, not wealthy men. In fact all too often Black politicians looked to their political posts as a major source of income and advancement. Sometimes leaders were bought off by pathetically meaningless posts in the political hierarchy. Before World War II, they could not become judges, city solicitors, district attorneys, or heads of major departments in the city administration. They remained at the mercy of the white party that gave them their positions. For this reason, many Black ministers in 1976 gave their support to Frank Rizzo, who at that time was generally viewed as the symbol of the white backlash.

The Black political organization in Philadelphia was the Citizens Republican Club, formed at Cape May, New Jersey, in 1884 by a group of Old Philadelphians and relative newcomers. Among the founders were William Warrick, the father of Dr. William Warrick, famous Black physician; Warley Bascom, a South Carolina–born caterer; W. Carl Bolivar, bibliophile and historian; J. W. Holland and A. Baptiste, caterers; Dr. James Howard; and Chris Perry, the founder of the *Philadelphia Tribune*. The club was chartered in 1895 to create an independent political group that could mediate between the Black masses and the holders of power.

The first headquarters of the Citizens Republican Club (CRC) was in the 500 block of South Broad Street. The club participated actively in the creation of Douglass and Mercy hospitals and was a source of monies for the Black Home for the Aged. Almost half the founding members of the organization were graduates of the ICY and many knew each other through church, business, and other organizations, including the Ugly Club, a small group that gathered for good dinners. In this case, the Old Philadelphians shared the power. At the time of its founding, the CRC had fifteen members. During the height of the migration it grew to one thousand members, only to drop to 350 members by the mid-thirties as our people around the country defected to the Democratic party.

Any Black who reached political prominence before 1930 owed his position to the CRC. In the late thirties, its historian was able to say that "of eleven Negroes who have represented this city in the House at Harrisburg, all except one were members of this organization. All the Negro magistrates, the Assistant Director of Public Safety, the Deputy Recorder of Deeds, the Negro representative on the Board of Revision of Taxes and a number of Negroes holding lesser political positions either have been or are members of the Citizens Republican Club."

The political maneuverings of our Black Philadelphia politicians seemed, on the surface, so opportunistic as to defy traditional political analysis. They moved from the Republican to the Democratic party and back again in such quick succession that it is almost impossible to designate Ed Henry, for example, or Marshall Shepherd, Sr., an upcoming North Carolinian, as either Democratic or Republican. It is possible that all the twisting and turning was an effort by them to maximize their leverage against both parties. Black political leaders, one scholar concluded, "disagreed over goals, tactics, personalities, and patronage rights. They also waged bitter and vituperative attacks upon each other."

The results of Black political activity between 1900 and World War II were meager. We had served on the city's elected governing board before 1920, but in that year the whites changed the method of election so that no Black held a post on the city council for another sixteen years. In 1932, there were twenty-five thousand city employees, of whom eight hundred were Black, and of these only eight held white-collar jobs. In that same year, in the "black majority Thirtieth Ward, jobs with salaries totalling $136,000 were dispensed among the party faithful. Negro workers received only $17,000."

On the positive side, some half-dozen Blacks were elected to the state legislature during the 1920s and 1930s. The most prestigious and meaningful reward, however, was the naming of Austin Norris to the city's Board of Revision of Taxes in the mid-thirties. From this position, both by the importance of the post and his own ability, Norris exercised unmatched power over Black politics in the city.

By the 1960s, things were little better. Blacks occupied many posts under the Democratic reform administrations of Mayors Joseph S. Clark and Richardson Dilworth, from 1951 to 1963. In 1963 a major reapportionment reduced the plurality in the only Senate district with a Black majority from eighty-one percent to sixty-nine percent and reconstructed the assembly districts so that the number of Blacks in the general assembly dropped from nine to eight afterward. Writing in the 1960s, a scholar pessimistically concluded that "when Blacks are appointed or elected to political office, the decision to give an office to a Black is made by whites and the Blacks are selected by whites. There has been no Black political organization in Philadelphia. Blacks work for whites in Philadelphia politics."

Yet we must try to understand that the political failure of our people in Philadelphia was an outgrowth of the trauma surrounding the migration into the city. Many Blacks distrusted the political process, and Southern immigrants in particular had reason to view the ballot as a charade. They came to Philadelphia in search of jobs, and found economic depression. Looking for a fair chance, they were up against whites who excluded them from real power. Political cohesion awaited the broadening of educational, economic, and housing opportunities. When all is said and done, the pioneering Black politicians probably did the best they could under the difficult circumstances in which they found themselves.

By the 1970s, second-generation Philadelphians like Hardy Williams, now a state senator, and Charles Bowser made the first initiatives toward preparing the city's Blacks for power. Wilson Goode, now the Democratic candidate for mayor, was one of the young politicians getting their feet wet in those campaigns. Goode, the son of North Carolina sharecroppers who migrated to Philadelphia, is the beneficiary of two events that welded the Black community together. The first was the attempt by former Mayor Rizzo in 1978 to have the city charter

revised to permit him a third term. Uniting with other dis-
affected elements in the city, the Black community, led by
church leaders, voted overwhelmingly to defeat that measure.
This movement carried over into an attempt by Charles Bowser,
a Philadelphia lawyer, to obtain the Democratic nomination
for mayor in 1979. He failed, but again that effort was centered
in the Black churches, which became the organizing grounds
for Wilson Goode's successful attempt to win the spring 1983
primary against ex-mayor Rizzo. It was a campaign marked
by considerable political maturity and restraint on the part of
both men. Goode, with the endorsement of Rizzo, became
Philadelphia's first Black mayor in the fall of 1983, winning
the election with 55 percent of all the votes cast.

Education

If creativity is produced by the clash of opposites, we would
expect to find something powerful taking place in the Black
Philadelphia schools. The teachers were Black, trained at the
Institute for Colored Youth and Jacob White's Vaux School,
and they served as a stabilizing, if conservative, influence on
the migrants. Black creativity in Philadelphia flowed from the
interplay of the ICY tradition and the Southern rural tradition.

Segregation in Philadelphia schools was illegal according
to a law passed in 1881. Nevertheless, by 1908, the system
was almost totally segregated—except on the high-school level,
where it was economically unfeasible—and those Black children who did attend white schools were assigned either to
a separate section of the class or an annex of the school.
The annex was almost always in a state of disrepair and
neglect when compared to the main school attended by the
whites.

Not only were Black children segregated from white, but
Black teachers were forbidden to instruct white children until
the 1930s. School authorities in the early 1900s devised a two-
list system for the assignment of teachers. On one list were
Black teachers who could be assigned only to all-Black schools,

and on the other were whites who could teach anywhere. The lists were not merged until 1938. Arthur Huff Fauset recalled that: "By the time I finished Penn with a Master's degree, the only thing I could become was an elementary school teacher— I could not even become a junior high school teacher." Eventually he became the principal of a segregated school.

Impact of the Migration

The migration changed the percentage of Black children in the elementary schools from eight percent in 1920 to twenty-three percent in 1940. In absolute terms, the number of Blacks rose from fourteen thousand to thirty thousand in the elementary schools and from twenty thousand to fifty thousand in the high schools. The process was so sudden that certain schools—the Arnold, the Allison, Meade, Stanton—that were still integrated in 1928 were all Black by 1940.

The children who flocked into these classrooms were overwhelmingly Southern. In North Philadelphia, more than one-fifth of all the school children—and nearly forty percent born outside of Pennsylvania—were South Carolinians. The fathers of many of the children were common laborers, but the most common occupation, according to a 1933 survey, was unemployment. Forty-four percent of the fathers of the children in South Philadelphia were unemployed, while in North Philadelphia, nearly sixty percent of the fathers were out of work. The young refugees were overage for their grade levels, so that sixth-grade students in North Philadelphia averaged thirteen years of age, nearly four years older than their classmates in other parts of the city.

The task of educating the migrants was left to the Old Philadelphians and to some of the earlier migrants who had come to the city with an educational head start. A directory of Black schoolteachers in the city shows that the teachers in 1910 were overwhelmingly either graduates of the ICY or of Jacob White's Vaux School. In one school, seven out of nine teachers fit this category, in another, three of six, in still another, two of two. And in every school there was a high proportion of such graduates.

Our people who went to school in those days remember well those Old Philadelphian teachers. Mabel Brady, whose family came from Virginia by way of Chambersburg, Pennsylvania, talked about Henrietta Edwards at the Joseph E. Hill School in the 1900s when "there was discipline. And they had a ruler and they made you hold out your hand. I know when I put my hand down, I couldn't use it for a mighty long time. You held it out, went back to your seat, wiped away your tears and waited till that numbness left your hands, then went right on. Nobody used profane language. A janitor could correct you." The Reverend Frank Mitchell, a student at the same school in the early twenties, also remembered "Henny" Edwards, "who lived to be almost one hundred years old. She couldn't stand dumbness and you knew that when you went into the room. You weren't supposed to be dumb." A powerful statement to be made to any Black child. Reverend Mitchell also recalled, "Miss Morris. She's an Old Philadelphian, but, oh, how she inspired kids to learn." The principal of the Hill School was also an ICY graduate.

William Duckrey, later a principal, remembered that his teachers were Frances Still, daughter of William Still; Clara Sadler; and Ella Titus, all graduates of the ICY. Recalling his childhood at a school at Twentieth and Jefferson, he said: "I started in the kindergarten there and it was adjacent to the main building which was an old brick structure of 1870 vintage. The kindergarten was an abandoned police station that had been leased by the Board of Education for a dollar a year and that's just what it was worth. There was just one big room that had been the main room of the police station, the roll call room, I guess. . . . There were actually jail cells in my kindergarten, only they were used for dressing rooms and so forth, but the iron bars were still there. It was an eight grade school run in the traditional fashion of the schools in those days, large schools with rather strict discipline. It was totally Black, Black principal, Black secretary, and the principal was Clarence Whyte."

Dr. Duckrey, who recently died, recalled that "I just felt as I was growing up that everyone around me was interested in improving the Negro and had a faith in education. They were always talking about how you have to get an education to succeed. I remember one time we were in seventh grade and we had a very strict teacher, Miss Junior [graduate of the Vaux School]. She was nice, but also strict and she was dissatisfied with the appearance of my homework paper and she said, 'William, you're going to be a hod carrier.' And I didn't know what a hod carrier was. I later learned it was someone who carries bricks up a ladder. I used to see these men sweeping up the street and I used to think they were hod carriers and I felt depressed and when I went home to my mother, she kept me in, and she said I'd be a hod carrier." Ralph Jones, onetime editor of the *Philadelphia Tribune*, recalled: "The teachers usually affiliated with churches. The teachers were active and they were community minded. It was different from what it is today."

For Jack Saunders, another former editor, and a migrant from Florida, the most influential teacher was Henry Jones: "He was a teacher as well as the coach of the athletic team, baseball team, and volleyball team. He became a world-famous artist." Jones, of an Old Philadelphia family, was indeed an artist of stature, and the author of several short stories, one of which appeared in O. Henry's annual collection. Saunders said that "practically everyone who went to that school amounted to something. There were very few who did not achieve."

Other important influences on the minds of Black Philadelphians—those who were fortunate enough to graduate from high school—were the Black colleges of the South, and nearby Cheyney State College (the name given to the ICY when it moved to the outskirts of the city in the early 1900s)—and Lincoln University. Obtaining a higher education in a Black milieu reintroduced many Black Philadelphians, who had graduated from white high schools, to the South, and forced them to understand themselves and associate with other Blacks. Links created in this process formed the basis for the leap in

Black conciousness after World War II. Just as the Old Philadelphians stimulated the achievement of many Southerners, so did the Southern Black colleges provide a sense of Black togetherness to those educated in the Northern high schools.

Arriving at Cheyney State College from his home in upstate Pennsylvania, Wade Wilson, the president of the college from 1965 to 1980, recalled: "I came here and on sight fell in love with the place. I couldn't think of anything outside the church being Black. So when I got off at Cheyney, I saw these dilapidated buildings. I walked in there, got a single room, learned the regulations, learned that there was going to be two sheet changes a week. You went down there and ate whatever they had. I could make it if I had just had bread and gravy."

A graduate of Virginia Union in the twenties recalls that "as soon as I got to Union, with its teams, its activities, I felt a part of it and that it belonged to me. Not like I felt at the white schools where all I did was go to classes. I really got my education at Union, not at Germantown High School. It was at Union that I learned to deal with people, to relax. Before, I simply felt tolerated."

A Black doctor describes a similar experience at Howard University: "We got the feeling that the reason the white man hated us so was because he knew that we were not inferior. That was indoctrinated into us very subtly. We called Howard University the capstone of Black education. As I tell my wife now, when she asks me how I do the *Times* crossword puzzle, I tell her that I went to a colored school."

There was much camaraderie and self-help as the Philadelphians tried to make their way through college. At Lincoln, a graduate of the thirties recalls that William Fontaine, later the first Black professor at the University of Pennsylvania, spent many late hours tutoring the students. At Union, self-help seminars were led by Henry Allen Bullock, the great writer on Black education: "On Monday night in that room, it was chemistry, on Tuesday, philosophy." At Cheyney, recalls Wade Wilson, who was tutoring math, "My job was to get them over the math hurdle. Somebody else was strong in drafting. It was a great family. For example, the choir was going on a tour somewhere. Woodson [the Reverend Howard J. of Trenton, New Jersey] had a brand new tux. In camaraderie, he calculated that we had enough money to buy one fare and he gave the tux to me."

Wilson describes the struggle to pay for an education: "I worked in the dining hall for two years, then I became the head janitor for Penn Hall for twenty-five cents an hour. Each time it snowed, I would be out snow clearing too." A former Lincoln man, born in Greenville, South Carolina, recalled that he owed two hundred and ninety dollars on the eve of graduation and that he could not receive his diploma without paying the money due the college: "I called Mom and told her. She said, 'Don't worry, son.' And brought that money up to me. She borrowed it from the Household Finance Company. I cried like a fool. She paid it back by taking in laundry. She washed by hand and ironed by hand for this wealthy white family up in Chestnut Hill."

The churches also helped. A member of Reverend Tindley's church, Ralph Jones, was the recipient on two occasions of special offerings raised by the congregation specifically to help him through college: "One time it was $200 and the next $300." The offering did not come without strings, for Reverend Tindley, the ex-slave who taught himself Hebrew, was more demanding than some of his teachers: "Every time I came home, he would say, 'Ralph, I want to see you in my study after service. And that man would quiz me on my subjects. When I started taking comparative anatomy, I thought I had him, but he took me into his office and quizzed me to death. When I made a mistake, he said, 'I don't want to hear any excuses. Now, you go on back to your books and two weeks from now I'm going to quiz you on your comparative anatomy study.' Now, that was a man who was self-educated. He used to say, 'This congregation is proud of you and I am proud of you.' "

Old Philadelphia families, as a rule, did not send their children to the Southern Black colleges. Instead, their children frequently attended white institutions. With the removal of Cheyney to the outskirts of the city in the early 1900s and the college's turn toward vocational education, the ICY lost its importance among the Old Philadelphians.

The Black refugees of the 1920s and 1930s received poor educations in comparison with those given to whites. They were taught in old schools with second-hand books and none of the amenities whites took for granted. But the de facto segregation of Philadelphia's schools had positive as well as negative effects. We had one of the best corps of teachers in the country, and they believed in teaching children about their heritage. So schoolchildren received an education in Black Studies at the same time they were learning their ABCs. Black pride and achievement were stressed at all of the schools, something that would not have been possible had whites directed the education of the Southern refugee children.

Chapter 18

THE CULTURE OF
MODERN BLACK
PHILADELPHIA

Folks, I come up North
Cause they told me de North was fine.
I come up North
Cause they told me de North was fine.
Been up here six months—
I'm about to lose my mind.

This mornin' for breakfast
I chawed de mornin' air.
This mornin' for breakfast
Chawed de mornin' air.
But this evenin' for supper, I got evenin' air to spare.

Believe I'll do a little dancin'
Just to drive my blues away—
A little dancin'
To drive my blues away,
Cause when I'm dancin'
De blues forgets to stay.

But if you was to ask me
How de blues they come to be,
Says if you was to ask me
How de blues they come to be—
You wouldn't need to ask me:
Just look at me and see!

"Evenin' Air Blues" by LANGSTON HUGHES

Life in South Philadelphia and the developing Black enclaves in North and West Philadelphia was rich in its complexity and variety and—to paraphrase Nikki Giovanni—mostly always singing a song. The melody of that tune had a million variations, but they were all elaborations on how Black people had managed to survive the Southern oppression and arrive safely in the Promised Land, the city of refuge, Philadelphia. But there was no rest for the tired of body, no way for the newly arrived refugee to sort out his or her life and plan the next thirty years. The city took over the lives of the country folk and sometimes channeled them in directions they did not want to go. Romantics may want to believe that there was a beauty in the very poverty and misery of the lives of Black Philadelphians, but there's no way that could be true. Certainly, there were moments and days of beauty, but there was dirt, unemployment, sickness, and death all around our community. Yet, through it all, and out of the very depths of human degradation, came a triumphant sense of certitude about the Southern Blacks' ability to survive the city, as they had surmounted the oppression. How else explain the frequency with which one hears those who grew up in the thirties and forties say that they never knew that they were poor, so great was the love that surrounded them.

Blacks may not have been a majority in the city, but by 1930 our numbers were great enough in both North and South Philadelphia to make Old Philadelphians feel that they lived in a Black community. Within it, Old Philadelphians and new influenced each other, sharing manners, styles, traditions, institutions, and ways of seeing the world. The Black nationalism of the Old Philadelphia intelligentsia was refined and shaped by contact with the Black masses. Out of that mixture, that clash, arose a form of Black expression that was epitomized by Alain Locke and Jessie Fauset in literature; Ethel Waters, Marian Anderson, and the Clara Ward singers in music; Judith Jamison in dance; Ed Bullins, Bill Cosby, Charles Fuller, and Larry Neal in drama; and Guy Rogers, Wilt Chamberlain, and Ora Washington in athletics.

Sports Galvanize the Community

Much of Philadelphia's Black community life centered around athletics. E. Franklin Frazier, the Black sociologist and author of *Black Bourgeoisie* (1962), condemned Black people's emphasis on sports and complained that the middle classes could think of nothing except athletics. It's difficult to believe that an observer as acute as Frazier could have failed to understand the importance of athletics in knitting together the Black community. Sports was the only arena in which Black people could act out their feelings against whites. Sports provided a socially accepted means of revenge that did not lead to the prison or the electric chair. We also recall that O. V. Catto and the Pythians had formed one of the country's first Black baseball teams. And by the turn of the century, the ICY had become a power in athletics. John P. Taylor, America's first Black Olympic gold medalist—he was a member of the winning sixteen-hundred meter relay team in 1908—and a graduate of the University of Pennsylvania was an object of adulation.

In Philadelphia, a great scholar was also supposed to be a great athlete. Jack Saunders, former editor of the *Philadelphia Tribune*, himself discovered on a basketball court by E. Washington Rhodes, says, "Without athletics, a whole lot of Blacks that we know today would never have finished school. Because first of all they didn't have the money to go and they wouldn't have been able to get scholarships. Athletics [was] a dominant part of every Black man who achieved anything. One way or another. Maybe he wasn't a participant, but because of what somebody else did, the door was opened for him."

In this context, where Jack Blackburn, the future manager of Joe Louis, was fighting, Joe Rainey, later a magistrate, won fame as the captain of Central High's track team, and the holder of the world's interscholastic record for the fifty-yard dash. Robert N. C. Nix, son of the dean at South Carolina State, and Philadelphia's first Black congressman, made his mark as an All-American football player at Lincoln University. People still talk about his exploits. William T. Coleman,

Jr., former secretary of transportation, became well-known in Philadelphia as the first Black on the University of Pennsylvania's swimming team. He was probably better known for that than for becoming the first Black on the Harvard Law Review. Indeed, most of the leading Black politicians in Philadelphia today were onetime athletic standouts.

Philadelphia was a relatively spacious city that, unlike New York and Chicago, nourished a child's desire to run far afield. Biographies of both Roy Campanella and Wilt Chamberlain note that as boys they never walked, but ran everywhere. Most people lived in homes and the city was spread out, with a vast network of parks and greenery. The whites could not segregate Fairmount Park—it was too big. Openness and an abundance of recreational facilities created an athletic ferment.

Athletics bound the city's youth together. It broke down the territorial boundaries they brought with them from the South, and attached them instead to recreation centers, such as the Wharton Center in North Philadelphia or the Seger Center in South Philadelphia. Playing in each other's territories was often physically dangerous, but the teams did it, and a youth's identity as a North Philadelphian or South Philadelphian became merged into an identity as a Black Philadelphian. Sports was the lifeblood of the community.

The same socializing effect took place as people engaged in high school athletics. Track meets, particularly the Penn Relays, allowed young people to represent the city's entire Black community as they went about defeating whites. When Ken Dixon of Germantown High School won the city's cross-country championship in the 1940s, it was considered a victory for our people since whites had long claimed that Blacks couldn't run distances—too lazy, they said. Watching Morgan State's great mile relay teams defeat every white team in the country gave a sense of triumph to the community. To see Reggie Pearman of New York University adjust his horn-rimmed glasses and take off, quicksilver colored brown, to win the anchor lap of the mile relay in the 1940s, was a unifying force for the Black people of Philadelphia, and the kids would go home excitedly describing to each other exactly how Reggie had wiped out the twenty-five-yard gap between himself and the white running the anchor leg for the other team.

It was the same in basketball. Down in South Philadelphia, Tarzan Cooper, Jackie Bethard, Bill Yancy, and Zack Clayton, running down the court, stopping, pivoting, driving, whirling, hitting, were so damn bad that they went on to play with the New York Renaissance. They formed the nucleus of the team that along with Pop Bell whipped the white champions of the world in 1939—the beginning of the end of white supremacy in basketball. Guy Rogers, Hal Lear, Earl Monroe, Wally Jones, Wayne Hightower, Walt Hazzard, and Wilt came on a little later to finish the job. The basketball feats were repeated in football by Herb Adderly of the Green Bay Packers, Em Tunnell and Wally Triplett of Ambler, Ed Bell of the Philadelphia Eagles, Bo Roberson of Cornell, and Leroy Kelley of the Cleveland Browns. During the 1920s and 1930s Philadelphia was also the center of the rise of our people in tennis. Ora Washington and Lula Ballard, both born in South Carolina, became National Negro champions. Washington, in the opinion of most experts, could have beaten any modern woman tennis player. Tennis provided both women with educations at Tuskegee Institute, from which place they together dominated tennis throughout the country. Nobody ever beat them in doubles.

Literary Growth

Philadelphia's Black culture was highly literary as well as athletic. Their tradition was that everybody worth his or her salt could read and write. The Old Philadelphia literary tradition also involved interest in and a sense of responsibility to other Black people in this country.

No one person so embodies the tradition of Philadelphia's intellectuals as Alain Locke, a leading figure in the Harlem Renaissance of the 1920s. Locke, a 1907 graduate of Harvard

University and the first Black Rhodes scholar, received his Ph.D. in philosophy from Harvard in 1918. Although he did not write much, he was the most influential force in the development of such writers as Countee Cullen and Langston Hughes. Locke saw himself as the "philosophical midwife to a generation of younger Negro poets, writers, and artists" rather than as a "professional philosopher." Locke is the most direct link between the Old Philadelphia tradition and modern Black American thought.

Locke's intellectual tradition—created outside of major universities or great presses—rested on a sense of moral outrage about the hypocrisy of the white American democratic tradition. Locke's introductory essay in *The New Negro* (1925) directly states this theme. Writing that the "deep feeling of race is at present the mainspring of Negro life," Locke went on to say that American democracy could only be fulfilled when the term was expanded to include Black people. Said Locke, "the great discrepancy between the American social creed and the American social practice forces upon the Negro the taking of the moral advantage that is his." He further states that Black people had begun to understand their role as one of "acting as the advance guard of the African people in their contact with twentieth century civilization." Locke emphasized that the galvanizing force for this new racial conciousness had been the migration out of the South into the North. Looking back at the Harlem Renaissance, we can argue that it represented the coming together of the Northern tradition and the Southern and African traditions. They merged in the person of Locke, and in the writings of Jean Toomer, Zora Neale Hurston, James Weldon Johnson, Claude McKay, Arthur Schomberg, and Langston Hughes, who are all represented in *The New Negro*, the book that signaled the beginning of the Harlem Renaissance.

Two other Philadelphia writers, Jessie Fauset and her brother Arthur Huff Fauset, were represented in that volume. Jessie Redmond Fauset was a 1905 Phi Beta Kappa graduate of Cornell and the literary editor of the NAACP's *Crisis*. She was also a novelist of some note. In her most famous work, *There*

Is Confusion (1924), about the thought and life of Old Black Philadelphia, a character remembers learning about Douglass, Vesey, Nat Turner, and the "great women . . . Harriet Tubman, Phyllis Wheatley, Sojourner Truth, women [who] had been slaves . . . but had won their way to fame and freedom through their own efforts." The young woman "could understand that the bravery and courage exercised by these slave women was a much finer and different thing from that exercised for instance by Florence Nightingale." The book also depicts the wrath of one Black family who felt that wealthy Quaker whites had risen on the backs of slaves. Defined politically, Jessie Fauset was a bourgeois Black nationalist, like Locke radical in racial matters, but conservative in her acceptance of the American economic structure.

Her brother Arthur Huff Fauset, the principal of the Singletary School, was the author of several works, among them *Black Gods of the Metropolis* (1944), an examination of the religious practices of Black storefront churches in Philadelphia. He also published, along with the stern principal of the Hill School, Nellie Bright, *America, Red, White, Black, and Yellow.* Far ahead of its time, the book was a multiethnic approach to teaching American history to elementary school children. Fauset was also a poet and a collector of the Black folklore of Philadelphia. And he also wrote a weekly column on religion for the *Philadelphia Tribune* in which he tried to make Christianity relevant to the needs of Black people. Today, well past eighty, he has almost completed a sweeping novel about the history of Black Philadelphians.

Philadelphia's William Gardner Smith was the first Black to publish a major novel in the post–World War II period, the *Last of the Conquerers*, in 1948. His books are full of themes of Black nationalism and his target, as often as not, is the bourgeois life of the Old Philadelphians. Smith typifies the creative reaction that emerged from the clash between the Old Philadelphia culture and the Southerners. Unable to solve the contradiction, Smith went into exile in Paris, where you could find him in the 1950s, sitting at the now-famous Café de Tournon, with James Baldwin, Richard Wright, and Chester

B. Himes, drinking white wine and talking about white people, and sometimes about the Old Philadelphians. He was glad to see me every time I came through and wanted to know how things were at home. He particularly enjoyed news about sports events and the kids he wrote about in his newspaper column for the *Philadelphia Tribune*. Smith became the cultural advisor to Kwame Nkrumah upon the founding of Ghana and left there upon Nkrumah's overthrow. He died in Paris a few years ago. Henry Jones, the teacher, was also a writer, and his hobby was the study of "African and Bantu" tribes. The tradition of literary excellence in Philadelphia finds its present-day expression in the works of Ed Bullins, the playwright, and Charles Fuller, the Pulitzer Prize–winning author of *The Brownsville Raid* and *A Soldier's Play*.

A Rich Musical Tradition Takes Root

In recent years one of the most popular forms of Black rhythm and blues has been the "Philadelphia Sound," and one of the most important Black singers, Teddy Pendergrass of Philadelphia. Music has a long-honored place in the culture of both Black and white Philadelphia. From the eighteenth century on, music lessons were popular in the city and many people believed that learning to appreciate music was an important part of education.

The classical artist most closely identified with Philadelphia is Marian Anderson, who was born (1902) and raised in the city and learned to sing in the choir of the Union Baptist Church where her father was an officer. The emergence of her career is another instance of collaboration between Old Philadelphia and the new Philadelphia of the Southern immigrants. Anderson took her church singing seriously: "I became convinced that my presence in the senior and junior choirs was not only a duty, but a necessity for the church and me, and I never missed a Sunday. The congregation made me feel that I was an indispensable part of what went on there. It was a stimulating experience." The church, as it had done for promising youth in the South, collected money to help her on her way—by collecting $17.02 at a time when she needed it: "I cannot put into words how grateful I felt to those good people at the Church." Anderson joined, as she was developing her talent, the Philadelphia Choral Society, a group of Old Philadelphia Blacks who sang classical music for "presentation to its large following." This group, too, collected money to help her. And at a critical point in her career, when she needed money for a first-class music teacher, "Mrs. Ida Asbury, who lived across the street from us . . . some other neighbors and friends arranged a gala concert at our church," raising $600. Mrs. Asbury, the wife of John Asbury, long-time political leader, was herself a graduate of the ICY, and a member of an Old Philadelphia family of long standing. Marian Anderson repaid the favor many times over. She even came to the elementary schools (including my own) to sing after she was famous.

One of the first Black classical composers—mixing classics with the music of Africa—was Carl Diton, educated in Philadelphia, and a graduate in 1909 of the University of Pennsylvania. He subsequently earned a Ph.D. in musicology at Columbia University. Marian Anderson's nephew, James De Priest, became a famous conductor, and Andre Watts has also sustained the tradition of achievement in classical Western music.

Besides Marian Anderson, Philadelphia's great contribution to the development of Black music in America is gospel music, for the city was its birthplace. Like the writing of Alain Locke and Jessie Fauset, gospel music symbolized the merging of the Old Philadelphia tradition with the Southern tradition. The Reverend Charles A. Tindley, from the Eastern Shore of Maryland, wrote the words, and ICY-educated F. A. Clark, who wrote sacred music and directed many Sunday school pageants, arranged the music. The result reflected both the Southern rural experience and the chaos that followed the move to the cold Northern cities.

An Ex-Slave Creates Gospel Music

Tindley understood the essence of the Black experience. Most of our people were poor, inadequately housed, and came from a place where if poverty didn't get them, the white man would. They had left the South for a city where they were scorned by many whites and some Blacks, a place that was full of temptation to the young, of invitations to death in the form of booze, gambling, and crazy brawls. Young country girls arrived at the train station in downtown Philadelphia, at the mercy of slick-talking street dudes who were ready to divest them of virtue and respect. It was a place where cops would call you nigger and beat your head without cause, and where straying into a white neighborhood might result in physical assault. And there were no jobs. Families disintegrated, and arguments broke out between husband and wife, parents and children, so that their whole worlds seemed torn and full of strife. And what do you do when your son of fifteen just flat out says, "I ain't going to school no more! Look at you." The music of Reverend Tindley became the refuge for those of us lucky enough to be in a church on Sunday morning to hear it. It spoke of the power of Black people to keep on keeping on, to ride on and never look back, as poet James Emanuel has written.

Tindley had the face of a prince of Benin. He was born a slave in Berlin, Maryland, about 1850. As a youth he watered stock and groomed horses and taught himself to read by sounding out words from newspapers. When he first came to Philadelphia in 1870, he took a job as a hod carrier, and then became a janitor in the church he later pastored, Calvary Methodist, now Tindley Temple. He never received a formal degree, although Bennett College in North Carolina gave him an honorary one. He didn't need a degree: "That he was one of the best read men of his denomination is attested by the thousands of books shelved in his residence at 1509 Christian Street, and the great philosophy of his sermons preached in nearly every section of the United States." His church was at one time the largest Black congregation in the country. One observer said that he had never seen a man like Tindley: "All he had to do was walk into the church, and the people would start applauding. Never saw anything like it in my life."

With the eye of a poet, Tindley had seen the storms over the ocean and the Chesapeake Bay, knew how thunder sounds like a battle of artillery raging around you, and had seen lightning so powerful that it seemed to be one continuous flow of jagged white power from on high. Tindley knew, because he had surely seen it, that the mightiest vessel afloat could be thrown about; that foamy seas would pick it up and toss it on its sides, like a man flicking a mosquito off his arm. He had seen the way a storm would pass over, and had experienced the plain quiet that said "Peace, be still." Tindley was at one with his God and the earth all about him.

This man was able to create a body of music and a philosophy that would comfort not only the people of the Eastern Shore, but those from Sumter, South Carolina, and Durham, North Carolina, and Staunton, Virginia—anywhere that Black people had been. Tindley was able to tell them, don't worry children, it will be all right. If they burned down your daddy's barn, it'll still be all right; if they drove the schoolteacher out of the town, don't worry; ain't got no rent money? don't be upset; if your child is dying of a T.B. hack, now don't you worry. No bread for tomorrow, well, God will make a way out of no way. For in the end, God will punish the transgressors, and Africa's spirituality will triumph over those who have made a religion out of money and called it Christianity. Yours, the way of the humble, the way of the oppressed, is Christianity, not theirs.

So this brooding giant gave a literature of song to the Black masses. He knew personal pain, for his wife died on the same day that he moved his congregation into a new church, and the white Methodists denied him a bishopric, but he persevered and became the catalyst for the creation of modern Black gospel music. Thomas A. Dorsey, who wrote "Precious Lord" and "Peace in the Valley" and is himself frequently identified as the father of gospel music, says that Tindley holds this place. Dorsey, the son of a Georgia Baptist country minister, penned his own great song shortly after the death of his wife in childbirth and still marvels at "the power of God to change sorrowful things into miracles of amazing good." The song, "We Shall Overcome" is directly derived from Tindley's "I'll Overcome Someday." His songs, "Nothing Between," "Leave It There," "Stand By Me," "Beams of Heaven," "The Storm Is Passing Over," and "We'll Understand It Better Bye and Bye" are the most powerful Black music. When James Baldwin wanted a hymn to symbolize the life in Harlem's Black churches, he chose Tindley's "Beams of Heaven."

Tindley saw the world as a battlefield with the forces of evil arrayed against the forces of good, and he was certain that if you kept the faith, if you took one day at a time, that hell could not prevail against you. No song portrays this better than the one about a boy lured away from home and tied to a stake at ebb tide, left to die when the tide rose. Well, wrote Tindley, the waves foamed and broke about the boy and there was "no way to quit that awful stake." But just as he was about "to yield and die"—like Mr. Harris praying at that tree in Phoenix—just then, a stranger's voice said, "I will help you," and with "one mighty stroke," he cut "that awful rope and brought me to shore." Tindley's theme was always the liberation from oppression.

In his most popular song, "We'll Understand It Better Bye and Bye," almost a staple of the Black service, Tindley wrote that we were a "tossed and driven" people, battered on a sea of time—that in this land of plenty, we Black people have "want of shelter and of food" and that for us it is a place of "thirsty hills and barren land." In the midst of this oppression, Tindley said, God is guiding us, and if we look neither right nor left, but trust in him, someday we will be given understanding. And on that perfect day, we will sit around and tell how we survived the guns at Wilmington, North Carolina, the burning of the orphanages in Philadelphia, and the journey from Barbados to Philadelphia. That day we'll tell how we overcame all those things and we'll shout out the victory.

Tindley's message was sung in his four-thousand-member church, and throughout the city and the country, so that by 1920, it had become the backbone of Black American church music. Philadelphia became a major center of such music, with the Clara Ward singers, newly arrived from North Carolina, coming out of Ebenezer Baptist Church—heavily populated by Abbeville County folk—with Sister Rosetta Thorpe, the Dixie Hummingbirds, and Marion Williams, originally a Ward singer, all contributing. Thomas Dorsey, who was the pianist for Mahalia Jackson from 1937 to 1946, discovered and encouraged the Ward Singers. There was enormous interaction between musicians and the music that poured from storefront churches.

Dizzy Gillespie's family had moved from Cheraw, South Carolina, to Philadelphia in 1935, and there he bought his first trumpet. And it was in Philadelphia that Dizzy got his first big band job, and where, as he says, he had some "baaad jam sessions." Up and down South Street, in clubs near the spot where Richard Allen had first declared the African nation, Dizzy and others were making what became the dominant music in the modern world. Bessie Smith made Philadelphia her home for many years after World War I. She was married there by Reverend Tindley and frequently performed at the theaters owned by Black impresario John T. Gibson. And when Bessie was brought back to Philadelphia in 1937 after her death on a Mississippi road, her body lay in state at the O. V. Catto Elks Lodge.

Rhythm and blues, the secular expression of the church's music, linked the Black people of Philadelphia. Joe Rainey became the city's first Black disc jockey, followed by "Jocko" Henderson and Georgie Woods. And into town in the twenties, thirties, and forties, came—and sometimes stayed—such greats as Billie Holiday and Billy Eckstine. Ethel Waters spent some of her childhood in "little Protestant churches" although raised a Catholic from age nine. Pearl Bailey, born in Virginia, was raised and educated in Philadelphia. Philadelphia-grown talent includes the O'Jays, Harold Melvin and the Bluenotes, Chubby Checker, Grover Washington, Jr., Patty LaBelle, and Lola Falana. It remains a city of great musical ferment.

The Dance

Essie-Marie Dorsey, a Marylander come to Philadelphia, opened a music dance school in 1926, one of the first in the city. She had studied Spanish dance and had been trained by William Dollar, the great choreographer and dance instructor. In the thirties, she sponsored lavish dance festivals for the Black children who were her pupils. She had great force: "This dynamic, glamourous woman could command an entire room without opening her mouth and whenever she did, everyone paid attention." Her philosophy was that "the worst colored dance teacher is better for a Black student than the best white teacher," because "of the love contained therein, the concern, the feeling, and rich inheritance." Among her protégés was Marion Durham Cuyjet, an Old Philadelphian who, with Essie-Marie's encouragement, opened her own dance studio in which dozens of Black girls received their instruction. The most famous of them is Judith Jamison, who combines the best of the classical and African traditions. Her parents came from South Carolina and worship at Mother Bethel A.M.E. Church.

Chapter 19

THE STRUGGLE CONTINUED

You got a right
I got a right
We all got a right to the tree of life

Traditional Black Spiritual

Making a Living in Black Philadelphia

Philadelphia industrialists, as we have seen, actively recruited Black workers from the South during World War I. After the war ended, Blacks lost many of these jobs. The cycle was repeated again during World War II. Most Blacks in Philadelphia who could find jobs were common laborers.

An important obstacle to Black employment in industry was the trade unions. Part of the reason was the racism of white workers. Also, early-twentieth-century unions tended to reserve jobs for the sons of their members. And finally, employers' use of Black workers as strikebreakers deepened the antagonism between white and Black workers. Not until the growth of the CIO in the 1930s were our people admitted to unions.

By 1933, over fifty percent of all Black Philadelphians were unemployed. They were shut out of textiles, electrical machinery, tool and die, plumbing, steam fitter, structural ironworker, printer, and machinist trades. The Depression wiped out any advances we had been able to make in the building, shipping, and construction industries. In 1939, a survey of two hundred and sixty factories with a total of forty-three thousand employees indicated that Black youth made up less than one percent of the total employed. The proportion of Black youth in the population at large was fifteen percent.

The outcome was predictable. Unable to find work, Blacks, who made up twelve percent of the city's population, were, by 1939, forty percent of the welfare case load. Recent studies of the effects of unemployment on white Americans show an increase in stress, family breakdown, and violent crimes. If this is the case, such long-standing denial of meaningful work to the Black population must be largely responsible for the destruction of our youth and the disasters in our family life— notably the rise of the single female-headed family.

Most Black women in the city who were employed outside their homes were domestic workers. Mabel Brady describes Black working-class life in Philadelphia: "My mother and grandmother and all those people they worked for a dollar and a quarter a day. I remember when they went to a dollar and a half. And the men [in Germantown] worked driving coal wagons. 'Cause wasn't nothing but coal heat then. You burnt a coal stove summer and winter.

"I married Richard Brady. It was hard times. He came to Germantown to work as a laborer. He could just about manage to write his name. He drove for Nolan's contractors down on Church Lane, drove a double team of horses and from there went to work for a coal contractor. Worked there for pretty near twenty-five years.

"Back in those days, they were glad for a girl to get married. We were poor. He was a hard-working man. My mother looked at him and said, 'Well, you're clean and change your shirt. You working now? You able to take care of my daughter?' And he was making nine dollars a week.

"I worked for a family, as a laundress for thirty-five years. Worked for mother and daughter. I worked the hard way. Wasn't no machines. You had to do everything with your hands. My hands were getting bad. And I washed, put the clothes in a tub, walked up the hill, and put them on the line, then go back. It was laborious work. Then my legs commenced to give out. It's no wonder I have no legs cause I wore them out working.

"One day my husband came home and said they were going to call him back. But they never called him back." Despite these circumstances, Mabel Brady managed to raise a family, and serve her church. She was a senior stewardess of Bethel A.M.E. Church fourteen years, a deaconess in the A.M.E. Church, a singer in the Senior Choir, and a successful fundraiser. She died on Christmas morning, 1979, at the age of ninety.

Her experience mirrored that of thousands of Black Philadelphia women. When Marian Anderson's father died, Anderson recalls: "Mother worked hard to support us—how hard we did not know then and can scarcely realize today. She went out to work by day and occasionally she took in laundry. Whatever mother did, she did conscientiously and well." So did the mother of Wilt Chamberlain. Ethel Waters's grandmother did the same thing. My grandmother from Greenville, South Carolina, also worked for white people and raised her family at the same time.

There were few successful Black businessmen—with the exception of lawyers and doctors—in Philadelphia by the mid-thirties. Certainly, there were no business successes such as those in some of the larger Southern Black communities. Most of the caterers who had formed the backbone of Old Philadelphia had long since been driven out of business or seen their trade diminished by competition from the whites. Black entrepreneurs were the exception. A Black might have a business in Reading Terminal, but that bustling center of trade had two hundred businesses—and the other 199 were owned by whites. There were other scattered examples of business enterprises, such as beauty shops owned by Blacks, but none of their proprietors became millionaires. Whatever their success, however, Black business and professional people could have little impact on the exclusion of most Black Philadelphians from the possibility of making a living.

Housing

Poor people—and practically all of us were poor—lived in houses cast off by the whites. Discrimination led to overcrowding, which was repeatedly noted in studies made of the Black population from 1914 to 1923. In one instance, a four-room house was occupied by four families, the smallest of which was composed of seven members. It was not uncommon for six newcomers to use two beds on a rotating shift, and in a room where "the windows were covered over by blankets, sheets, or rags to keep the drafts from coming in through the sills and around the sashes." Sometimes families would hang blankets on ropes in a room to get some privacy. Lodging houses catered to single men who had come to the city to make some money before sending home for their families. Their loneliness made them prey to all kinds of vice. In a city where the average white population density was 28.2 per acre, the average population density for Black neighborhoods was 111 per acre, with some areas, particularly in South Philadelphia, having a density of nearly 170 per acre.

The overcrowding was caused not only by the policy of the realtors, but also by the need of the newcomers for companionship and the tendency of people from the same towns to crowd together. But whatever its cause, overcrowding often resulted in death. In the mid-twenties the death rate from T.B. among Philadelphia Blacks was four times as high as the white rate; from pneumonia, nearly three times as great; and for infant deaths, twice as great.

Two major building collapses occurred during the thirties. In the aftermath of these disasters, Black agitation led to the construction of the first two housing projects in the city, the James Weldon Johnson Homes in North Philadelphia, and the Tasker Homes in South Philadelphia. A member of the Better Housing Council, which led the campaign for the Johnson Homes, recalled: "My group selected the spot. . . . It was a cemetery. All the graves had to be dug up and taken out. A lot of people won't live there now because they remember the cemetery." By 1940, in the heart of the Greenwood section of

Philadelphia at Ninth and Poplar streets, the Richard Allen Homes were built. These were the first projects in the city to result in the demolition of a slum. Urban renewal had come to the city.

All of our people did not live in slum houses. Black building and loan associations flourished during the 1920s—some thirty-six by 1923—under the aegis of the churches. For some thirty years George W. Mitchell worked heroically to coordinate the activities of such organizations. In the mid-thirties the median value of homes owned by Philadelphia Blacks was $4600, the highest of any city with a Black population of more than 50,000. Black Philadelphians owned about 8000 homes, Black Washingtonians 7300, and Black Chicagoans, 5700.

It was clear that in this "City of Homes" "nowhere [was] the desire for home ownership as pronounced as among the Negroes." Despite poverty and economic deprivation, the Black community was focusing on values centered around the home, a reflection of the rural values of the newcomers and their desire to achieve stability for themselves and their families. The Black people of Philadelphia can best be described as "poor, but respectable." The rural peasantry was bourgeois and transmitted bourgeois values to its children. Even the very poor in Philadelphia lived in rented homes—not apartments— and their aspirations were always to own a home.

William Gardner Smith, remembering South Philadelphia, wrote about

> the little house on the tiny street with much dirt
> and horse manure and the house with four rooms
> and a toilet outside in the back yard and the dirty
> little children that ran outside the house all day and
> half of the night playing games and writing dirty
> names on the wall . . . homes packed so tightly to-
> gether that they were not homes, but shelters from
> the rain and wind. . . . With big cracks in the plaster
> and the paper sagging and spotted in the ceiling from
> the rain that leaked through the roof. . . . With the
> little bedbugs that you could not get rid of though

you sprayed day after day . . . walls so dirty that you walked in the halls straight and with your shoulders pulled in so that you would not touch the walls.

Self-Help

The Black community in Philadelphia had a long history of organizing. The Masons, as we have seen, were founded by Richard Allen and Absalom Jones. The Odd Fellows had been started in 1844 by members of the Philadelphia Library Company who were active members of the Underground Railroad. By the turn of the century, the Public Waiters Association, the Private Waiters Association, and the Hotel Brotherhood— all of which had both social and economic functions—had come into existence.

Migrants from Virginia, Delaware, and Maryland created places where they could socialize together. Because they were not welcome in white bars and clubs, they needed institutions of their own. The Elks were one such institution. The first lodge of the Elks in Philadelphia was organized in 1903 and named for O. V. Catto. By the mid-twenties it had five thousand members, several bands, a woman's auxiliary, and a "junior herd" of more than one hundred boys, and it grew even larger in the 1930s. The Elks provided a measure of self-respect. One observer said: "A lot of the members who were Elks began to take a little personal pride. I mean they wanted to dress good. They wanted to make good public appearances."

The Elks concentrated on personal uplift. Other organizations focused on economic improvement. Thus Eloise Fickland-Spencer, the Georgia-born daughter of an A.M.E. minister and his Atlanta University graduate wife, organized, along with William G. Smith, a Citizens Consumer Cooperative with eighty members in the mid-thirties. The cooperative began a milk distribution business with its headquarters in North Philadelphia. A "buying club" held meetings every Friday so that members could plan their purchases for the week ahead. "The first thing we sold was soup and cake," Eloise Fickland recalled. Even earlier, under the leadership of G. B. Anthony, the "possessor of remarkable organizing ability," the United Consumers Cooperative succeeded to the extent of winning a federal grant of $13,000. By the early thirties, its membership numbered over four hundred people.

Still other groups directed their efforts toward young people. Sam Evans, described as a "tall earnest Negro who . . . devot[ed] time, energy, and meager funds with a fanatical devotion to his people" was born in Florida and had seen five lynchings before he was ten. He came to North Philadelphia looking for opportunity in 1917 and instead found "poverty, broken homes, vice, habitual corner lounging and crime." In response, he established a program for Black kids from twelve to twenty. At its height, the organization enrolled 900 members and had its own building at 1717 North Twelfth Street, in the center of the territory to which Greenwood's refugees had come. Evans organized Youth City, which had its own courts, its own penalties for the use of profanity, and its own mayor. This group, centered around the building of "self-pride and discipline," was a precursor of today's community action programs.

Another youth organization, the Royal Bears Club, was founded by Russell Allen at 1312 Oxford Street, not far from George Bailey's store. Its thirty members, ranging in age from sixteen to twenty-five, had "baseball, football, and basketball camps." Using their own materials and funds, the young men renovated an old building for a clubhouse, laying "a wooden floor in the cellar about six inches above the ground. Upon the side walls and ceiling, beaver board had been placed, and upon that, wallpaper." Said an observer, "All in all the boys through their own money, time, and labor have made their clubhouse look just as cozy and comfortable as it would be on an upper floor."

The Wissahickon Boys Club in Germantown did significant work around the community, and created Camp Emlen, a summer camp which featured a so-called country week for poor Black children from Philadelphia. Located in Pennsylvania Dutch country, the camp was an oasis for children trying to escape the wet Philadelphia summer heat, and is remembered fondly by thousands of Black Philadelphians despite the apple butter sandwiches that frequently were the entire evening's meal: "All the apple butter and bread you can eat" was the motto. The Wissahickon Boys Club gave Bill Cosby material for his skit about the basketball court so small that there was no out-of-bounds line, so it was legal to bounce the ball off the walls to a teammate. The problem for visiting teams was that they were never shown the imaginary dividing line on the wall between the legal and illegal zones. The Wissahickon Speed Marvels practically never lost a game. The boys club was sponsored by John T. Emlen, a white philanthropist, and directed by a Marylander, W. T. Coleman. His chief assistant for some time was Allen Ballard, Sr., born in Greenville, South Carolina, of a father born and raised in Greenwood.

In Philadelphia self-help groups were sponsored by both Blacks and whites. The YWCA and YMCA were, in a large measure, funded by the Black community. The Wharton Center in North Philadelphia and the Wissahickon Boys Club in Germantown were jointly sponsored by the Black and white communities. Would these institutions be integrated or segregated? Controversy raged. The Old Philadelphia tradition was staunchly integrationist. The Southern migrants, however, had no experience of integration and were more inclined to favor Black institutions—and that's what most recreation centers became. At the same time, the migrants opposed segregation.

The daily operation of several of the recreational facilities reflected these contradictory attitudes toward whites and toward separate institutions. Behind many of the problems was white control over the institutions. Thus, letters from a YMCA official in 1936 tells how the whites "had planned a new building for the Colored back in 1926 when we had a campaign for our own building, but unfortunately not enough was secured to do both." As a result, there were two YMCAs, one a modern building with a swimming pool and all the accoutrements of a modern health spa, while our YMCA around the corner consisted of one room with a big Ping-Pong table in the middle of the floor and a one-net basketball court outside. The whites praised the director of the Black YMCA, who opposed the "one or two men on his committee of the modern type who think there should be no segregation and one YMCA building for both races. . . . He does not share this idea with them, but thoroughly believes in a work of, for, and by the colored." The director was a Black South Carolinian, and the men on his board who favored integration were Old Black Philadelphians, including Dr. William Warrick, among the first of his race to finish the University of Pennsylvania. The Black South Carolinian did good work among the young people, but they would have been a lot happier if they could have used the facilities around the corner. It made them mad every time they walked past the new building with its big columns.

The Black South Carolinian and his successor were both underpaid and much set upon. Thus, in the mid-thirties, the South Carolinian suggested that the Black children of the neighborhood have access three evenings a week to the gym of the newly built white elementary school which had a "fair-sized gymnasium, shower baths, wonderful auditorium, and plenty of classrooms." A nearby white community center had been given this privilege, free of charge. A white Y official conveyed this suggestion to the school authorities. The request was denied and Black youth for years had to climb over the fence of the schoolyard to play baseball in the summer. Finally, the school authorities put barbed wire on the fence to keep the Black kids out. One time, when four or five ten-year-olds slipped into the school building after hours to stare at the equipment, the white authorities called in a policeman to tell them they would be locked up if they ever set foot in their school again. Every day, for years, the Black children passed that modern white school on their way to the old building that honored Joseph E. Hill.

An example of more successful Black and white collaboration in a self-help project was the Whittier Centre of South Philadelphia. Its director, Susan P. Wharton, was a white Philadelphian with a sense of mission who, in the early part of the century, did much to focus attention on the health needs of Black people. In 1914, the center declared that its major concern would be illness among poor Blacks. In collaboration with the Phipps Institute, a medical clinic, the center supported both the development of a special T.B. clinic for Blacks, directed by Dr. Henry Minton—whose father, an ICY graduate, had been in South Carolina during the Reconstruction—and a special effort to provide services for T.B. patients at the Jefferson Hospital. The center also hired Black social-medical workers, understanding that "to really get behind the scene requires a visitor in sympathy with the race. Other things being equal, a Negro is better than a white visitor."

Dr. Minton was aided by Dr. Charles Lewis, who "while a medical student at the University of Pennsylvania . . . [was] unwilling to accept the teachings of its medical course lectures that Negroes were more susceptible to the dreaded disease [T.B.] primarily because of color." After finishing medical school in 1912, Dr. Lewis solicited funds from the University of Pennsylvania's president—he collected $75.00 from Lincoln University, where he was physician to the students—and personally made a survey of the Blacks in the area between Bainbridge and Fitzwater streets and Twelfth and Thirteenth streets. He showed that the reason for the high Black T.B. rate was the "deplorable conditions under which Negroes were forced to live," and "improper nourishment," not the color of our skin.

By 1920, the work of the Whittier Centre had attracted contributions by Black donors: "The colored people themselves have begun to support the ever increasing work. Two hundred and fifty-four persons have already given one dollar each for a special nurse." That year the center also provided $1,120, the full salary for the head of the school of nursing at the Mercy Hospital, a Black-run institution.

Protest Organizations

In the twentieth century as in the nineteenth, the most important self-help for Philadelphia Blacks was the struggle against discrimination and oppression. Black Philadelphians formed a large number of organizations, differing in composition and in strategy, but sharing this common goal. The principal organ of Black protest in the city was the National Association for the Advancement of Colored People (NAACP), first organized in 1913. Among its members were Addie Dickerson, the Wilmington, North Carolina–born wife of a militant Black attorney; Jessie Fauset; Mrs. S. W. Layten, founder of the Protective Association for Colored Women; Dr. Nathan Mossell, an activist physician who frequently was on picket lines; Archdeacon Phillips; Bishop Benjamin T. Tanner of the A.M.E. Church; George White, the ex-congressman from North Carolina; and Isadore Martin, its primary leader during the early years. The group also had some white members.

The NAACP was sometimes criticized by militants as being an instrument for the protection of middle-class Black rights. But the record indicates that the NAACP campaigned successfully to have white newspapers capitalize "Negro" and complained when local radio stations used such terms as "nigger" and "darky." It protested the violent response of some whites to the movement of Blacks into their neighborhoods, the arrests of Blacks for sitting in unauthorized sections of movie theaters, the compulsory vaccination of Black children in elementary schools, and the attempt to segregate Black teams at the Penn Relays. It managed to have arrested a group of white men who had assaulted a Black woman and thrown her from a car. The NAACP was also a constant force in the fight for a state equal rights bill. Among the presidents of the NAACP were Charles Dorsey, a dentist; Herbert Millen, a future magistrate; and Joe Rainey. By the mid-thirties, under Rainey's leadership, the NAACP had a membership of fourteen hundred persons. It maintained a reputation for conservatism until the arrival in the mid-fifties of Cecil Moore, West Virginia–born ex-marine whose militant stance ultimately split the NAACP into several branches. The branch he founded, in North Philadelphia, is still considered the most militant of the organization.

Important also as a protest organization was the Colored Protective Association, created in 1918 to respond to the white attacks on Blacks seeking homes in white neighborhoods. Primarily composed of clergymen, including R. R. Wright, an A.M.E. minister and future bishop, and Tindley, its membership included William Henry Moses, pastor of Zion Baptist Church, who was afterward to be prominent in the Garveyite movement. This organization was one of many ad hoc groups that sprang up to deal with specific problems, and then disappeared. The Inter-Racial Committee set up an "Anti-Lynching Committee" in the mid-twenties, headed by Anne Biddle Sterling. Arthur Fauset and Reverend Tindley participated in this organization as well.

Philadelphia was also a center of the Garveyite movement during the 1920s. Garveyism, named after its leader, Marcus Garvey, a Jamaican who espoused a "Back to Africa" movement as the sole means of surviving white oppression in America, was especially popular among the Black masses newly come from the South. But there are some indications that middle-class Black Philadelphians were also involved in the movement. Also, another member of the Colored Protective Association, James Walker Hood Eason, an A.M.E. Zion minister from North Carolina, rose to high office in the Garveyite movement and was mysteriously assassinated in January 1923. The Reverend George Alexander McGuire, an assistant for four years to Archdeacon Phillips, became an important force in the movement. In August 1922, the Garveyites gave Bishop Heard the title of "His Grace, the Duke of Niger because of the great work done by him in Africa among the native people there." Indeed, R. R. Wright, Jr. himself was very sympathetic to the Garveyites.

The Educational Equality League, headed by Floyd Logan, a North Carolinian, fought for and ultimately achieved in the late thirties the merging of the two separate lists for Black and white teachers. In addition, there were such local activist groups as the Philadelphia Civic League, formed by the dentist Dr. John Rice, in 1933, which fought for a job for a Black cashier at North Philadelphia's Jewel Theatre, and established play streets for children. There were occasional ad hoc protest organizations such as the Philadelphia Committee for the Defense of Ethiopia, founded by Eloise Fickland-Spencer, the organizer of the Consumers Cooperative Association. Other members of that group were Arthur Huff Fauset and Raymond Pace Alexander. Mrs. Fickland-Spencer, along with the wife of Joseph Rainey, was also a member of the Better Housing Council which agitated for the construction of the James Weldon Johnson Homes in North Philadelphia. Fickland-Spencer's activities included the Negro Work Committee of the Socialist party where she served with A. Phillip Randolph, and she conducted literacy classes "to give . . . the basics of socialism and show how a socialist government would be much better than the government we had." She was also an organizer of Local 192 of the laundry workers.

After the controversial conviction of the so-called Scottsboro Boys in Alabama in the mid-thirties, Black Philadelphians organized a Scottsboro Defense League whose board included Old Philadelphia names like Arthur Huff Fauset and the first wife of Eugene Rhodes, and new Philadelphians like the Reverend Marshall Shepherd and Clarence Whyte. Austin Norris, Fauset, the Elk leader Hobson Reynolds, and Reverend Shepherd all joined together to protest against General Franco and the Spanish Fascists. Philadelphia, by the mid-thirties, had an estimated three hundred Black members of the Communist party. Their activities remain to be explored.

Despite frequent protest, the levers of economic and political power remained in the hands of the whites, who were not about to give them up. William Gardner Smith sums up the situation in these words:

> The leaders were very elegant in their big cars and fine clothes, and they talked a lot about how oppressed the Negro was and how Congress ought to do something to prove that this great country of ours was truly a country for ALL THE PEOPLE. There was one Negro leader in the ward where I lived. He was in City Council. He was picked by the ward leader of the party and was not a bad fellow. My mother told me that he gave more than half of his

salary from the City Council to the ward leader, who kept him in office. This leader in City Council never said much up at City Hall, although I read a lot of statements he made in the colored papers about the future of the Negro in Philadelphia. The statements were very fine.

Chapter 20

CONCLUSION

I feel all right, no condemnation
Feel all right, no condemnation
Well, I feel all right, no condemnation,
No condemnation in my soul

Traditional Black Spiritual

Nothing is gained by condemning the dead. To understand them is another matter. I've tried to focus on the lives and fates of South Carolina and Philadelphia Blacks in such a way that makes clear that even in their sharpest moments of misunderstanding, they had more to unite them than to divide them. Nobody ever said that a people's history need reflect unanimity of purpose.

Black people have been divided by color, hair, dress, and geography. Neither the texture of hair, nor the shape of the nose, nor where we live is something over which most of us have had a choice. It is not surprising, living in a country where a recent poll of Ivy League graduates at their twenty-fifth reunions showed that less than half agreed that Blacks were as intelligent as whites, that we would take on some of these attitudes. Prejudices against one another have been the most dangerous and persistent obstacles to our development as a people and have led to vicious conflicts in institutions as diverse as Sunday schools, fraternal orders, and labor organizations.

Black intellectuals have been buffeted by the same waves that have tossed the rest of our people about. The Black situation in America has been in as much flux as the society around it. Wars don't leave it alone and depressions don't pass it by, any more than delta floods only drown whites. Those Blacks who do wish to describe and transmit our cultural tradition are often distracted by other activities that seem to offer more immediate payoffs for the race. And this is, after all, a people barely more than a hundred years out of bondage. This writer was born sixty-five years after its end. When I was young, errant children were still told that if they didn't behave, they would be sold back into slavery. There has been little time to gather our forces and trace the steps that have brought us to our present condition. Few Black men or women have ever had enough of a quiet place.

It takes a conceptual leap to pass over our differences and fasten onto the truth that the Black community has developed a surprising degree of cohesiveness, forged by a common experience of oppression. Indeed, throughout the history of the United States our community has prevented the country from becoming far more conservative than it is. The impact of President Reagan's program on the white middle class has made it clear that what harms Black people also destroys the very essence of the American dream—a society where every man and woman has a chance to live a decent life. As the old folks say, "You can't keep a man down in a ditch lessn' you get down there with him."

If a sense of oneness, the unique and precious quality that while dividing us one from the other also unites us, defines a community, then it is clear that we are a community. If by chance we find ourselves at a party in a strange town on Saturday night, we can be certain that the people there will play the same music, dance the same rhythms, and speak with the same inflection as they do in our hometowns. On a Sunday, a New Yorker can enter an A.M.E. Church in York, Maine, and find the same service, hymns, and kinds of people that he or she left at home. Few are the regions of this land without their indigenous outposts of the Black community. Where early American history did not place us, later migrations have.

Our community is sustained by a strong and positive tradition. Its marrow is a fierce determination to survive and overcome the injustice that assails us. Black music hints at this, but there is no culture without institutions, and music and rhythm are not institutions. They can't organize, feed people, resist or speak out against injustice. They provide a social cement, but any argument that depends on music to prove the existence of a Black community is doomed to fail.

I have tried to show how, out of a multitude of nations, a people was created in the United States with a unity that could not, because of colonialism and national histories, exist in its native continent. It was here, and not in Brazil, Jamaica, or Africa, that the most prolonged Black-white confrontation took place. The United States became the center stage on which the racial conflict between European colonialists and Blacks was played out. Out of the very tenacity of the white grip on power and resources was forged, by necessity, an African people. I don't think it a matter of chance that William Gardner Smith of Philadelphia became the cultural advisor to Kwame Nkrumah, an embodiment of African nationalism.

In Philadelphia, we found the beginnings of the written tradition of Black protest. The same city yields the beginnings of two major underpinnings of the Black nation, the Masons and the Black Church. Before white Americans had finished writing their Constitution, Philadelphia Africans had bent to the task of creating a new nation here. Black caterers and Black hod carriers were one in their perception of the need to institutionalize protest. Because they could not continue to observe their African religions, they Africanized the white religion. Understanding that any Black person's freedom was precarious as long as one remained a slave, they helped to build an Underground Railroad. When Garrison orated and John Brown rode to Harpers Ferry, the funds to support them were furnished by Black Philadelphians. When guns were raised against them and their churches, they armed for self-defense. But most of all, they busied themselves with political and intellectual protest.

On the other hand, in South Carolina, we see the development of a tradition of violence, physicality, and strong communal and family ties. Love bound us together. Our people in South Carolina, with few exceptions, had little time to write. They were caught up in a struggle against whites and nature. Food, protection of self and family, and shelter were uppermost in their minds. Yet in the midst of the storms and the fires, they built on the voluntary organizations and the church founded by their Northern brethren. At the same time, they brought forth leaders firmly rooted both in the Black masses and in the church.

Most Blacks remained in the South until World War I, and most lived in situations similar to those in South Carolina. Thus, a distinctly Southern Black political and social amalgam emerged, and was brought to the Northern cities during the Great Migration. The tradition, predictably, clashed with that of the Northern Black community, weakening for a time the Black ability to cope with the miseries and dislocations caused by the modernization process. The clash also obscured the continuities and similarities in the Northern and Southern Black traditions, and the remarkable ability of institutions and ideas to survive adversity. Our people developed institutions that enabled them to survive repeated assaults on their homes, churches, and persons, and retain the most important human quality—compassion.

Finally, we must look at the work of E. Franklin Frazier, the great scholar whose book on the Black family contains much rich material, but who lashed out at his own people in *The Black Bourgeoisie.* Few books on Black people have been as often cited as this one, whose thesis is the moral corruption of the Black middle class formed after the Great Migration. Frazier said that they had lost their Southern peasant roots but had rejected the Puritan way of the Northern and Southern Black elites. So the Black middle class, neither white nor Black, engaged in conspicuous consumption and forgot the Black masses. Frazier presented no data to support this thesis and indeed, later in life, regretted that he had written the book. But his thesis has been eagerly picked up by a number of scholars. Some, writing from a left perspective, use Frazier's thesis to castigate Black leaders for not doing what perhaps they could not do. Others, like Thomas Sowell, appropriate it for an opposite purpose, to argue that the Black middle class does not represent the Black poor.

Sometimes the distance between middle class and poor, urban and rural, North and South, Old Philadelphian and new, seemed impossibly far. It was easy for the migrants to lash out at an Old Philadelphia family for putting on airs. And the Old Philadelphians could never understand the roughness and peasant ways of many of the Southern migrants. In such circumstances, members of one group sometimes identified with whites and considered members of the other group as "them" rather than "we." The hostility that should have been directed outward was frequently turned inward. In the process, Old Philadelphians or Southern immigrants could not always see that they were linked together, that they were helping one another, and that together they were forming a dynamic and powerful new force in American society. What becomes apparent in our study is that the division is not that simple. Black Philadelphians have a "twoness," formed by the merging of the nineteenth century and the Southern Black traditions. Frequently both cultures are at war within one person.

From that ferment came the basis for much of American music, and an intellectual environment that would feed the modern Black protest movement. During the twenties and thirties Philadelphia was a major base for the conquest of the sphere of athletics by Black people and for achievement in the arts. And much of the thought about the nature of American racism was emerging from the classrooms, bars, and churches of Philadelphia in this period. The Black people of the city were getting it together and didn't know it sometimes.

Fierce struggles for leadership and power took place, but we did not seem to have learned the lesson that leadership is imperfect because people are not perfect. It was easy to label a person a "Tom" or a "demagogue," and such excess was encouraged by the intensity of the experiences that Black Southerners had undergone. In the same way, we frequently demanded consistency and steadiness from our leadership when the struggle had burned them out. The great capacity of Black people for forgiveness should be first extended to our own.

The argument here has been that the social butterfly in Old Black Philadelphia circles may have been at the same time a mighty inspirer of the young through her readings of Afro-American poetry. The courtesy and dignity of the Old Philadelphians were good models for any people to follow. Their moral rectitude and tradition of protest added to the strength of the Black Southerners' tradition. All Black Philadelphians had been subjected to white hostility and all had reacted to it in their own ways. In both cases of the Old Philadelphians and of the newcomers, Black mutual self-help was part of that reaction. The response of the Black guerrillas at Phoenix is as much a part of the tradition of self-help as the formation of the Afro-American History Society in Philadelphia in 1901. The role of the leaders of Abbeville-Greenwood County in helping their own was paralleled by the work in Philadelphia of similar organizations. For they were of those people, and how can you turn your back on yourself?

It has always seemed to me that official white America— I'm thinking in particular of history texts published before 1970, but there are many other examples—tried to deny the existence of a Black tradition. It was, after all, to the advantage of whites if Blacks believed that every event was discrete, and that each Black person was alone and vulnerable. Yet, every white American has two traditions. Color is the passport to the tradition of John Paul Jones, the cherry tree, the Alamo, and damn the torpedoes. Then there is the ethnic tradition, which connects the white American to Europe—to Poland, Italy, or Ireland.

Even today, some whites are uncomfortable when Blacks claim either tradition—the American, or their own. Some whites cannot believe that Blacks are really Americans. On the other hand, the Black tradition of protest and struggle seems to them hostile. This book puts forward a claim to both.

Chapter 21

EPILOGUE

Lord help the poor and needy
In this land
In the great getting up morning we shall face another sun
Lord help the poor and the needy
In this land, in this land

Traditional Black Spiritual

It would make a perfect ending to our story if we could proclaim that the strength and spirit of Philadelphia's Black tradition had produced a miracle; that, despite the odds, poverty had been banished, or that housing was adequate, education top-notch, and the quality of life decent. But that would declare the battle over when it is still raging. By the 1980s, Blacks accounted for forty percent of the city's inhabitants, from a level of ten percent in 1930. But the unemployment rate is the highest of the major cities, holding steady at twenty-one percent, three and one-half times the rate for whites. In some neighborhoods, the unemployment rate for Black men reaches fifty-six percent, and it is close to seventy percent for teen-agers. In 1974, over half of Black tenth-graders failed to graduate with their classes. Our people occupy eighty percent of the city's 120,000 public housing units. Two-thirds of teen-age pregnancies occur among Black adolescents. The infant mortality rate of Blacks is twice that of whites. A Black youngster has a fifty percent chance of being arrested before he reaches age thirty. Blacks made up eighty-five percent of the prison population.

Consider the differing fates of the whites and Blacks in Abbeville-Greenwood who bore the names Cothran, Perrin, Talbert, Ballard, and Logan. The descendants of the whites occupy prestigious positions in American society. The names of the Blacks who were their slaves can be found in undue proportions on the welfare rolls and prison rolls of the city of Philadelphia. Not many of them can be found on the rolls of the Chamber of Commerce, or the board of trustees of a bank or corporation. For American history has not been good to us.

There are, to be sure, positive achievements. Thus, in line with the nationwide increase, the percentage of Blacks who completed high school rose from eight percent in 1940 to seventeen percent in 1950 and twenty-four percent by 1960. Home ownership by Black people in the city remains around forty percent. Significant improvements in political representation have occurred. Blacks made up close to one-third of Philadelphia's delegation in the two bodies of the state legislature. The head of the city council and the mayor are Black. And in the city, Blacks control six major unions with a total membership of 43,000 workers, the largest of which is the municipal union with some 18,000 members.

The community, moreover, has continued to struggle against oppression, and, in the years after World War II, made some gains. In 1964, the Reverend Leon Sullivan marshalled the collective strength of the Black churches and led a boycott that broke down many employment barriers. The "Lion of North Philadelphia," Cecil Moore, a lawyer, directed the movement that ended segregation at Girard College, a boys' school in North Philadelphia. Interestingly enough, both Sullivan and Moore were newcomers to Philadelphia. Moore ran for mayor and then for Congress against Robert Nix. The congressman's son, in turn, became the first Black member of the state supreme court, and is in line to become the chief justice.

Yet, despite this progress, racism persists. A Black life is still not secure in Philadelphia. Even a casual look at Philadelphia's newspapers reveals such events as the killing of a Black youth, a graduate of the O. V. Catto school, by a policeman in the summer of 1980; the shooting of another youth by police as he stood in handcuffs; the beating to death of a crazed Black man who stood and threatened police with a knife. A white man cruised the streets in the early hours one morning and killed one Black and sniped at others. The Philadelphia police force in 1980 listed 387 officers of the rank of captain and above. Of these, 5 were Black. In 1967, Blacks accounted for twenty-seven percent of new recruits to the force. In 1980, the percentage was seven percent. As a writer for the *Philadelphia Tribune* said: "The tune remains the same, sad and melancholy. The characters remain the same; Black men killed by the blistering lead from an officer's revolver."

But if race hatred persists, so do the links that bind the Black community together. Thus, every year, on Founder's Day, the people of Mother Bethel A.M.E. Church walk in remembrance from St. George's Methodist Church to Mother Bethel. The Old Philadelphia Club still meets, although it is now full of Virginians and South Carolinians. A Minton, related to Dr. Minton, throws a fiftieth wedding anniversary party and the names of the guests mirror the Old Philadelphia past, with Dorseys, Abeles, and Duckreys in attendance. Zoar, the first Black Methodist church, holds a reception for its 186th anniversary and the guest speaker is Sam Evans, who founded Youth City among the refugees in North Philadelphia. A ceremony commemorating the ordination of the third Black woman Episcopal priest takes place at a church whose pastor is among the most radical leaders in the city. He can be seen in pictures with Ben Chavis of the Wilmington Ten and Imari Abubakari Obadele, the president of the Republic of New Africa. Present at the ceremony is Pauli Murray, the first Black woman priest, and the granddaughter of an ICY man. The new priest grew up in a church founded by Archdeacon Phillips. The songs sung at the ceremony are the gospel favorites, "He's Sweet I know," "Sign Me Up," and "Close to Thee." Saint-Simon, another church founded by the archdeacon, had a ceremony in 1974 honoring its priest who is a member of the O. V. Catto Elks Lodge, and 32nd Degree Mason, and a member of the Boule. Vaux Junior High School, whose student body is all poor and Black, produced a chess team that for three years in a row has won a national championship. That was the way Jacob White expected the school to be. In 1980, Berean Church honored its founder, Matthew Anderson. The present pastor is a director of the Wharton Center, and active in the Black Unity movement. A Philadelphia news-paper also notes that the city's first Black police captain, born in Dillon, South Carolina, is retiring. His retirement is marked by an invocation given by the pastor of St. Thomas Episcopal Church, the church of Absalom Jones and James Forten.

The South Carolina influence still lives. On December 19, 1980, the *Philadelphia Tribune* featured stories on two men who had lived to be a hundred. One had been born in Edgefield County and remembered that "my folks farmed corn, cotton, potatoes, greens, hogs, chickens and cows." He had come to Philadelphia in the 1923 wave of migrants. The other cente-narian had been born on a plantation near St. George, South Carolina, in 1872 of "parents who had been slaves only eight years earlier."

The Greenwood connection remains tight. In June 1977, after nearly fifty years, the congregation of Morris Chapel Church of Greenwood, South Carolina, traveled to Philadel-phia to worship with Morris Chapel Church of Philadelphia. Hughsey Childs, who had been a member of the church in both places, was honored on this occasion. Each year, the Holiday Inn in Greenwood is flooded with Philadelphians re-turning home for reunions. If these reunions ceased, the motel would probably go out of business. The *Philadelphia Inquirer* of February 20, 1977, featured a story on a Black Philadelphia dentist, born in Greenwood, who decided to leave Philadelphia with its crime and its dirt and return to the pastoral quiet of Greenwood. The story is illustrated with a picture of the den-tist fishing from a boat. There is a satisfied smile on his face; he is home. Greenwood has outlived its past. The guns are silent now; the people are courteous; and the town seems well on its way to an era of peaceful cooperation and mutual respect between Black and white.

No term so clearly describes what happened in the United States as does "colonialism." You could point your finger to spots on the map and say Britain dominated India or Kenya. American colonialism, like the Russian variety, has been invisible because it took place in a contiguous territory, but it is no less real for that. Vestiges of the colonialization and exploitation of Black people are still evident everywhere. In Philadelphia, whites control the banks, real estate, government, school system, universities, police, newspapers, TV, and health and welfare bureaucracies. Of late they have made an effort to bring some of the Blacks into the system. But these measures have been thwarted by other whites, who feel that they have earned everything they have and that we had the same chance as they did to make it in this society. Now their self-righteousness finds an echo at the highest levels of government. The sooner they are disabused of this notion, the sooner will this country move into a time of peaceful and healthy internal development. Such a course is critical to the survival of the United States.

> Walk together, children
> Don't you get weary
> Talk together, children
> Don't you get weary
> Sing together, children
> Don't you get weary
> There's a great camp meeting in the Promised Land

Traditional Black Spiritual

When I cry when I'm singing, I'm not sad like some people think. I look back where I came from and I rejoice.

MAHALIA JACKSON in *Black Song: The Forge and the Flame* by John Lovell, Jr.

NOTES

CHAPTER 1: *Linking South Carolina and Philadelphia*

Some Old Philadelphians

Jean-Pierre Burr: A family document in the possession of my cousin, Miriam Burr Mitchell Cooper, refers to Burr and his "colored wife." Another document—transcribed by Cooper's mother, Mabel Burr Cornish, in 1935, claims that "Jean-Pierre Burr's mother was an East Indian woman, born in Calcutta, who went to Haiti and became housekeeper to Aaron Burr's children." Cornish was the granddaughter of Jean-Pierre's son, John Emory Burr. My mother claimed that, as a child, she saw a copy of Aaron Burr's marriage license, but that my grandmother subsequently destroyed it.

CHAPTER 2: *At the Beginning*

Antigua, Saint Christopher, and Anguilla: Basic sources on slavery in Pennsylvania and Philadelphia are Deborah Newman, "They Left with the British: Black Women in the Evacuation of Philadelphia, 1778," *Pennsylvania Heritage*, vol. 4, 1977, pp. 20–24; Darold D. Wax, "Negro Imports into Pennsylvania, 1720–1766," *Pennsylvania History*, vol. 32, 1965, pp. 254–88; Darold D. Wax, "Quaker Merchants and the Slave Trade in Colonial Pennsylvania," the *Pennsylvania Magazine of History and Biography* (hereafter PMHB), vol. 86, 1962, pp. 143–60; Gary B. Nash, "Slaves and Slave-owners in Colonial Philadelphia," *William and Mary Quarterly*, series III, vol. 30, 1973, pp. 223–56; Darold D. Wax, "The Demand for Slave Labor in Colonial Pennsylvania," *Pennyslvania History*, vol. 34, 1967, pp. 331–45. Darold D. Wax, "Negro Import Duties in Colonial Pennsylvania," vol. 47, 1973.

Quakers and the Slave Trade

six slaves directly: Wax, "Imports," p. 254. labor shortage: Wax, "Quaker Merchants," p. 144. Jonathan Dickinson: Ibid., pp. 148, 149. Samuel Carpenter, for example: Gary B. Nash, *Quakers and Politics in Pennsylvania, 1681–1726*, Princeton University Press, 1968, p. 61. Old Philadelphians ... slave merchants: Wax, "Quaker Merchants," p. 158. "Weightiest

Quakers": Ibid.; see note on Tolles. trade of commodities: Wax, "Quaker
Merchants," p. 146. "Parcel of Five Negroes": Wax, "Imports," pp. 261 ff.
for some lists. One hundred Africans: Newman, p. 21. "odious spectacle":
John F. Watson, *Annals of Philadelphia and Pennsylvania in the Olden
Times*, vol. 2, 1857, p. 265. "to go naked": Wax, "Quaker Merchants,"
p. 154.

Early Philadelphia
Philadelphia like Europe: Carl and Jessica Bridenbaugh, *Rebels and
Gentlemen: Philadelphia in the Age of Franklin*, Reynal and Hitchcock,
1942. As quoted, p. 11. "finer mansions": Carl Bridenbaugh, *Cities in the
Wilderness*, Ronald Press, 1938, p. 416. "for their upkeep": Ibid., p. 254.
"pleasures of the table": Frederick B. Tolles, *Meeting House and Counting
House*, University of North Carolina Press, 1948, pp. 109, 131, 135. William
Shippen: Ibid., p. 49. "self-designing": Ibid., p. 37. "burdened by a reserve":
Harry Emerson Wildes, *The Delaware*, Farrar and Rinehart, 1940, p. 84.

Philadelphia a Cultural Capital
"great taste for books": Tolles, p. 10. "grand tours" to Europe: Bridenbaugh, *Rebels*, pp. 150 ff. Poverty, disease: Ibid., p. 225. "gentleman . . . Church of England": Ibid., p. 182. separate schools: Ibid., p. 18 ff.
clubs and jobs: Ibid., p. 236 ff.

Early Blacks and Philadelphia Culture
Friends' Public School: Ibid., p. 254. distressed Black people: Ibid. "pub-
licly catechized": Frank J. Klingberg, "The African Immigrant in Colonial
Pennsylvania and Delaware," *History Magazine of the Protestant Episcopal
Church*, vol. 11, 1942, pp. 126–53.

CHAPTER 3: *Black Philadelphia Leaders*
The Legacy of Philadelphia's Black Leadership
"Colored American": *Philadelphia Tribune*, November 22, 1913. Bolivar wrote under the pen name "Pencil Pusher."

Origins of Black Philadelphians
several languages: Edward Raymond Turner, *The Negro in Pennsylvania, 1639–1861*, Arno Press, 1969, pp. 50–51. "in their own tongue": Watson, vol. 2, p. 265. gourds: Ibid., p. 220. peanut candy cakes: "Pencil Pusher,"
Philadelphia Tribune, May 10, 1913. "Metizo ladies": Watson, vol. 1,
p. 181.

The Life of Early Blacks
"ventilation, consumption": Turner, pp. 201–02. the law was different:
This summary of the state of the law in Pennsylvania is drawn from Turner

and A. Leon Higginbotham, Jr., *In the Matter of Color*, Oxford University Press, 1978, pp. 267 ff. too much trouble: Turner, p. 114. "keenness and intelligence": "Pencil Pusher," *Philadelphia Tribune*, May 17, 1913. a viable community: Turner, p. 127. "a people pinioned": As quoted in Benjamin C. Bacon, *Statistics of the Colored People of Philadelphia*, 2nd ed., Philadelphia Board of Education, 1859, p. 16.

James Forten, Sailmaker

"traitor to her interests": Ray Allen Billington, "James Forten: Forgotten Abolitionist," *The Making of Black America*, vol. 1, August Meier and Elliot Rudwick, eds., Atheneum, 1973, pp. 289–302. Unless otherwise noted, descriptions of Forten come from the above and from Esther M. Douty, *Forten the Sailmaker*, Rand McNally, 1968. "timely remittance": Benjamin Quarles, *Black Abolitionists*, Oxford University Press, 1975, p. 20. "Arthur and Lewis Tappan": Ray Allen Billington, ed., *The Journal of Charlotte L. Forten*, Dryden Press, 1953. See his introduction, p. 11.

Richard Allen—From Slave to Bishop

"damn fool thing": The description of Richard Allen's life is taken from Charles H. Wesley, *Richard Allen: Apostle of Freedom*, Associated Publishers, 1935, and Carol V. R. George, *Segregated Sabbaths*, Oxford University Press, 1973. "apostle of human freedom": Reverend William J. Simmons, *Men of Mark*, Arno Press, 1968, p. 493.

Absalom Jones, A Singular Man

born a slave: The description of Absalom Jones's life is taken primarily from George Freeman Bragg, Jr., *History of the Afro-American Group of the Episcopal Church*, Church Advocate Press, 1922. This rare volume was a gift to the author from the late Arthur Huff Fauset.

Robert Purvis, Black Abolitionist

portraits show . . . defiance: The best description of Purvis is found in Joseph A. Boromé, "Robert Purvis and His Early Challenge to American Racism," *Negro History Bulletin*, vol. 30, 1967. Professor Boromé was kind enough to share his information on Purvis with me. slaves on their way to Canada: Joseph A. Boromé, "The Vigilant Committee of Philadelphia," *PMHB*, vol. 92, 1968, pp. 320–52. "weary are at rest": Billington, *Journal*, p. 15. always be counted in: William Still, *The Underground Railroad*, Johnson Publishing, 1970, p. 737.

William Still, Underground Railroad Conductor

William Still himself: The description of Still is found in Simmons, p. 149 ff. John Brown's brave band: Ibid., p. 159.

O. V. Catto, Scholar and Activist

O. V. Catto: The description of O. V. Catto's life is from Henry C. Silcox, "Nineteenth Century Philadelphia Black Militant: Octavius V. Catto (1839–1871)," *Pennsylvania History*, vol. 63, 1977, pp. 53–77. "white pillagers": Mifflin W. Gibbs, *Shadow and Light, An Autobiography*, Arno Press, 1968. Quotation is from pp. 22–23; other information is from pp. 19 ff.

CHAPTER 4: *The Black Church*

The Church and the Free African Society

"wavering step": W.E.B. DuBois, *The Philadelphia Negro: A Social Study*, Schocken, 1970 (orig. 1899), p. 19. DuBois claimed: Ibid., p. 197. "subscribed . . . toward the furnishing": Richard Allen's description of the event is in Bragg, pp. 47–52. "soar out of their slavery": William L. Douglass, *Annals of the First African Church in the United States of America*, King and Baird, 1862, p. 11.

The First African Church Is Founded

Cyrus Bustill: Quote is from Ibid., p. 52, and description from Eslanda Goode Robeson, *Paul Robeson, Negro*, Victor Gollancz, 1930, p. 22. "Quaker disgust": as quoted in Linda Perkins, "Fanny Jackson-Coppin and the Institute for Colored Youth," Ed. D. thesis, University of Illinois, 1978, p. 76. Dr. Perkins kindly shared this manuscript with me. succeeding priests knew: For account, see Bragg, pp. 63 ff. "white race within their midst": Ibid., p. 54. "feasting and dancing": Ibid., pp. 56–57. "stimulating influence of St. Thomas": Ibid., pp. 74–75. "foremost in good work": W.E.B. DuBois, p. 199, note. Of another Episcopal church, DuBois observed that it "especially reaches out after a class of neglected poor whom the other colored churches shun or forgot and for whom there is little fellowship in white churches" p. 217.

Influence of Episcopalians and Presbyterians

"Black bourgeoisie": See, for example, Theodore Hershberg, "Mulattos and Blacks: Intra-Group Color Differences and Social Stratification in Nineteenth Century Philadelphia," unpublished paper delivered at annual meeting of Organization of American Historians, April 1974, p. 36. Frazier differentiated the old elite with their puritanical ways from the Black bourgeoisie. Hershberg recognized this in the revised edition of his paper appearing in his *Philadelphia: Work, Space, Family, and Group Experience in the Nineteenth Century*, Oxford University Press, 1981, p. 427.

Payne and Williams meeting: Daniel A. Payne, *Recollections of Seventy Years*, Arno Press, 1969, pp. 42, 46. Also see remarks of Reverend William Douglass as quoted in Bragg, p. 84. *"character"*: Sketch of Crummell in Simmons, pp. 530 ff. Text of speech in Bragg, pp. 262 ff; quote on p. 265.

"lapse of time": Simmons, p. 533. Peter Levington: Bragg, pp. 91 ff. Frederick Douglass and St. Thomas: Douglass called it a "corrupt old pro-slavery hag" in Quarles, p. 83.

Richard Allen Founds the A.M.E. Church
"most remarkable": DuBois, p. 21. "undisciplined minds": Douglass, William, p. 2. "set thee apart": Payne, p. 17. Morris Brown quote: Ibid., p. 94. "must be a ring": All these incidents are recounted in Payne.

The A.M.E. Church Takes Root
an escaped slave: Milton C. Sernett, *Black Religion and American Evangelicanism*, Scarecrow Press, 1975, pp. 157–58. "certain parts of Maryland": "Pencil Pusher," *Philadelphia Tribune*, June 28, 1913. Sarah Allen: George, p. 130. Quinn Chapel: Quarles, p. 84. First Presbyterian Church: Boromé, p. 327. Churches in Underground Railroad: Charles L. Blockson, *Pennsylvania's Black History*, Portfolio Associates, 1975. Susquehanna riverboatman: *The Negro in Montour County*, unpublished WPA manuscript in public library of Danville, Pennsylvania. I thank my cousins, the Young family of Danville, for bringing this manuscript to my attention. "great sympathy with slaves": R. R. Wright, Jr., *Encyclopedia of African Methodism*, 2nd ed., 1947, p. 566. First African Presbyterian Church: See Benjamin Brawley, *A Social History of the American Negro*, Macmillan, 1970, p. 70; Blockson, p. 129. Lists of church membership for 1864, 1871, and 1876 can be found in the Leon Gardiner Collection of the Historical Society of Pennsylvania. "Union Baptist . . . Virginia servant girls": DuBois, p. 204. "dark-complexioned": Hershberg, *Philadelphia*, p. 425. picnic: In Gardiner Collection. shattered African tribe: DuBois, pp. 197, 201. "manhood": Bragg, p. 303.

CHAPTER 5: *Black Education*
First Schools for Black Pupils
Anthony Benezet: Turner, pp. 129 ff., has information on early Black education. Also see DuBois, pp. 83 ff. "beset any Negro": Turner, p. 133.

Unequal from the Outset
Early nineteenth-century education: Harry C. Silcox, "Delay and Neglect: Negro Public Education in Antebellum Philadelphia," in *PMHB*, vol. 82, 1973, pp. 444–65 is source, unless otherwise noted, of information on public school system. put them in jail: See quote of Robert Vaux, Ibid., p. 451. "ignorant degradation of our people": Ibid., p. 453. voluntarily accept segregation: Ibid., quoting the *Jones Report of 1917*, p. 464.

The Black Community Creates Its Own Schools
private schools: Bacon, p. 8. Black school population: Ibid.

Black America's First High School

The institute: The best account of the ICY is found in Perkins. Also important is Fanny Jackson-Coppin, *Reminiscences of School Life, and Hints of Teaching*, A.M.E. Book Concern, 1913. The title is misleading; it's a fine history of the ICY and its graduates. "never his superior": Payne, p. 48. "Then up! Awake!: Simmons, p. 110. Ebenezer Basset: Jackson-Coppin, p. 140. as was O. V. Catto: Perkins, p. 71; also see "Proceedings of the State Equal Rights Convention of the Colored People of Pennsylvania, held at Harrisburg, February 8, 9, 10, 1865," Afro-American History Series, Collections, Scholarly Resources, Inc. "Toussaint L. Martin": ICY program for December 12, 1867 in Gardiner Collection.

Three-quarters of . . . teachers: Figure obtained by matching names of graduates with lists of teachers in R. R. Wright, Jr., *Philadelphia Colored Directory*, 1908. Black in color: All pictures in Jackson-Coppin.

Literary Clubs Supplement Formal Education

"defense of their race": "Pencil Pusher," *Philadelphia Tribune*, January 18, 1913. Dorothy Porter: "The Organized Educational Activities of Negro Literary Societies, 1828–1846," in Meier and Rudwick, p. 282. "habits and necessities of literary men": Document of 1860, n.d., but addressed to president of the Banneker Institute by St. George R. Taylor and William G. Minton in Gardiner Collection. intellectual training . . . a waste: Letter of Charles Dorsey, July 14, 1858 to the Banneker Institute, in Ibid. white observer: In 1833 as quoted in Porter, Meier and Rudwick, pp. 280–81. "American slavery": "Minutes of American Moral Reform Society Meeting Held in the Presbyterian Church in Seventh St. Below Shippen, August 14–19, 1837," Afro-American History Series, Collection 6, Scholarly Resources Inc.

CHAPTER 6: *Self-Help and Protest*

Helping One Another—The Institutions

caterers and waiters: Broadsides for these organizations are scattered throughout the Gardiner Collection and the Jacob C. White, Jr. Papers, Historical Society of Pennsylvania. Theodore Hershberg of the University of Pennsylvania has broken down these lists so that they can be analyzed by a computer, but his interpretation of the data leaves something to be desired, particularly his insistence that well-to-do Blacks did not help poor, immigrant Blacks. Stephen Smith: Blockson, p. 112. John Trower: Unpublished paper by Robert Ulle, n.d., on Germantown Black community, p. 8. Mr. Ulle kindly shared this paper with me. Pythians: Score cards and letters are in Gardiner Collection. Reference to South Philadelphia is in an August 7, 1869, letter signed by Abraham Brown. Harrisburg: Communication by Raymond Burr, dated December 18, 1867, in Gardiner Collection.

Notes

Antislavery Organizations

Richard Allen: See Allen and Absalom Jones, "A Narrative of the Proceedings of the Black People during the Late Awful Calamity in Philadelphia," in Afro-American History Series, Collection 1. "baddest, meanest": Phillip S. Foner, ed., *The Voice of Black America*, Simon & Schuster, 1972, p. 267. "countenance from this House": Douty, pp. 87, 91. "ties of consanguinity": Brawley, p. 161. "ten great moments": Lerone Bennet, *Wade in the Water*, Johnson Publishing, 1979. Two Black men . . . Declaration of Principles: Quarles, p. 24. Black convention movement: Howard H. Bell, "National Negro Conventions of the Middle 1840's" in Meier and Rudwick, pp. 315–27; and John H. Cromwell, "The Early Negro Convention Movement," Occasional Paper no. 9 of the American Negro Academy, 1904. The late William P. Duckrey kindly shared the latter with me. William Whipper: Cromwell, p. 11. Purvis and "exclusive": Quarles, p. 55.

Underground Railroad

Purvis and Vigilant Committee: Boromé, "The Vigilant Committee," is best source on these activities. See especially his list of the members of the committee. Female Vigilant Association: Ibid., p. 323. Philadelphia women . . . fugitive slave movements: Quarles, p. 158. Still and Harpers Ferry: Larry Gara, "William Still and the Underground Railroad," in Meier and Rudwick, p. 330. "howlings": "Pencil Pusher," *Philadelphia Tribune*, August 17, 1912. Charlotte Forten and Fourth of July: Billington, *Journal*, p. 5. "hollow-headedness": August 9 report to the institute in Gardiner Collection. "arming the Institute": J. Wesley Simpson, "Report of the President," January 9, 1861, in Gardiner Collection. Black Philadelphians protested: "An Appeal to the Colored Citizens of Pennsylvania," in Afro-American History Series, Collection 5. white man's "heart": Ibid.

Direct Self-Help: Fighting in the Union Army

54th Regiment: See Luis F. Emilio, *A Brave Black Regiment, A History of the Fifty-Fourth Regiment of Massachusetts Volunteer Infantry, 1863–1865*, Arno Press, 1969, p. 9. light-complexioned Charlestonians: "Pencil Pusher," *Philadelphia Tribune*, March 7, 1914, adds that two Black men from Philadelphia served as majors in white regiments. Pauli Murray in *Proud Shoes*, Harper & Row, 1956, 1978, also notes this phenomenon of Blacks serving in supposedly "white" regiments, pp. 116–17. 6th and 8th Regiments: Frederick M. Binder, "Pennsylvania Negro Regiments in the Civil War," *Journal of Negro History*, vol. 37, 1952, New Market Heights: Horace Montgomery, "A Union Officer's Recollection of the Negro as a Soldier," *Pennsylvania History*, vol. 27, 1961, pp. 156–87, gives an account of this action. Robert Forten's death: From a memorandum of Leon Gardiner to Orrin Evans, July 1, 1933, in Gardiner Collection.

Intellectual Tradition

"our mother-country": Wesley, p. 220. history of Egypt: *Egyptian and African Rulers,* in Gardiner Collection. The author was identified by "Pencil Pusher" in the *Philadelphia Tribune,* December 23, 1912, as John H. Johnson. Purvis, "The Almighty," and natural rights: See "An Appeal to the Coloured Citizens" and *Minutes* of Moral Reform Society, August 1837. "we being in fact Americans": Purvis to Parker T. Smith, February 22, 1867, in Gardiner Collection. "from amongst the white people": Douty, p. 118.

CHAPTER 7: *The Philadelphia Oppression*

"fierce . . . hatred": Turner, p. 165.

Race Hatred Widespread in the Cities

seven cities: see Leonard P. Curry, *The Free Black in Urban America, 1800–1850,* University of Chicago Press, 1981, p. 98. Cincinnati and New York riots: John Hope Franklin, *From Slavery to Freedom,* Knopf, 1980, p. 174; and Robert Ernst, "The Economic Status of New York City Negroes, 1850–1863," in Meier and Rudwick, p. 256. On Chicago riots see St. Clair Drake and Horace R. Cayton, *Black Metropolis,* Harper & Row, 1962, pp. 42–43. "most serious . . . Pennsylvania": Franklin, p. 174. "pushed from the sidewalk in Boston": Curry, p. 93. "most anti-Negro city": Phillip S. Foner, "The Battle to End Discrimination Against Negroes in Philadelphia, Part I" in *Pa. History,* vol. 40 (1973), p. 261. "Box" Brown: Ibid., p. 262. Douglass: Ibid., p. 266. John Brown and other anti-Black feeling: Ibid., pp. 262–263.

The Terror Begins

onslaught of white mobs: Unless otherwise noted, my sources on the riot are Elizabeth M. Geffen, "Violence in Philadelphia in the 1840's and 1850's," *Pennsylvania History,* vol. 36, 1969, no. 4, pp. 381–411; John Runcie, "Hunting the Nigs in Philadelphia: The Race Riot of August, 1834," in *Pennsylvania History,* vol. 39, 1972, pp. 187–218; Emma Jones Lapsansky, " 'Since They Got Those Separate Churches': Afro-Americans and Racism in Jacksonian Philadelphia," unpublished paper kindly shared with me by the author; Turner, DuBois, and Wildes. some friendly farmers: Geffen, p. 387. "thugs and pro-slavery firemen": "Pencil Pusher," *Philadelphia Tribune,* December 23, 1912. Black population remained at 18,000: Geffen, pp. 388–89. force the Blacks out: Curry, p. 109. lack of growth . . . terror: Runcie, p. 213. "commercial and financial elite": Russell F. Weigley, "A Peaceful City: Public Order in Philadelphia," in Allen F. Davis and Mark H. Haller, eds., *The Peoples of Philadelphia,* Temple University Press, 1973, p. 160. anti-Black tone: Ibid., pp. 160–61. Quakers "savors of pity": Foner, "The Battle," p. 264. Friends' anti-slavery journal: Ibid., p. 263. One historian attributed: Turner, pp. 149, 152. "communal pathology": Dennis Clark, "Urban Blacks and Irishmen: Brothers in Prejudice," in Miriam Ershkowitz and Joseph Zikmund, eds., *Black Politics in Philadelphia*, Basic, 1973, p. 22. "the Irish favor slavery": Nicholas B. Wainwright, ed., *A Philadelphia Perspective: The Diary of Sidney George Fisher—Covering the Years 1834–1871*, Historical Society of Pennsylvania, 1967, p. 439. Irish unrealistic expectations: Runcie, p. 199. "efficient industry": Turner, p. 158. James Forten, "annoyance over rumour": Lapsansky, p. 9. "debauchery and dissipation": Turner, pp. 149, 152. "gaiety, music and dancing": Ibid., p. 140. "thousands of Black children": Ibid., p. 195. interracial marriage: Lapsansky, p. 9.

The Struggle for the Vote
attack on their legal rights: Material on the fight for the ballot is from Turner, and Ira V. Brown, "Pennsylvania and the Rights of the Negro, 1865–1887," in *Pennsylvania History*, vol. 28, 1961. Forten and the polls: Curry, p. 220. O. V. Catto, martyred: Material on the assassination from Silcox, "O. V. Catto," pp. 73–74. Details further verified by phone conversation with Silcox, June 17, 1983. My thanks to him. Also see DuBois, pp. 40–41. Catto's poem: Silcox, "O. V. Catto," p. 58. scattered shots: Brown, p. 53. "pride of his race": Silcox, "O. V. Catto," p. 72. "spirit of mobocracy": DuBois, p. 40. "Oh, Mr. Catto": *Public Ledger*, October 14, 1871. Information on Kelly, courtesy Harry C. Silcox, June 17, 1983 phone conversation. two policemen: *Public Ledger*, October 14, 1871. "Kelly escaped": Conversation with Silcox. O. V. Catto's funeral: *Public Ledger*, October 17, 1871.

Blacks Denied Right to Ride on Streetcars
Streetcars: This account is drawn, unless otherwise noted, from Foner, "The Battle," Parts I and II. "I arraign Philadelphia": Ibid., Part II, p. 370. "one hundred little white boys": Ray S. Baker, *Following the Color Line*, Harper & Row, 1964 (orig. 1908), p. 124. race riot in July 1918: A detailed account is found in an unpublished paper by Marion Stepansky for a seminar in social history by M. Haller at Temple University. Paper is in Temple University Urban Archives. *The Records of the WPA Historical Survey*, Pennsylvania State Archives, Harrisburg, also contain a good account of the riot. "a white man wouldn't take the job": Firman Hopkins was interviewed on November 30, 1976. Quotes from tape in possession of author. " 'Jump!' ": Hopkins tape. Four Black men were beaten: *Public Ledger*, August 21, 1904. In 1915, a policeman . . . with a fractured skull: *Public Ledger*, October 18, 1915. "vast majority . . . unskilled capacities": Hershberg, *Philadelphia*, p. 409. "Nothing . . . innately inferior and undesirable": Curry, p. 241.

CHAPTER 8: *South Carolina Before the Civil War*
"Southern Road": Dudley Randall, "Southern Road," *Poem Counterpoem*, Broadside Press, 1966. Barbados: Peter H. Wood, *Black Majority*,

Knopf, 1974, p. xiv. Other sources on the Black entry into South Carolina are W. Robert Higgins, "The Geographical Origins of Negro Slaves in Colonial South Carolina," *South Atlantic Quarterly*, vol. 70, 1971, pp. 34–48; W. Robert Higgins, "Charleston: Terminus and Entrepot of the Colonial Slave Trade", in Martin L. Kilson and Robert I. Rotberg, eds., *The African Diaspora*, Harvard University Press, 1976, pp. 114–32. Also see *South Carolina: Resources and Population, Institutions and Industries*, State Board of Agriculture of South Carolina, 1883, p. 370. "infusion of white blood": See *South Carolina*, p. 373; on general race mixing in South Carolina, see Joel Williamson, *New People*, Basic, 1980. Charlotte Forten and the African singing: Billington, *Journal*; for her other feelings on South Carolina, see pp. 133, 183, 137, 195. "oh Graveyard": See Billington, *Journal*, pp. 128, 142–43. "way back to Africa . . . songs": N. S. Shaler, "An Ex-Southerner in South Carolina," *Atlantic Monthly*, vol. 36, 1870, pp. 53–61.

Slavery in South Carolina

"bare heads exposed": Willie Lee Rose, *A Documentary History of Slavery*, Oxford University Press, 1976, p. 304. "this generally carries of[f] great numbers": Ibid., pp. 55–56. "he put de Nigger dog": George P. Rawick, ed., *The American Slave: A Composite Autobiography*, vol. 2, Greenwood Publishing, 1972, pp. 191–92. slitting the nose: H. M. Henry, "The Police Control of the Slave in South Carolina," Ph.D. dissertation, Vanderbilt University, 1914, p. 119. "cat o' nine tail": Rawick, p. 21. run away to the woods: Ibid., p. 184. "De nigger trader": Henry, p. 56. One historian believes: George M. Fredrickson, " 'Masters and Mudsills': The Role of Race in the Planter Ideology of South Carolina," *South Atlantic Urban Studies*, vol. 2, 1978, p. 40.

Urban Slaves and Free Blacks

Bishop Henry M. Turner: Early life drawn from Simmons, pp. 805–19. "Some other free Black men . . . owned slaves: Joel Williamson, *After Slavery: The Negro in South Carolina During Reconstruction, 1861–1877*, University of North Carolina Press, 1965, pp. 370–71. Some . . . became slave owners: E. Horace Fitchett, "The Traditions of the Free Negro in Charleston, South Carolina," in Meier and Rudwick, pp. 206–16. betrayed . . . Denmark Vesey: Ibid., p. 212. "custodian": Ibid.

Religion

"very genuine fear": Susan Markey Fickling, "Slave Conversion in South Carolina," M.A. thesis, University of South Carolina, 1924, p. 1. Charles C. Pinckney: Ibid., pp. 12–15 is almost complete text of his speech. Great Awakening: Wood, pp. 133 ff and Fickling, pp. 12–14. "seats . . . for house servants": Fickling, p. 32. Charleston Episcopal church: Thomas D. Clark, ed., *South Carolina, the Grand Tour*, University of South Carolina Press, 1973, pp. 218, 257. Loss Goode: J. E. Hunter, *A Nickel and a Prayer*, Elli

Kane Publishing, 1940, p. 18. "knocked out the side of the church": Annie Hughes Mallard, "Religious Work of South Carolina Baptists Among the Slaves, 1781–1830," M.A. thesis, University of South Carolina, 1946, pp. 27–28. "that God was working for their deliverance": Broadside signed by Robert Grier, October 1, 1850, in South Carolina Library. taking masters to church: For this and other information see Mallard, pp. 23, 75, 79–80. Forty-three white Methodist missionaries: Fickling, p. 45. base for the African Methodist Episcopal Church: For information on this transformation see Leon F. Litwack, *Been in the Storm So Long*, Knopf, 1979, pp. 455–69. "could answer every question": Fickling, p. 46. On church membership: Ibid., pp. 49–50; and see *South Carolina: Resources and Population*, p. 524.

From Resistance to Freedom
armed insurrections: See Henry, pp. 121, 122, 149–151; and Wood, pp. 285–326.

CHAPTER 9: *The Reconstruction in South Carolina*
Reconstruction: A good summary of the Reconstruction is in Franklin, pp. 227–50. A longer treatment is James M. McPherson, *Ordeal by Fire: The Civil War and Reconstruction*, Knopf, 1982.

Reconstructing the Reputation of Reconstruction
"inexhaustible reservoir": Page Smith, *Trial by Fire: A People's History of the Civil War and Reconstruction*, vol. 5, McGraw-Hill, 1982, p. 990. "chasten white arrogance": Ibid., p. 989. "mixed legacy": George Brown Tindall, *South Carolina Negroes, 1877–1900*, Louisiana State University Press, 1966, p. 10. Summary of Reconstruction: Williamson, *After Slavery*; Alrutheus Ambush Taylor, *The Negro in South Carolina During Reconstruction*, Association for the Study of Negro Life and History, 1924; Francis Butler Simkins and Robert Hilliard Woody, *South Carolina During the Reconstruction*, University of North Carolina Press, 1932. Jonathan C. Gibbs: See Gibbs, pp. 11–12. Pliny Locke: Information on these men and women unless otherwise noted from Jackson-Coppin; Gerry Majors, *Black Society*, Johnson Publishing, 1976; "Pencil Pusher," *Philadelphia Tribune*, January 31, 1914; Robert Morris, "Reading, Riting and Reconstruction: Freedmen's Education in the South, 1865–1870," Ph.D. dissertation, University of Chicago, 1976; diverse communications in Gardiner and Jacob C. White, Jr., Collections. Data on the Philadelphians in South Carolina also comes from the indispensable books of Lawrence C. Bryant, *Negro Senators and Representatives in the South Carolina Legislature, 1868–1902*, 1968; *Negro Legislators in South Carolina, 1868–1902*, self-published, 1967; *South Carolina Negro Legislators*, 1970; and *Bills and Resolutions Proposed by Negro Legislators in South Carolina*, 1967, all published by Lawrence C. Bryant; and Thomas Holt, *Black Over White: Negro Political Leadership in South*

Carolina During Reconstruction, University of Illinois Press, 1977. Bryant was of great assistance in tracing some of the movements of the Philadelphians. John Wesley Cromwell: Morris, pp. 145–46. "secret order affiliation": "Pencil Pusher," *Philadelphia Tribune,* January 31, 1914. Rainey, Smalls, and Elliot: Summaries of the lives of these three legislators can be found in the excellent *Dictionary of American Negro Biography,* ed. Rayford W. Logan and Michael R. Winston, Norton, 1982. My account of these men's lives also draws on Peggy Lamson, *The Glorious Failure: Black Congressman Robert Brown Elliot and the Reconstruction in South Carolina,* Norton, 1973, and on Simmons. just as soon shoot: Williamson, *After Slavery,* p. 256. He adds that Blacks committed their share of violence too. cut the Black man: Litwack, p. 278. "white police chief . . . absolved": Ibid., p. 290. Information on militia units: Allen W. Trelease, *White Terror, the Ku Klux Klan Conspiracy and Southern Reconstruction,* Harper & Row, 1971; and particularly Otis A. Singletary, *Negro Militia and Reconstruction,* University of Texas, 1957.

Some Black Military Leaders

The Black captains: John S. Reynolds, *Reconstruction in South Carolina, 1865–1877,* State Company, 1905, pp. 138, 145. white marshall . . . attempted to arrest: Ibid., p. 183. Klan . . . "run their horses": *The Ku Klux Klan Conspiracy: Testimony Taken by the Joint Select Committee to Inquire into the Condition of Affairs in the Late Insurrectionary States,* vols. 1–4, Government Printing Office, pp. 1580–94, is an account by Black eyewitnesses. See particularly p. 1582, which describes how the Klan left so fast that they lost the sheets and flour bags that covered their horses' heads; also see pp. 1590–91. "bold and aggressive": Reynolds, p. 189. "other captains . . . cowards": *Ku Klux Klan Trials at Columbia, South Carolina, U.S. Circuit Court, November term, 1871,* Negro Universities Press, p. 337. "have a whole plantation": Ibid., p. 339. "old field and fight": Ibid., p. 351. "hung him to a tree": Reynolds, p. 190. "had they found a leader": Trelease, pp. 367–68. Tennant and "large bodies of rifle companies": Julian L. Mims, "Radical Reconstruction in Edgefield County," M.A. thesis, University of South Carolina, 1969, p. 62. Also see Reynolds, p. 272, for account of this action. "one hand full of cartridges": Reynolds, p. 272. disband both forces: Letter from Paris Simkins to Governor Moses, September 21, 1874, as quoted in Mims, p. 62. Captain Tennant . . . took his guns back: Reynolds, pp. 301–02. one of Tennant's lieutenants: *Greenville Enterprise,* May 12, 1875. "where the ambush took place": Reynolds, p. 380. They may also have been from a Captain Bullock's company. the Hamburg riot: Reynolds, p. 344 ff; Mims, *passim;* Williamson, *After Slavery,* p. 267. General Butler said: Reynolds, p. 346. shot dead while talking: Williamson, *After Slavery,* p. 269. "meanest characters": Matilda A. Evans, *Martha Schofield, Pioneer Negro Educator,* p. 45, a remarkable account of the riot. "most prominent": Williamson,

After Slavery, p. 264. guards could shoot them: Ibid., p. 269. Evans says they fired over the men's heads, p. 47.

The End of the Armed Conflict

Captain Simon Coker: Reynolds, p. 377. Coker . . . was captured: Ibid., pp. 377–78; Evans, pp. 57–59. unsympathetic Southern writer: William Arthur Sheppard, *Red Shirts Remembered,* Ruralist Press, 1940, p. 144. "Coker . . . passed from earth": As reported in Evans, pp. 57–58. "resisted . . . armed Negroes": Reynolds, p. 392. Captain Daniels: Hampton M. Jarrell, *Wade Hampton and the Negro,* University of South Carolina Press, 1950, pp. 69–70. "Hamburg . . . reversed": Williamson, *After Slavery,* p. 272. Wade Hampton cried: Ibid. Black policemen: Reynolds, p. 391. Church expulsion and women: Singletary, p. 25; Reynolds, p. 374. "Scores of newspapers": Foner, *Voice,* pp. 445–47. Delany: Holt, p. 223. Honky-Dory Clubs: WPA Writers Project, *South Carolina: A Guide to the Palmetto State,* Oxford University Press, 1941, p. 41; also see Simkins and Woody, pp. 525–26.

CHAPTER 10: *The Black Church in South Carolina*

Morris Brown had planted the seed: *Minutes of the Twelfth Session of the South Carolina Annual Conference of the A.M.E. Church Held at Charleston, South Carolina from February 1 to February 10, 1876,* Walker, Evans, and Cogswell, 1876. Remarks of Reverend A. T. Carr, p. 9. A.M.E. membership: A good source on the early days of the church is Nancy Vance Ashmore, "The Development of the A.M.E. Church in South Carolina, 1865–1965," M.A. thesis, University of South Carolina, 1969, particularly the first pages, and p. 67. Ministers served . . . in legislature: See Bryant, *Glorious Success,* p. 39. There were also nine Baptist ministers, one Presbyterian, one C.M.E., and three M.E.'s. "solid phalanx": Williamson, *After Slavery,* p. 369.

The A.M.E. Church's Many Tasks

"or even church edifices": *Twelfth Session,* p. 22. "bedrock of knowledge": Ibid., pp. 6–7. qualified teachers: Ibid., p. 23. "pure air": *Minutes of the Tenth Session of the South Carolina Annual Conference of the A.M.E. Church Held at Newberry, South Carolina from February 6 to February 16, 1874,* Republican Printing Co., 1874, p. 27. Wilberforce University: *Minutes of the Seventh Session of the South Carolina Annual Conference of the A.M.E. Church Held in Bethel A.M.E. Church, Columbia, South Carolina from January 28, 1871 to February 6, 1871,* John W. Denny, 1871, p. 7. Payne Institute: Ibid., p. 32. "best orchards": *Tenth Session,* p. 28. "deeds": *Seventh Session,* p. 29.

Some Preachers Who Would Die for Their Faith

"nothing intelligible": ed. Bishop W. Arnett, *Proceedings of the Quarto-Centennial Conference of the African M.E. Church of South Carolina at*

Charleston, South Carolina, May 15, 16, 17, 1889, Adline Printing House, 1890, pp. 110, 113. "purpose of organizing the African Methodist Church": Ibid. Reverend James J. Baker: *Minutes of the First, Second, and Third Sessions of the Abbeville Singing Convention of the A.M.E. Church,* Hugh Wilson, 1889. This includes Joseph I. William, "A Sketch of the Life and Work of Reverend James T. Baker with Some Facts of the Early History of the A.M.E. Church in South Carolina," pp. 11–16. "will not let you die": Ibid., p. 16. "old Greenwood": Ibid., p. 13. "new God and a new Bible": Ibid., p. 14. "church into a political club": Simkins and Woody, p. 393. "but God was with us": William, "Life of Baker," p. 14. Bishop Turner . . . camp meetings: Ibid., pp. 14–15. Colored Alliance: The speaker was A. L. Ford. *Abbeville Singing Convention,* p. 5; Thomas W. Kremm and Diane Neal, "Challenges to Subordination: Organized Black Agricultural Protest in South Carolina, 1886–1895," *South Atlantic Quarterly,* vol. 77, no. 1, 1978, p. 106. "no other one to send": *Quarto-Centennial Conference,* Remarks of Weston, p. 110. "poor wayfaring men": Ibid., also see p. 71. "C.M.E. Church with 1,600 members": Ibid., p. 71. "suffered from the suspicions": Tindall, p. 192. "Amid all the danger": *Quarto-Centennial Conference,* Remarks of R. C. Irvin from Cokesbury, p. 115. "we made up our church": Ibid. Wade Perrin . . . memorialized: *Seventh Session,* p. 33. "God give us strength": *Quarto-Centennial Conference,* pp. 116–17. "redheaded African": Ibid., Remarks of Reverend Silas H. Jefferson, p. 112. "Weston signed the certificates": Ibid., p. 115. Membership in Abbeville: *Tenth Session,* Appendix. Tradition of Baptist local autonomy: Simkins and Woody, pp. 388–89. Reverend Brawley: Simmons, pp. 908–12; Tindall, p. 188. Organization of Baptists: Tindall, p. 189. Alexander Bettis: Ibid., p. 189. closeness of the ties: Holt makes a contrary argument.

Chapter 11: *Black Education in South Carolina*

"reduced literacy": Williamson, *After Slavery,* p. 238.

Educating the Freedmen

"rural Blue Ridge South Carolina": Lewis K. McMillan, *Negro Higher Education in the State of South Carolina,* Private printing, 1952. "unlettered Negro Baptists": Ibid., p. 31. "humble" place: Ibid., p. 29. Hancock: Raymond Gavins, "Gordon B. Hancock: A Black Profile from the New South," *Journal of Negro History,* vol. 59, 1974, pp. 202–28. "word came that he would be lynched": Ibid., pp. 212–13. "forsaken poverty-stricken": Mc-Millan, p. 38. "stringy short-leaf pine saplings": Ibid., p. 36. "could not write his name": Ibid. "Pleasant Grove Church": Ibid., p. 37. "Willow Swamp, Bushy Pond, and Allen Chapel": Ibid., see account of founding, pp. 65–72. "no fun in doing easy things": Elizabeth Evelyn Wright to Booker T. Washington, June 6, 1898 in Louis R. Harlan, ed., *Booker T. Washington Papers,* vol. 4, 1895–1898, University of Illinois Press, 1975, p. 433. Benedict College: McMillan, p. 117. "stately black derby": Ibid., pp. 117–18. "set up their State Convention": Ibid., p. 118. "hammer and saw": Ibid., p. 136. "mass adult education": Ibid., p. 134. "tens of thousands": Ibid., p. 135. Nelson Cornelius Nix: A. B. Caldwell, *History of the American Negro,* A. B. Caldwell Publishing, 1919, pp. 186–87. Howard High: McMillan, p. 119. ten dollars on each white child: *Negro Education: A Study of the Private and Higher Schools for Colored People in the United States,* vol. 2, Government Printing Office, 1917, pp. 471, 473. "I am opposed": Gov. Cole L. Blease, inauguration speech of January 11, 1911, in McMillan, pp. 258–59.

Education in Abbeville County

Reverend Stark's description: McMillan, p. 11. "Greenwood, and Due West": Paul Knox, "The Development of Education in Abbeville County, South Carolina," M.A. thesis, University of South Carolina, 1929, p. 36. Brewer Academy: American Missionary Association Manuscripts, South Carolina, Roll 5, H7696–H8400, Amistad Research Center, Dillard University, New Orleans, Louisiana (hereafter AMA). Communication to Mr. E. M. Cravath from Trustees of School District no. 2, Greenwood, South Carolina, July 23, 1872. Black community found "gratifying": Ibid., G. W. Rouse School Trustees to Cravath, October 5, 1872; J. D. Backenstose to Cravath, November 13, 1872. School description and worry over students: Ibid., Backenstose; Backenstose to Cravath, November 28, 1872; Backenstose to Cravath, December 13, 1872. "a dollar a month": Ibid., Backenstose to Cravath, December 6, 1872. "make money out of the people": Ibid., Backenstose to Cravath, January 16, 1873, and December 19, 1872, and November 28, 1872. "obliged to return to their homes": Ibid., Backenstose to Cravath, April 16, 1873. "trifling compensation": Ibid., Backenstose to M. E. Strickby, June 13, 1876. In 1916, the Academy: *Negro Education,* p. 493. Ferguson Academy: McMillan, pp. 56–59; Tindall, pp. 225–26; *Negro Education,* p. 522. Reverend Williams . . . "Afro-American" school: *Negro Education,* p. 522. "husband's work might bear fruit": McMillan, p. 57. Reverend Thomas A. Amos and "unpardonable sin.": Ibid., pp. 57–59. Also see Inez M. Parker, *The Rise and Decline of the Program of Education for Black Presbyterians of the United Presbyterian Church, U.S.A., 1865–1970,* Trinity University Press, 1977, pp. 168–69. "land of my most enraged enemies": W.O.B. Hoitt, May 12, 1869, to Governor Scott, Governor's Papers, South Carolina Archives (hereafter G.P.). Six thousand Blacks: These and other statistics from Knox, p. 5. Figures on Abbeville from Ibid., pp. 84, 87, 88, 93, 94, 95. Expenditures in Greenwood County from *Negro Education,* p. 493.

CHAPTER 12: *The Oppression in Abbeville County, Part One*

"left for the city": Benjamin Mays, *Born to Rebel,* Scribner's, 1971, p. 25.

Notes

Abbeville County

vast brakes of cane: Sources on early days in the county are Robert D. Bass, *Ninety-Six: The Struggle for the South Carolina Back Country*, Sandlapper Store, 1978; Margaret Watson, *Greenwood County Sketches*, Attic Press, 1970; H. T. Cook, *The Hard Labor Section*, Attic Press, 1979 (orig. 1923). "to support two families": Bass, p. 22. White Hall: Watson, p. 46. Hard Labor Creek: Cook, p. 27. "kind, industrious people": Ibid. Cherokee nation: Bass has a good description of this. Long Cane battle: Watson, p. 174; Cook, pp. 6, 38. Destruction of Cherokee: Cook, p. 19. "Strum": Watson, p. 45; Cook, p. 11. "Of whom 11 were slaves": Watson, p. 87. in one graveyard: Ibid., p. 77. William P. Dorn: See Cook, pp. 57–59 for these descriptions. "14 rooms": See Watson, pp. 153, 170, 189, 194, 203, 271, 284, 290, and *passim* for specific information on the slaveholders. "twenty-two fireplaces": Ibid., p. 344. department stores in Greenwood: Ibid., p. 379. "Virgil, Cicero and Horace": *South Carolina: A Guide to the Palmetto State*, p. 457. All five were killed: Watson, p. 380. Thirteen thousand casualties: Simkins and Woody, pp. 10–11. "Jamaican Revolution": *Abbeville Press*, January 5 and March 16, 1866. "alien whites and native blacks": Simkins and Woody, p. 112. Union Leagues . . . special targets: Simkins and Woody, p. 77. For gerrymandering and filling of positions see Williamson, *After Slavery*, pp. 343–47. "to ratify the new constitution": Williamson, *After Slavery*, p. 343.

The Terror Begins

federal army officer reported: *Military Records, Office of Army Continental Command; Record Group 98, 393, 1867—Letters Received*, September 30, 1868, Report of W. F. DeKnight, p. 273. report of October 27, 1868: Ibid., pp. 554, 555. Aiken's background: Claudio Hornby Pritchard, Jr., *Colonel D. Wyatt Aiken, 1828–1887*, Private printing, 1970, p. 3. "small boy with a hoe": Ibid., pp. 22–23. Aiken's wealth: Ibid., p. 21. well-treated exslaves: Ibid., pp. 42, 45. "to oppress" the whites: Ibid., p. 49. His biographer specifically denies that he counseled violence. A state investigating committee . . . charged Aiken: *Reports and Resolutions, South Carolina, 1869–1870, Report on the Evidence Taken by the Committee of Investigation of the Third Congressional District Under Authority of the General Assembly of South Carolina* (hereafter *RRSC*), p. 621. "not leave one on the face of the earth": Ibid., Testimony of Henry Nash, p. 1094. Nash is testifying before Robert Smalls, who had taken over the Confederate gunboat.

The Assassination of a Black Leader

directly implicated in the murder of B. F. Randolph: Ibid., p. 621. The committee concluded that "D. Wyatt Aiken, no doubt, laid the plan to kill him." Also see Williamson, *After Slavery*, pp. 205–06. "shall live together or not": *Proceedings*, Constitutional Convention of South Carolina, March

272

5, 1868, vol. I, Arno Press, 1968, p. 747. "piece of land, four foot by six": *RRSC*, p. 625. For a summary of the evidence against Aiken, see p. 621. at one train station Aiken accosted Randolph: Aiken's biographer, a relative, says of this encounter that "A spirited argument ensued between the Congressman [sic] and the Colonel with the former being invited to withdraw from the campaign. . . . Furthermore D. Wyatt advised him that it would not be safe to repeat such remarks in Abbeville County lest his life be endangered." Pritchard, p. 50. Aiken also is reported to have called Randolph a "damned black son-of-a-bitch." The "son-of-a-bitch" comment is from the eyewitness account of Hutson A. Lomax, a member of the state legislature and head of the Union League in Abbeville. Randolph . . . proud of Black blood: *RRSC*, p. 1091. Tolbert description "leader of a band": From letters to Scott from A. Burton, November 11, 1868 in G.P. would be recognized as "patriots": J. A. Leland to Scott, January 5, 1869, in G.P. Joshua Logan and John West Talbert gave themselves up and made this confession as part of a deal to turn state's evidence against William K. Tolbert. They then escaped and took off for Texas. William K. Tolbert was caught, attempted to escape, and was finally shot and killed on December 23, 1869. This information in Communication to Scott, December 23, 1869, in G.P. This is testimony of William K. Tolbert, one of the confessed murderers of Randolph. He admits to committing the murder and explains in detail how he and two others did it. See *42nd Congress 2nd Session, Report no. 41, Part 3, Testimony Taken by the Joint Select Committee to Inquire into the Condition of Affairs in the Late Insurrectionary States, South Carolina* (hereafter *JSC*), Government Printing Office, 1872, Appendix no. 7. Testimony of William K. Tolbert, pp. 1256–59. On Hodges' role and remaining details of the murder day: *JSC*, Appendix, p. 1258, testimony of Tolbert; *RRSC*, Testimony of Aaron Mitchell, p. 1101. The questioner was J. J. Wright of Pennsylvania. For Hodges' remark about "blood flowing," see *RRSC*, p. 109. For the before-the-night planning, see remarks of Henry Nash, Ibid., pp. 1091–93; Mitchell's remark on p. 1101; testimony on p. 1090 corroborates Mitchell's story. For the "cut-him up" remarks, see Tolbert, *JSC*, p. 1259.

Guns at Polling Stations
KKK, led by Boozer: Tolbert identified J. G. Boozer, Creswell Fletcher, Hodges, Langdon Conners, as members of the KKK. He specifically denied knowing D. Wyatt Aiken. See *JSC*, p. 1260. From the testimony of the Abbeville coroner, there were "about twenty or more violent murders in that county to his certain knowledge," *RRSC*, p. 620. Aiken was arrested on November 9 as an accessory before the fact in the Randolph murder. He was released on $5,000 bail paid by Wade Hampton, the future governor of the state. The case was never brought to trial; Pritchard, p. 51. "took him off into Georgia": *Military Records*, July 2, 1868 complaint in *Abbeville*

Complaints. rumored to be a Republican: *Abbeville Complaints,* 1868. coffin-shaped paper: Ibid. "Briscoe and Curtis": Griffin to Scott, January 22, 1869 in G.P. "very disloyal": Same Military Records Group, but *Press Copies of Letters Sent,* vol. 98, Hart to Walker; April 11, 1868, p. 356. "five times with a strap": See testimony of Joshua Wardlaw, *RRSC,* p. 1057. colored man . . . as a poll watcher: *RRSC,* pp. 1217, 1219. " 'all men are born free and equal' ": From *Mercury,* January 20, 1868, as quoted in Carl M. Logue, "Racist Reporting During Reconstruction," *Journal of Black Studies,* vol. 9, no. 3, March 1979, pp. 335–49. novelist Ralph Ellison: Petition Union League of Abbeville to Scott, April 20, 1870, in G.P. "kill them, shoot them": See Tolbert's testimony in *JSC,* p. 1260. Dr. Moses Taggart: See *RRSC,* pp. 622, 1063, 1098–99, 1180. For the full military report on the election violence, see DeKnight to Stone, November 6, 1868, in G.P. It also contains the election results. Biographical information on Dr. Taggart is from Watson. "system of intimidation": *RRSC,* p. 622. "in fear and trembling": DeKnight to Stone, November 6, 1868, in G.P. At Greenwood itself: Ibid. "ruinous affect": Guffin to Scott, April 5, 1869, in G.P. "strong disposition": Military Records Group, but DeKnight to Neide, July 31, 1868, *Press Copies of Letters Sent,* vol. 99, South Carolina. "use all their exertions": Hollinshead to Scott, July 17 and 22, 1869, in G.P. in a local bank: Citizens to Scott (James A. Norwood, the head of the citizens), August 12, 1869, in G.P. woman by her breasts: *JSC,* pp. 295, 296. "three times in the back": *South Carolina in 1876,* Abbeville County, Senate Committee, 2nd Session, 44th Congress, p. 422. The father of one of the murderers had been elected to the state legislature. Everidge Cain: Bryant, *Negro Senators and Representatives,* p. 2.

Bravery Amid the Terror

"get out of the way": *South Carolina in 1876,* Testimony of Vance, pp. 417–23, is source of all information here. "bullets . . . in the door": Ibid. "walked every bit": Lewis Waller's testimony in Ibid., pp. 423–26. A. M. Heard: William H. Heard, *From Slavery to the Bishopric in the A.M.E. Church,* Arno Press, 1969; and *South Carolina in 1876* is source of all information in this section. See especially Heard's testimony in that volume, pp. 322, 327–39, which recounts at great length these events. influenced by Bishop Turner: Heard, pp. 89–90. "even if they kill me": *South Carolina in 1876,* pp. 332, 433. "ran up and surrounded me": Ibid., Testimony of Lewis Clay, p. 432; Heard, Ibid., p. 329; for the "picking up" of Heard, see testimony of R. A. Dunlap, Ibid., p. 413. "but they refused me": Heard, p. 332. "republican from principle": Ibid., p. 339. "not to scratch their ticket": *South Carolina in 1876,* pp. 422, 423. their political opinions: Ibid., p. 520. Richard Greener: Dorothy Sterling, ed., *The Trouble They Seen: Black People Tell the Story of Reconstruction,* Doubleday, 1976, p. 79. "Big Tuesday": Rachel Hemphill Minshall, *WPA Papers, Abbeville Historical Papers,* South Carolina Writers Project, Archives Division, pp. 42–43.

CHAPTER 13: *The Oppression in Abbeville County, Part Two*

Patrick Bradley: Biographical information in Cook, p. 35; Watson, pp. 160–61. General M. C. Butler: Cook, p. 35.

Stockade No. 5

"stay in the house if you didn't have a job": Hughsey Childs tapes. Childs was interviewed on April 2, July 14, 27, August 3, 11, 18, 24, September 8, and December 1, 1977. All tapes in possession of author. "stockade no. 5": Best general account of this incident in Tindall, pp. 268–72. Where I have used other sources, they are specified. planning a revolt: *Reports and Resolutions,* South Carolina, 1879–1880, Report of Superintendent Lipscomb, September 2, 1879. "caused by the vermin": Ibid., Report of Surgeon Trezevant, August 30, 1879. "diseased impressions": *Reports and Resolutions,* p. 925. packed into a room: Ibid. "so badly burned" and other descriptions: Ibid., pp. 910, 931, 936. J. J. Cahill: Ibid., p. 965. "waste places of our country": Ibid., p. 941. "careless and indifferent": Ibid., pp. 909, 910. "carefully kept from me": Ibid., p. 942. "to attack the guard": Ibid., pp. 898–99. never really ended: Albert D. Oliphant, *The Evolution of the Penal System of South Carolina from 1866 to 1916,* 1916; also see Daniel A. Novack, *The Wheel of Servitude: Black Forced Labor After Slavery,* University Press of Kentucky, 1978. "lifers could be put to work": Tindall has a good discussion of this, pp. 272–76; also see Oliphant, pp. 8–12.

A Race War Over the Ballot

Phoenix riot: The basic sources on the Phoenix riot are Tom Henderson Wells, "The Phoenix Election Riot," *Phylon,* Spring, 1970, pp. 58–69; James A. Hoyt, "The Phoenix Riot," 1938; Bruce Lee Kleinschmidt, "The Phoenix Riot," *Furman Review,* vol. 5, no. 1, Spring, 1974; Tindall, pp. 256–58; Mays, pp. 328–35. In addition, I have used the *Greenwood Index, Abbeville Medium, Columbia State,* and *Greenville News.* Black people in Philadelphia, in particular Hughsey Childs, provided me with much information with which to round out the events. Other sources are indicated. Watson's *Greenwood County Sketches* was invaluable for pinpointing the white participants and their relationships to each other. "go back and shoot the white folk": *Greenwood Index,* December 1, 1898, has all the above comments. They were made at the so-called inquest by Dr. J. L. Ward, who apparently was taking the testimony of one London McKinney, who had been with the guerrillas. It has the ring of truth, since they did ambush the whites that night. For "our women stood," see the *Greenwood Index,* November 24, 1898. Also see *Columbia State,* November 11, 1898. McKinney had a rope around his neck during this "inquest" and was wounded from the action at Phoenix. I am unable to tell whether this is the same "Wade Hampton McKinney" listed as among the dead. "every Republican shall leave the land": Wells, p. 62. "closed behind the . . . buggy": Ibid., p. 63.

"underground militia": Ibid.; also *Greenwood Index*, November 18, 1898, for mention of the Winchesters. "what they had, they shot": All reports state that the ambush took place. The report of the barbed wire is from Hughsey Childs; it may have been tangled brush. train to Columbia: Wells, p. 66; Hoyt, p. 9. "killed him for vengeance": Childs tapes.

Some Atrocities

anybody they could get: Hoyt, pp. 8, 9; also *Columbia State*, November 9, 1898, which claims that a posse of 100 armed whites decided not to attack the armed band of Blacks at the Tolberts. that rainy Wednesday and Thursday: The men, as best I can ascertain, were Wade Hampton, Wade Hampton McKinney, Charlie White, Robert Daniel, Lum (Lunford) Jackson, Jessie Williams, Drayton Watts, George Logan, Essex Harrison, Ben Collins, Jeff Darling, and Gaines Williams. "who were immediately lynched": See *Columbia State*, November 10, 1898; *Greenwood Index*, November 10, 1898. "one hundred and fifty shots": *Greenwood Index*, November 10, 1898. Essex Harrison: Childs tapes. Also see *Greenwood Index*, November 17, 1898, which condemned ". . . the unnecessarily brutal scene at Reheboth" but then says, "It is not fair to call the best part of our people savages because there were some fools in the crowd." "pile of already dead Negroes": *Columbia State*, November 11, 1898; Hoyt, pp. 11–12. "almost endangered each other": Hoyt, p. 11. "That man could pray better": Childs tapes. "seen to fall and crawl off": *Greenwood Index*, November 10, 1898. Eliza Goode: Hoyt, p. 12; *Greenwood Index*, November 17, 1898. Mays's earliest memory: Mays, p. 1, "Come fifty or sixty": Childs tapes. "well-known and highly respected": *Greenwood Index*, December 8, 1898. Abbeville whites . . . violent: Watson is full of such violence. For general discussion of white Southerners and violence, see John Hope Franklin, *The Militant South, 1800–1861*, Harvard University Press, 1956; the more recent Bertram Wyatt-Brown, *Southern Honor: Ethics and Behavior in the Old South*, Oxford University Press, 1983; the fine work by James Oakes, *The Ruling Race: A History of American Slaveholders*, Knopf, 1982; and W. J. Cash's classic, *The Mind of the South*, Knopf, 1960 (orig. 1941).

The White Terror

"upper bracket because they rented": Childs tapes. "shiftless white trash": Wells, p. 59; *Greenwood Index*, January 12, 1899. "Negroes in the other end": *Greenwood Index*, January 12, 1899. "rise up and put a stop": *Greenwood Index*, November 17, 1898; May 4, 1899; March 2, 1899. "I do not believe in disenfranchising": *Greenwood Index*, May 4, 1899. "it is an unwritten law": *Greenwood Index*, November 17, 1898. White reactions: *Greenwood Index*, March 12, 1899; November 17, 1898. white bands roamed: *Greenwood Index*, December 22, 1898; January 5, 1899; January 12, 1899; February 1, 1899. Lynchings: Jack Simpson Mullins, "Lynching in South

Carolina, 1900–1914," M.A. thesis, University of South Carolina, 1961, pp. 128, 129, 132, 143–45. ears, fingers: Mullins, p. 120, p. 45.

Another Black Leader Is Lynched

Anthony Crawford: Sources are untitled piece by Roy Nash, *The Independent*, vol. 18, 1916, pp. 456–62; biographical sketch of Walter C. Crawford, the son of Andrew Crawford in Caldwell, pp. 319–21; sketch of Walter C. Crawford in Wright, *Encyclopedia of African Methodism*, 1947, p. 574. For description of land, see Nash, p. 458. Black Masons: Elizabeth Clark, "History of Reverend William H. Clark," obituary, kindly given to this writer by Ruby Boyd of Philadelphia. "kicked him": Nash, p. 456.

There Is a Balm in Gilead

"cartridges": Ibid., p. 458. Family must vacate: Ibid., pp. 458–60. Alfred Ellison: *American Writers*, Supplement II, Part I, Scribner's Sons, 1981, p. 222. have to have a lynching: Nash, p. 460. element of jealousy: Ibid. Obituary: Clark, obituary. Walter Crawford: Caldwell, p. 319–21; Wright, *Encyclopedia*, p. 574.

The Chain Gang

2,660 Blacks: Sarah Hamnet Johnson, "The Negro Offender in South Carolina," M.A. thesis, University of South Carolina, 1926, particularly pp. 4–5, 27; quote is from Childs tapes. Also see mention of chain gang in *Greenwood Index*, December 22, 1898. "White men used physical force": Mays, p. 28. sisters to Sunday school: Childs tapes. "dangerous to argue": Mays, p. 23. "They did not mention": Ibid., p. 17. Migration to Mississippi: *Greenwood Index*, December 22, 1898.

CHAPTER 14: *On the Eve of the Migration*

"loved the farm": Mays, p. 4. "Oh, . . . good times": Rosa Moragne was interviewed on June 16, 1977. Tapes in possession of author. "fried the fish": Childs tapes.

Farming Was Their Livelihood

Both races . . . one means: Discussion of economics primarily drawn from Simkins and Woody, pp. 224–66, and Tindall, pp. 92–53. "little pieces of ground": Ibid., p. 229.

Life Centered About the Churches

"Old Mount Zion": Mays, p. 13. "prayed you through": Moragne tapes. "revival": Childs and Moragne tapes. Methodists: Childs tapes. James Foster Marshall: Caldwell, p. 692. "the best preacher": Mays, pp. 14–15. Promised Land: There is a detailed description of this community in Beth Bethel,

Promised Land, Temple University Press, 1981. Bethel was kind enough to share her page proofs with me prior to publication of her book.

Social Status in the County
"didn't like no dark persons": Childs tapes. Church segregation: Childs tapes. Cohesiveness: Childs and Hatcher tapes. W. "Jip" Hatcher was interviewed on June 30 and July 20, 1977. Tapes in possession of author.

CHAPTER 15: *Going to the City*
How They Moved to Philadelphia
"They come up in groups": Childs tapes. George Bailey, Sr.: From his obituary, 1904–76. George Bailey was buried at Bright Hope Baptist Church, March 26, 1976. Obituary courtesy of Jip Hatcher.

A Greenwood Church Becomes Many Philadelphia Churches
"Let's name a church": Account after Childs tapes and Hatcher tapes.

Greenwood's People Enter Other Churches
letters of transmittal: Courtesy of Historical Commission of Mother Bethel A.M.E. Church. One of the trustees of Weston Chapel A.M.E. was A. J. Pool, who had testified about the shootings during the election of 1876. Reverend Williams poem: From Mother Bethel's archives. "Prophet Cherry": From Childs tapes; and his remarks about "worse than hell" and " 'Who in hell is this?' " are from Arthur Huff Fauset's *Black Gods of the Metropolis,* University of Pennsylvania, pp. 33 ff. Volume courtesy of Arthur Huff Fauset.

Strains of City Life
Farmer into trashman and minister and alcohol: Childs tapes. "policeman in this bar": Hatcher tapes.

Adjusting to City Life
"wrong conception of it": Hatcher tapes. "throw dishwater": Childs tapes.

CHAPTER 16: *The Great Migration*
By 1910 . . . 2.4 percent: *Negro Population in the United States, 1790–1915,* Arno Press, 1968, p. 91.

The Migration's Impact on Philadelphia
nearly two-thirds of them: Ibid., pp. 74, 77, 84, 93. rise from six percent: Housing Association of Delaware Valley, *Statistics, 1870–1961,* in Temple University Urban Archives (hereafter *HADV* and TUUA). School registra-

tion statistics: Study of 486 pupils in sixth grade of separate schools in Philadelphia, June 1933, Urban League Papers, TUUA. Doughtery: Marquette to Gilman, January 27, 1917, in *HADV*. Midvale Steel Plant: Sadie Tanner Mossell, "The Standard of Living Among One Hundred Negro Migrant Families in Philadelphia," Ph.D. dissertation, reprinted in *Annals of Academy of Science and Political Science*, November 1926, p. 6. Copy in TUUA. Anderson's Employment Agency: *Public Ledger*, July 14, 1923. hired to break strikes: Cf. the *Philadelphia Tribune*, June 13, 1917; Ira De A. Reid, "Negro Membership in American Labor Unions," National Urban League, 1930, pp. 165–69 especially; and Florette Henri, *Black Migration*, Doubleday, 1975, pp. 150–55. 186,000 unskilled laborers: *Public Ledger*, August 2, 1918. "Racial violence . . . the Ku Klux Klan": Daniel M. Johnson, Ray R. Campbell, *Black Migration in America*, Duke University Press, 1981, p. 84. See page 85 for comment on lynching, and the assertion almost as many people left the South because of mistreatment by police as because of lynching. Henri, pp. 57–59, ultimately seems to agree that the oppression was the overriding cause of the migration. Crawford murder . . . cause: Emmet J. Scott, *Negro Migration During the War*, Arno Press, 1969, p. 47. Among the refugees: Letter of Thomas E. Miller to *Public Ledger*, June 23, 1923. Miller was an ex-congressman from South Carolina. "steady, reliable": William D. Fuller, "The Negro Migrant in Philadelphia," June 1, 1924. This 100-page study is an indispensable starting point for study of the migration. Copy in *HADV*. these studies: *Negro Migrant Study*, Papers, Report of July 1, 1923. Copy is TUUA.

Reaction to the Migration

asked his counterparts for information: A series of communications for June 1917 is in the *HADV*. City Club: See *Public Ledger*, November 28, 1925. Forrester Washington, *Philadelphia Tribune*, February 3, 1917. Washington's remarks were made at a conference in New York and referred to the migration to Detroit, where he was then the head of the Urban League. Sadie Pace Alexander: Mossell, p. 9. A.M.E. journal: *Christian Recorder*, May 31, 1917.

CHAPTER 17: *North Meets South*

Class and Color

"petty and vicious": Ralph Jones was interviewed on March 26, April 13, May 31, June 15, and July 29, 1977. Tapes in possession of author. "one of the most vicious": Jack Saunders was interviewed in Philadelphia on May 20, 1975. Tape in possession of author. "social clubs were crushing": Jones tapes. Eastern Shore: Reverend Frank Mitchell, Jr., was interviewed on May 24 and May 27, 1974. Tapes in possession of author. "Yellow Daffodils": Mabel Brady was interviewed in Philadelphia on December 18, 1976; February 22 and March 26, 1977. Tapes in possession of author. Arthur Huff

Fauset was interviewed on April 10, June 13, June 27, and August 8, 1977. Tapes in possession of author. Description of Old Philadelphia: "The Negro in Philadelphia," *Records of the WPA Historical Survey*. Originals in Pennsylvania State Archives, Harrisburg (hereafter *WPA-Philadelphia*). This uncompleted work is unpaginated in many sections. The late William Duckrey brought the existence of this rich archive to my attention. A.M.E. bishops: Charles Fred White, *Who's Who in Philadelphia*, A.M.E. Book Concern, 1912, pp. 131–41.

Black Leadership in Philadelphia
"so hard has been the lives": DuBois, pp. 317–18, 392–93. Marian Anderson: *Public Ledger*, June 9, 1926; March 8, 1933; July 23, 1933.

Politics in Modern Black Philadelphia
Citizens Republican Club: Good description in *WPA-Philadelphia* of its founding. This account, unless otherwise noted, is taken from that source. "vituperative attacks": John Hadley Strange, "Blacks and Philadelphia Politics: 1963–1966," in Ershkowitz and Zikmund, pp. 109–45, p. 111. "Negro workers . . . $17,000": Eugene A. Hatfield, "The Impact of the New Deal on Black Politics in Pennsylvania, 1928–1936," Ph.D. dissertation, University of North Carolina, 1979, p. 54. in 1963 . . . reapportionment: Strange, p. 111.

Impact of the Migration
"from eight percent . . . to twenty-three percent: Vincent P. Franklin, *The Education of Black Philadelphia*, University of Pennsylvania, 1979. See tables, Appendix 2. Statistics on Southern children: See "486 Negro Pupils in 6th Grade Classes," June 1933, Urban League Papers. Copy in TUUA. William Duckrey: Duckrey was interviewed in Philadelphia on November 1, November 15, November 29, December 6, and December 14, 1976. Tapes in possession of author. Wade Wilson: Wilson was interviewed on June 16, 1975. Tape in possession of author. Virginia Union: Clarence Jenkins was interviewed in Philadelphia on May 1, 1975. Tape in possession of author.

CHAPTER 18: *The Culture of Modern Black Philadelphia*
Sports Galvanize the Community
E. Franklin Frazier: *Black Bourgeoisie*, Free Press, 1962. Campanella and Chamberlain: Roy Campanella, *It's Good to Be Alive*, Signet, 1959, p. 45; Wilt Chamberlain and David Shaw, *Wilt*, Macmillan, 1973, p. 30.

Literary Growth
Locke . . . "philosophical midwife": Alain Locke, ed., *The New Negro*, Arno Press, 1968. Introduction of Doxey Wilkerson. "moral advantage":

Ibid., p. 13. "advance guard of the African people": Ibid., p. 14. Jessie Fauset's most famous work: *There Is Confusion*, Boni and Liveright, 1924. "the great women": Ibid., p. 14.

A Rich Musical Tradition Takes Root
Marian Anderson and Union Baptist Church: Marian Anderson, *My Lord, What a Morning*, Viking Press, 1956. "a stimulating experience": Ibid., p. 24. $17.02: Ibid., p. 31. Philadelphia Choral Society: Ibid., p. 33. "Mrs. Ida Asbury": Ibid., p. 49.

An Ex-Slave Creates Gospel Music
Charles Albert Tindley: The best available work on Tindley is Ralph H. Jones, *Charles Albert Tindley, Prince of Preachers*, Abingdon Press, 1982. Also see Wayne D. Shirley, unpublished manuscript on Tindley, Library of Congress. A copy was given this writer courtesy of Maryanne Tyler. There is a complete obituary of Tindley in *Public Ledger*, July 30, 1933. James A. Emanuel: *Black Man Abroad: The Toulouse Poems*, Lotus Press, 1978, title page. Dorsey credits Tindley: See Shirley. Tindley's songs: Reverend Tindley's collected songs were given to this writer by Marie Watson of Bordentown, New Jersey, a long-time congregant at Tindley Temple. I thank her. The Jones book has a fine collection of the songs and also several sermons. Dizzy Gillespie: Dizzy Gillespie with Al Fraser, *To Be or Not to Bop*, Doubleday, 1979, p. 58.

The Dance
Essie-Marie Dorsey: Article by Joan Myers Brown, executive director of Philadelphia Dance Company, in undated clipping from *Philadelphia Tribune*, 1978. Marion Durham Cuyjet: *Philadelphia Tribune*, December 11, 1976.

CHAPTER 19: *The Struggle Continues*
Making a Living in Black Philadelphia
"fear of competition": *WPA-Philadelphia*. jobs for the sons of . . . members: Ibid. Also see "Industrial Opportunities for Negro Youth in the Manufacturing Industries of Philadelphia," October 1939, a school district document in Urban League Papers, pp. 8–9. over fifty percent . . . unemployed: *WPA-Philadelphia*. 1939, a survey: "Industrial Opportunities," p. 7. welfare case load: Ibid., p. 13. domestic workers: Anderson, p. 18; Chamberlin, p. 8; Ethel Waters, with Charles Samuels, *His Eye Is on the Sparrow*, Doubleday, 1951, p. 21. None of their proprietors became millionaires: *WPA-Philadelphia*.

Housing
noted in studies: The first important one was Bernard J. Newman, "Housing of the City Negro," The Whittier Centre, 1914. In *HADV*. two

beds: Fuller, p. 50. hang blankets: Bernard J. Newman, "Housing in Phila-delphia," Philadelphia Housing Association, 1923, p. 19. In *HADV*. popu-lation density: T. J. Woofter, Jr. and Madge Headley Priest, "Negro Housing in Philadelphia," Philadelphia Housing Association, p. 6. In *HADV*. Death rates: Ibid., p. 21. Johnson Homes: Eloise Fickland-Spencer was interviewed in Philadelphia on January 20, February 4, March 7, March 18, and April 4, 1977. Tapes in possession of author. George Mitchell: *WPA-Philadelphia*. values centered around the home: Woofter, p. 28. William Gardner Smith: *Last of the Conquerers*, Farrar, Straus, 1948.

Self-Help

O. V. Catto lodge: *WPA-Philadelphia*. G. B. Anthony: Ibid. Sam Evans: *Philadelphia Record*, June 24, 1941, in *WPA-Philadelphia*. Russell Allen: Ibid. "unfortunately not enough": Carlton Harrison to William H. Crown, December 19, 1936, Rittenhouse YMCA. Copy in TUUA. "work . . . by the colored": Ibid., William Crown to C. E. Shirk, December 21, 1937. access to the gym: Ibid., William Crown to Charles H. Woodward, July 8, 1937. Whittier Centre . . . illness among poor Blacks: Whittier Centre, *Annual Report for 1914*. Copy in TUUA. "a Negro is better": Remarks of Dr. H. R. M. Landis in Whittier Centre, *Annual Report for 1919*. TUUA. Dr. Charles Lewis: *WPA-Philadelphia*. Two hundred and fifty-four persons: Whittier Centre, *Annual Report for 1920*.

Protest Organizations

Colored Protective Associations: Some documents are in TUUA and in *WPA-Philadelphia*. William Henry Moses: For Garveyites and Black reli-gious leaders, see Randall K. Burkett, *Garveyism as a Religious Movement*, Scarecrow Press, 1978, and Burkett, *Black Redemption*, Temple University Press, 1978. For Moses, see *Religious Movement*, p. 117; for McGuire, see p. 72; for award to Heard, p. 139. For James Walker Hood Eason, see *Re-demption*, p. 51 ff. For Wright, see *Religious Movement*, p. 139. "The leaders were very elegant": Smith, p. 80.

CHAPTER 21: *Epilogue*

Blacks now account: taken from *The State of Black Philadelphia*, Urban League of Philadelphia, 1981, unless otherwise noted. Also transcript of Ed Bradley's CBS report on Philadelphia, July 25, 1979. Copy of transcript furnished by Bradley. "blistering lead": *Philadelphia Tribune*, August 29, 1980. new priest . . . ceremony: *Philadelphia Tribune*, October 28, 1980. Berean Church: *Philadelphia Tribune*, July 4, 1980.

INDEX

283

Index

285

Index

Greenville, S.C., 3, 9, 10
  (*See also* Abbeville County, S.C.;
  Abbeville-Greenwood, S.C.)
Greenwood, S.C., 3, 9–15
  (*See also* Abbeville County, S.C.;
  Abbeville-Greenwood, S.C.)

Hall, James S., 175–176
Hall, Prince, 63
Hamburg Massacre, 107, 110–113
Hampton, Wade, 107, 111, 112
Hancock, Gordon Blaine, 123–124,
  161
Harbison Academy, 128
Harlem Renaissance, 56, 222–223
Harper, Frances E. W., 63
Harris, Edward F., 61–62
Harris, William, 153
Harrison, Essex, 152–153, 155
Heard, A. M., 143–144, 204, 242
Hodges, Fletcher, 137–138, 139
Holland, J. W., 207
Hopkins, Firman, 85
Hotel Lux, Moscow, 12
Housing conditions, Philadelphia, 234–
  235
Howard, James, 207
Howard High School, 126
Hughes, Langston, 217, 222
Humphreys, Richard, 55

Industrialization, modernization, 85–
  86, 183, 184–186, 231–232
Institute for Colored Youth (ICY), 55–
  58, 61, 211–212, 213
Integrationists, 73–74
Irish immigrants, 75–79, 81, 84, 135,
  207
Italian immigrants, 196, 207

Jackson, Jesse, 10
Jackson, Mahalia, 229
Jamison, Judith, 16, 230
Johnson, John H., 72–73
Johnson, Terry, 194
Jones, Absalom, 5, 28, 32, 34–35, 39–
  41, 63, 65, 72, 200
Jones, Henry, 213, 224
Jones, Ralph, 199
Jordan, Leroy, 194

Kelly, Frank, 82
King, Martin Luther, 161
Kinship networks, 167, 181–182

Ku Klux Klan, 106, 108–113, 135, 138–
  145, 185–186

Latimer, David, 153
Leadership, Black, 167, 169–170, 204–
  206, 249–250
  Black Philadelphian, 206–210
  (*See also specific churches and lead-
  ers*)
LeCount, Caroline, 80–81, 82, 84
Legal rights, white vs. Black, 30, 155,
  165
Levington, Peter, 43–44
Lewis, Charles, 240
Literary clubs, Black, 58–62
Literacy rates, 22–23, 34, 45, 122–123,
  130
Locke, Alain, 56, 57, 201, 204, 222–223
Locke, Ishmael, 56
Locke, Pliny I., 57, 105
Logan, Alice, 11
Logan, Floyd, 242
Lomax, Hutson, 139
Louis, Joe, 197, 220
Lynchings, 10, 13, 108–109, 152, 170

McCoy, Jim, 150
McCrummell, James, 67
McGuire, Archdeacon, 242
McMillan, Lewis K., 123, 124, 125
Malcolm X, 9
Manly, Alexander, 186
Marriage, interracial, 78, 79, 91, 166–
  167
Marshall, James Foster, 170
Martin, James, 139
Masonry, Black, 63–64, 77, 167, 187,
  196–197, 247
Mays, Benjamin, 14, 126, 130–131, 153,
  160, 161, 162–163, 166, 168, 169–
  170
Migration, Great, 12, 14, 162–188, 209
  African culture in, 181–182, 203
  Black reaction to, 187–188, 198–199
  causes of, 162–171, 184–187
  education and, 210–212, 215–216
  impact of, on Philadelphia, 184–187,
  198–204, 211–216
  recruitment for, 173, 185
  role of church in, 174–178
Minton, Henry, 240
Minton, Theophilus J., 62, 105
Mitchell, Aaron, 138
Mitchell, Frank, 212

286

0-595-31802-9